THE SOCIAL BRAIN
AN OPERATOR'S MANUAL

WRITTEN AND ILLUSTRATED BY MUHAMMAD AL-ADO

The Social Brain

Tellwell Talent
www.tellwell.ca

ISBN
978-0-2288-3554-7 (Hardcover)
978-0-2288-3553-0 (Paperback)
978-0-2288-3555-4 (eBook)

Disclaimer: This book is not intended to diagnose or treat any medical conditions. Any medical intervention you seek to adopt from this book has to be agreed upon by and discussed with your physician prior to making any change.

The topics discussed in this book are based on basic medical knowledge and the author's observations. Many of the characteristics attributed by the author onto the social centers in the brain are based on his personal views and his own medical experience.

TABLE OF CONTENTS

INTRODUCTION

After practicing medicine for many years and dealing with many patients on a daily basis, I was struck by the complexity of the human brain and its wonders. This intricacy has fascinated me, and more importantly, humbled me, as I was able to sense it from observing human behavior and reading about the scientific discoveries related to brain function. This complexity has left me with a flexible perspective on many issues in science, philosophy and psychology. This book is an attempt to open a tiny window into the social centers of our brains, allowing these centers to reflect the light onto our minds in the form of knowledge.

As a pediatrician, I am able to watch the developing psyche of my patients. Along with this privilege, comes the responsibility of providing parents with solutions for their children's behavioral problems. After long days at work, it is hard to go back home and enjoy the rest of the day, being burdened by these children's ailments. For that, I would like to dedicate this book to my patients and my fellow humans.

I hope this book will inspire others to write similar books and share their expertise, so together we may improve the lives of our children, and hence our planet. So, I would like to welcome you to a modest guide of the social brain. The brain has a special status compared to the rest of the organs in our body. When you try to approach it, it starts behaving like the outer galaxies in the universe, defying the Newtonian laws. The closer you get to it, the more mysterious it becomes. Other body organs, like the kidneys, for example, are a little bit easier to approach.

The brain involves the ever-elusive reality of consciousness that begs us to ask: Who are we? Who is truly experiencing the neurochemicals in the brain after they mediate the electric signals from one nerve cell to another? Who understands the words on this page when we are done reading it? Consciousness nags us frequently for an explanation of these phenomena.

BECOMING A BRAIN RESEARCHER

Even though it is hard to understand brain function, it is easy to become a brain researcher; but not through the classical means, so do not take that task so seriously! We will not need any sophisticated laboratory or fancy goggles. All we need to do is hatch out of our ego-shell, our ever-protective mental armor, and look at the social world with the aid of inquisitive eyes. This step improves our ability to observe our thoughts, and the thoughts of the people around us while we are interacting with them.

For the sake of understanding this book, we must peer into a few of the brain's key centers. Do not worry, I am not going to put you through learning any complicated brain circuits; that is beyond the scope of this book anyway. Sometimes words may not easily describe all of the ideas we are discussing, so there will be a few helpful diagrams to aid in understanding the social brain centers. This could be helpful for those who are visual thinkers, like me, without trying to make the book too long.

Before we begin, I would like to give thanks to all of the work humanity has done over the past centuries to discover the mysteries of the human body which have led to our current achievement in managing many diseases. I would also like to give thanks to the animal kingdom, which has provided us, patiently and generously, with great creatures to learn from. Lastly, I would like to give thanks to modern scientists and their dedication to discovery, which have led us to where we are now and to a promising future.

Neuroscientist and Noble Prize winner, Eric Kindle, studied memory and proposed sharing findings with the public via the daily news. In my opinion, this is a great idea.

Sharing knowledge about the brain may allow us to see that we have a lot in common, more so than where we live, what political system we belong to or other aspects of our lives. We share the greatest intricate machine, which dictates our interpretations of how we are experiencing the world. We can learn more about the brain by opening our eyes to the social world around us. This environment can provide us with a huge laboratory and with ample subjects to observe, including ourselves. This lab is yours for the easy payment of zero dollars per month and is available every minute of the day.

Welcome brain researchers. Let us begin this journey.

Here is our itinerary. We will be traveling through the brain in this order:

1. Introduction to the social brain and the general function of the limbic system
2. The reward system of the brain and its famous chemical dopamine, as well as the famous node, the nucleus accumbens
3. Depression
4. Anxiety
5. Peer interaction
6. The ego
7. The thinking box
8. Drug addiction
9. Sexuality and the social brain
10. Eating disorders
11. Sleeping concerns
12. Meditation and the interest in theology in the twenty-first century
13. Consciousness
14. Complexity in biology
15. Creating a brilliant brain
16. Opinions and arguments
17. Earth matter
18. The brain of Isaac Newton

STOP 1

INTRODUCTION TO THE SOCIAL PART OF THE BRAIN

In reality, the entire brain influences our social behavior, but we are going to focus on the parts of the brain that seem to have a main role in forming our social and emotional behavior. As we are learning from the neuroscience findings of the past century, the lead centers of the social brain are mainly the combination of four systems:

1. The limbic system
2. The frontal cortex
3. The natural reward system
4. The hypothalamus

We will also discuss three other systems, due to their influence on the social centers, but without assigning them separate chapters. These three systems are the autonomic, the hormonal and the arousal.

For the sake of simplifying the subject, we will couple these four main sections and call them the *social brain*. Therefore, when we are discussing the social brain in general, all these systems are included, and often we may use the limbic system as a representative of the social brain. It may not be a bad idea that you read the introduction twice if you are not familiar with the general brain anatomy.

We will separate the natural reward system and assign to it a separate section to make it easy to deal with, even though it is a core part of the social brain.

Although the activity of the entire brain influences our behavior, the limbic system takes the lead role. When we happen to be occupied by emotion, for example, sadness, by remembering something tragic that happened years ago, the limbic system will require a larger volume of blood flow at that moment, burning more calories and working more intensely. When we are doing something not so emotional, like working on a math equation, the limbic system will not be working so hard.

This observation is based on the study of the functional MRI or fMRI. We are all familiar with the MRI, which is the magnetic resonance imaging used to locate visible abnormalities in any body organ. When an MRI is taken as a motion picture, it allows us to see second to second the changes in the metabolic activity in the area of interest. Changes in blood flow and the consumption of glucose and oxygen lead to different images on the MRI scan. With the help of a computer, a live movie is generated before our eyes, revealing which parts of the brain are more active. The term "light up" is often used to describe the increase in metabolic activity in the area of study.

Does the brain burn many calories?

The brain consumes twenty-five percent of our caloric intake, even though it consists of only two percent of our body weight, and does not do any visible mechanical work. It consumes calories and generates heat, like computers, through the use of ample electrical circuits allowing communication between the brain cells, using a massive amount of wiring.

During mental activities like solving a math equation, the social part of the brain may become less active, but from time to time still sends signals to the rest of the brain. For example, while doing a math problem, we may remember a future social gathering, making it difficult for us to focus. During any emotional state, the social brain will light up on the fMRI and become more active. The same will happen when we solve the math problem and become excited about our success.

The social brain centers are trying to make sense of all the information coming to us from our senses: visual, acoustic, touch, language understanding, and variable modes of sensation from any place in our body. Then, these centers influence our responses to all that is around us.

When the limbic system is handling the information coming from our senses, it is trying to make sense of them socially and emotionally, for example, is the situation threatening or friendly? Does it induce happiness? Is it worth remembering? If someone has commented on something that we did, our limbic system will be tuning in carefully to see if these comments are going to hurt or going to support our ego, for example.

The limbic system is putting all of the social interactions we are handling every second into a unified mental entity called the emotional us, or the self. Even though this is our reality in life, this entity is far more philosophical and mental than materialistic or neurologic. This entity seems to have a massive gravitational pull on the rest of the brain's activities. This forces other centers in the brain to assume an orbiting role, so the idea of "us" becomes emphasized and strengthened.

As we will see, this social part of the brain is going to let us maneuver through our complicated social situations with thousands of social interactions every day.

A functional and balanced limbic system is what makes the human being able to survive, look for food and shelter, have friends, have a spouse, take care of a child, and look into the eyes of other humans.

The metabolic activity emanating from the social part of the brain could overwhelm the rest of the brain and influence it positively or negatively. For example, our psychological state influences the quality and the quantity of work we are committed to doing, and how we are performing. Furthermore, this social system of the brain is interacting with the autonomic nervous system and the hormonal system. These systems affect the body function, with or without our direct awareness, as they can change the heart rate, bowel movements, sweating, sleep, blood pressure, and many other functions.

The Limbic System

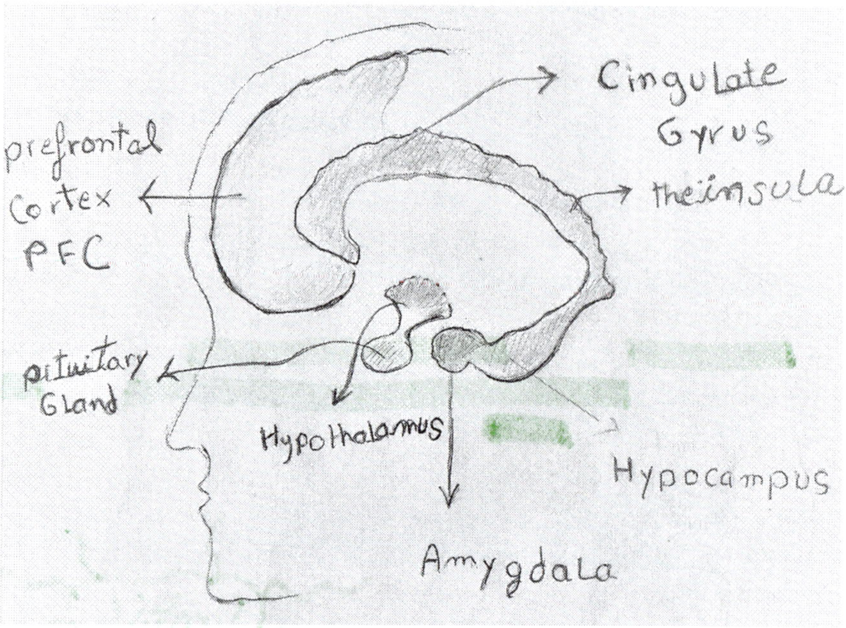

As I mentioned earlier, even though there is no consensus among neuroscientists on the definition or the theory of the limbic system, we will use this term for the purpose of this book to study this area of the brain in view of human behavior.

Where did the limbic system name come from? It came from the way it is shaped. If the limbic system has to communicate with the rest of the brain, then it must be shaped in a way that will make it easier to do that. The limbic system's iconic features include an elongated strip, which swings around to create an unfinished oval stretch, which then is lodged into an extremely crowded area. Note that there are two limbic systems, one for each side of the brain. The limbic system is further organized into separate centers or nodes; these nodes are composed of a collection of brain cells taking on particular functions. For example, if you are very happy, a certain node of the brain will become more active. A smile is known to be the physical manifestation of happiness. It is the product of muscular movements provoked by nerves and activated by a particular area in the motor center, which is in the cortex of the brain. This smile is triggered by a special area in the limbic system, which is more active while the emotion of happiness is taking place.

The Location of the Limbic System

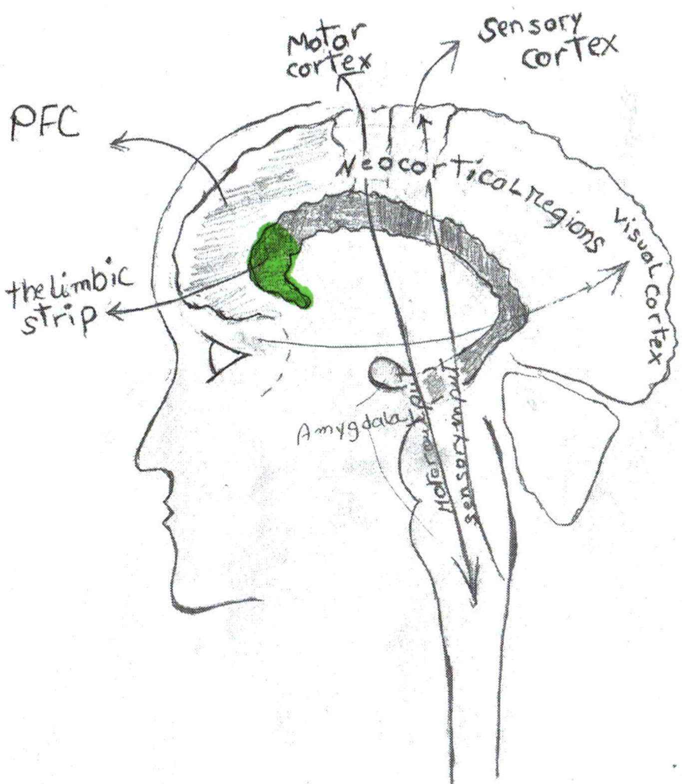

The limbic system sits in the middle of many centers in the brain. What does that mean? It means it sits between the cortical motor, sensory, and thinking or neocortical centers in the top layers of the brain, called the cortex, and the movement coordinating centers in the base of the brain.

This location is significant because it is sitting in the way of our sensory input. The path of sensory input starts with the nerve endings, on the skin of our hands for example, and ends in the higher cortical areas that are involved in processing the physical sensation. This will enable the limbic system to screen our sensory input and give it an emotional dimension. Also, this location allows the limbic system to influence our body movements to keep them in tune with our emotional state.

This social part of the brain is much more mature in mammals compared to other animals, like reptiles for example. As you can see from the illustration above, it occupies a very prime location. As they say in the real estate business, location is key. Obviously, location is important when you want to efficiently reach different areas by not spending a long time trying to get to where you need to go. Because the brain is trying to economize every single function it is doing, it is designed to perform its tasks with the least amount of caloric expenditure. Fewer steps mean fewer synapses. Fewer synapses mean fewer layers of brain cells transmitting the electric signals between each other. This improves the efficiency of the limbic system and its ability to strategically communicate with the rest of the brain.

If we take a moment to look into the premise of our behavior, and the behavior of animals, we will find what drives a large section of our reality is the fear of pain and the desire to experience pleasure, either physically or psychologically.

However, if we control our desire for pleasure, we may yield an even greater reward. When we are able to delay pleasure to a more appropriate time, when we are free of other obligations, it will allow the human brain, in its complexity, to organize our life and make it more functional.

For instance, when we adopt a religion while engaging in worship we may experience pleasure in two ways: part of the pleasure is derived from the activity itself, and part is derived from the concept of waiting for the reward to happen in the future after death. This will make the concept of the future for the human being very complicated.

This means that we are trying to calculate our position at all times, concerning what we should do over the next five minutes, with respect to what would be an appropriate interaction in the parameters of our environment. When we are not calculating, we are still trying to seek pleasure. We may be taking time to drink a cup of coffee or enjoying a phone call with a friend. But when our ability to cruise through the events of the day is dysfunctional, we may use a cigarette or other vice to alleviate the psychological ailments caused by our daily lives.

Psychiatric diseases are powerful ailments in our lives. They have the ability to disrupt the reward centers and the limbic system. Psychiatric diseases are observed by those who know the person who is hurting. We, the sufferers, may report our description of our illness in a variety of ways. Sometimes we can take the role of an observer in our psychological illness, and sometimes we cannot take this role, and we will be engaged in our illness in a more dysfunctional way.

Now, let us talk about the limbic system in some details.

The Prefrontal Cortex (The PFC)

The front part of the brain is called the executive center of the brain and is also called the prefrontal cortex.

The prefrontal cortex is known as the CEO (chief executive officer) of the brain. The prefrontal cortex supervises the limbic system to align our behavior with the accepted norms of the society we are living in. How do we know that? We know that the prefrontal cortex carries this responsibility by observing the behavior of people who have damaged prefrontal cortex areas, whether by illness or accidents. The result of that is obvious bizarre behavior, which deviates from the social norms, can lead to deterioration in interactions with others, and ultimately affects the wellbeing of the person.

The prefrontal cortex helps the limbic system concentrate on areas of interest, providing us with the ability to focus on tasks. This is especially true when the social brain is begging us to be engaged in activities different from what we should be doing at a certain time. For example, the prefrontal cortex helps us ignore a text message and stay on task, which may seem difficult due to the influence of our social lives on us.

The prefrontal cortex interferes when our environment pushes us to behave in a direction that deviates from what is considered appropriate. For example, when someone urges us to cheat to make more money, the prefrontal cortex may intrude to align our behavior with the ideal social norms.

There are times when the prefrontal cortex will not interfere when cheating is an option for us to take because we have no desire to obtain the extra amount of money through cheating. The activity of the prefrontal cortex as you can conclude is increased when our desires are not in line with societal norms. A powerful prefrontal cortex will allow us to crush our desires or subdue them, and to go with the rational and wise path.

Once the prefrontal cortex sets the plan for the rest of the brain, and the plan is followed, the prefrontal cortex will act as an observer, watching from a distance. Also, the prefrontal cortex helps us evaluate the realism of our thoughts and will let us know if this is a realistic thought or just an illusion. This function is affected in patients with schizophrenia because when reality becomes overwhelmed with hallucinations, the voices of the mind become true voices coming from hidden people.

The prefrontal cortex was trained in and graduated from the school of life, the one you are currently enrolled in. Psychologists sometimes refer to this part of the brain as the higher brain and it is doing what society has asked it to do. At times it may get exhausted, frustrated, or even numb, when the rest of the limbic system is acting out of control. The function of the prefrontal cortex becomes reversed, from being the CEO to becoming a server for the reward centers. Therefore, when the prefrontal cortex becomes weak and disabled, it loses its role in impulse control.

The prefrontal cortex normally plays a major role in controlling the lower centers of the brain. These centers are contributing to human behavior concerning anxiety. The prefrontal cortex evaluates our social situation, then prevents these centers in the limbic system from going out of control by warning us about a potential danger. It allows us to use rationality while examining a potentially threatening situation.

Humans with generalized anxiety disorder (GAD) have a disproportional estimate of how dangerous a situation may be in comparison to reality. A strong prefrontal cortex will be able to control the lead anxiety center, its neighbor, the amygdala. The prefrontal cortex tries to push the brake on the disproportionately hyperactive amygdala and forces it to slow down. This allows us to have a functional life.

The frontal lobe is also one of the main centers of consciousness. This term consciousness is used by spiritual teachers, neurologists, and philosophers. However, consciousness, used here in the neurological sense, is different from consciousness in the spiritual and philosophical sense. In the neurologic sense, it refers to our ability to be awake, alert, and aware of our surroundings, thoughts, feelings, and sensations. It also refers to our ability to report to others about our experiences.

Attention-deficit/hyperactivity disorder (ADHD), is often linked to a decline in the function of the prefrontal cortex. Sometimes it is blamed on genetic predispositions, meanwhile, the environmental factors are too numerous to count.

On average, my daily number of prescriptions of ADHD medications may exceed six, and my practice is an average-sized pediatric office.

The behavior of these children with ADHD is not in harmony with what society is asking of them. Teachers want the children seated while they are talking. They want students to be cooperative in doing their assignments in the classroom. Society tells us we should be tuning in to the activities we are handling. Our focus, concentration or attention, should be on the matter we are managing, but the focus becomes dysfunctional in the case of ADHD. Then the prefrontal cortex is unable to control the lower centers of the brain, which could be directing the child toward other fun activities.

Also, in ADHD, the neocortex, the functional and analytical part of the brain used to do science and math, becomes hijacked by the lower part of the brain. This lower part of the brain directs the energy of the neocortex toward playing videogames full time, for example.

The prefrontal cortex is consulting with memory storage areas and evaluating past experiences. It calculates an appropriate decision and action for us to take. Its function is slower than the lower parts of the brain, namely the amygdala and other areas connected closely to it. These lower parts of the brain are designed to make very quick decisions to change the direction of the organism in case of possible but unconfirmed danger.

The decisions made by the prefrontal cortex are calculated and wise but are slower, requiring a delicate estimation of the situation.

As you can see, for the prefrontal cortex to do its work, it is essential to be able to evaluate every sensory signal coming into our brain and to be able to contribute to our response. The response should be appropriately calculated to help us survive and succeed as an active member of the social community. As we will see, other parts of the limbic system are doing the exact thing the prefrontal cortex is doing, which is tuning in to every sensory experience. But the purpose of this tuning is different. For example, the amygdala is concerned with the emotional significance of every sensory input, and these sections of the brain are practically functioning as brains themselves inside of our brain. They are taking the role of reception, evaluation, and responding!

While discussing the prefrontal cortex, I would like to introduce the term *conscience.* In a highly functional and ideal society, a fair number of its members must have conscientiousness. These members are aware of their mental state and will navigate through experiences to become more empathic, hardworking, and honest in dealing with others. In any major aspect of philosophy, you will find ethics. Most philosophers do not disagree much about their views on ethics, despite ethics belonging to the world of metaphysics. To summarize ethics is to say that we should treat any human as an end by himself or herself and not as a means to another end, and also treat to him/her as we want to be treated.

To have conscientiousness is to take the general ethical ideas to heart and apply them to someone's actions and behavior. Some elements of conscientiousness include having honor, taking responsibility seriously, being honest, supportive, and altruistic.

Conscientiousness frees the human from self-seeking behaviors and diminishes the ego. Most of us have conscientiousness but are unaware of it. We can use it to evaluate our behavior and disengage from our needy self. We can then clearly see our deficiencies while dealing with others. This honest evaluation of the self may reveal how our values are sometimes the products of our struggles and a response to the dysfunctional society we are living in. The prefrontal cortex here plays a significant role in aligning our actions with the ethical standards of our lives. However, as you can see from our discussion about the prefrontal cortex, the prefrontal cortex cannot do this alone. Other centers in the brain must work with it, and this adds more complexity to the brain's function.

What I am getting at is that ethical behavior cannot be a mere byproduct of the material function of the brain. In reality, physical structures in the brain have to be assigned to this function. Survival of the fittest here offers no easy explanation for the creation of these centers, as we will be discussing later, unless you would say the fittest is the one with the most ethical traits.

We live in a society today where the traits of social wellness mentioned above are rarely a focus, and the brain is taking note of that. Due to this lack of attention, cultivating conscientiousness becomes difficult. Nevertheless, developing ethical characteristics is extremely important, since, at the end of the day, all of us would like to find someone with these positive characteristics, especially when we are looking for someone to marry, do business with or create a friendship with.

Lack of conscientiousness does not have to mean breaking the law, but it can also mean losing yourself to physical desires. For example, excessive eating is a physical desire which may result in self and societal harm. Obsession with sex is another physical desire that may define a person's life and character, potentially leading to self and societal harm.

As we continue, we will begin discussing the reward system. To do this, we must remember our previously explored friend, the prefrontal cortex.

Phineas Gage, a supervisor working on a railway track had a tragic accident. A metal pole went through his head and destroyed part of his prefrontal cortex. Phineas had a profound personality change, which was overall inappropriate in the eyes of society.

The Cingulate Gyrus

The cingulate gyrus is a strip of cortical matter sitting almost on top of the limbic system. The cingulate gyrate works socially and mediates "ideal" behavior, permitting feelings of empathy and understanding from the perspective of others.

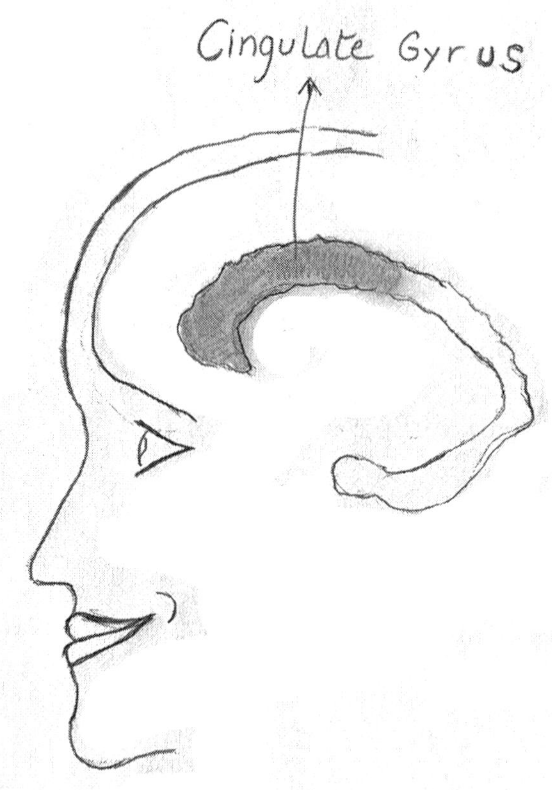

The cingulate gyrus helps us fine-tune our behavior to improve our rapport with a specific audience. It also helps us change our tone of voice and facial expressions to reflect our willingness to show others that we do in fact understand them and want to cooperate with them. It supports us in avoiding aggression and arguments. The cingulate gyrate is also essential in helping us move out of sad moods in a timely fashion. This is important in avoiding the pits of depression. It also helps us acquire new good habits and escape bad ones like addiction. The cingulate gyrate neurons communicate continuously with the rest of the limbic system. While communicating with the frontal lobe, the prefrontal cortex may need to take a back seat when we are meeting with a friend and the setup is relaxing and friendly, like at a café. The frontal cortex may interrupt to remind us to leave the café to make it to a business meeting or whatever we have scheduled for later.

At the café, the cingulate gyrate helps us keep our etiquette in check. If we think that our friend who is eating with us made an obvious mistake when quoting something, our cingulate gyrate advises us not to correct the mistake. It enables us to wink at this matter, smile, and continue the conversation. If we are driving a car and someone wants to go in front of us, we slow down and let them go before us. When the neighbor needs help with something, we do not think twice before offering a hand.

The cingulate gyrus is located right underneath the neocortex. The latter is continuously busy working on solving problems, creating new ideas and studying the world. During our daily living, we are constantly moving from one activity to another. Imagine the way we are working on solving one problem to find ourselves stuck in this activity for hours then days and ignoring everything else! Moving from one experience to another requires emotional flexibility. The cingulate gyrus gives us this ability to maneuver through ideas, thoughts and activities. Its anatomical location allows it to intimately interact with the neocortex in an amazingly miraculous pulse.

The positive social environment composed of parents, friends, relatives, and neighbors, encourages more blood flow to the area of the cingulate gyrus and decreases the amount of blood flowing to other areas in the brain that are active when we are stressed, like certain stress nuclei inside the amygdala, as we will discuss. The health of the cingulate gyrus also is connected to the conditioning of the reward center and the rest of the limbic system.

If the reward center is stimulated by supportive and friendly social interactions rather than materials and physical pleasure during a critical time of our childhood, then this will make social interactions the ultimate pleasurable experience. Positive social scenarios facilitate honesty and integrity in our behavior. For that to be a pleasurable experience, the reward system must be programmed to be pro-social and to induce pleasure from the pure social interactions, which are free from materially related thinking. This interaction needs to be free of other intruding thoughts like watching a movie, which does not fulfill the criteria of pure social interaction; even eating dinner might interfere with this purity. Pure social interaction means pure conversation or laughing.

On the other hand, when the social environment is unfriendly in the child's surroundings, the child will grow up feeling that being around humans is not a pleasant experience. The child will grow and carry with him/her some doubts about the entire experience of being among others. When the child is abused, this may make the situation even worse for the cingulate gyrate.

On the contrary, if the child has a rich spiritual environment, proper social upbringing, and favorable social circumstances, the child will not be as vulnerable to her/his genetic predisposition since it may carry negative traits.

Children bearing harsh environments, such as in wars, will experience a break in social development. Subsequently, they will have difficulty seeing the world as friendly. In addition, when a child is living in a home where the parents are continuously fighting, this will decrease the proper development of the cingulate gyrus. Fighting will limit her/his ability to have genuine and positive interactions with parents. Frequently, we see different kinds of hardships created artificially by the media. These experiences become embedded heavily in the collective psyche of what humans tend to describe as nations, tribes, or ethnic groups. The media could load our life with stories from the past, describing misery, wars, persecution, discrimination and other sad situations. Even though we are not actually living through these miserable scenarios, the bombardment of the social environment, using sad stories on our mind will create an immature cingulate gyrus. It will be disabled in its ability to help us survive life's difficulties by pulling us out of sad situations or depression. A healthy cingulate gyrus can divert our attention away from fear and anxiety and allows us to be a mature and balanced creature who is able to enjoy life and allow others to enjoy our company.

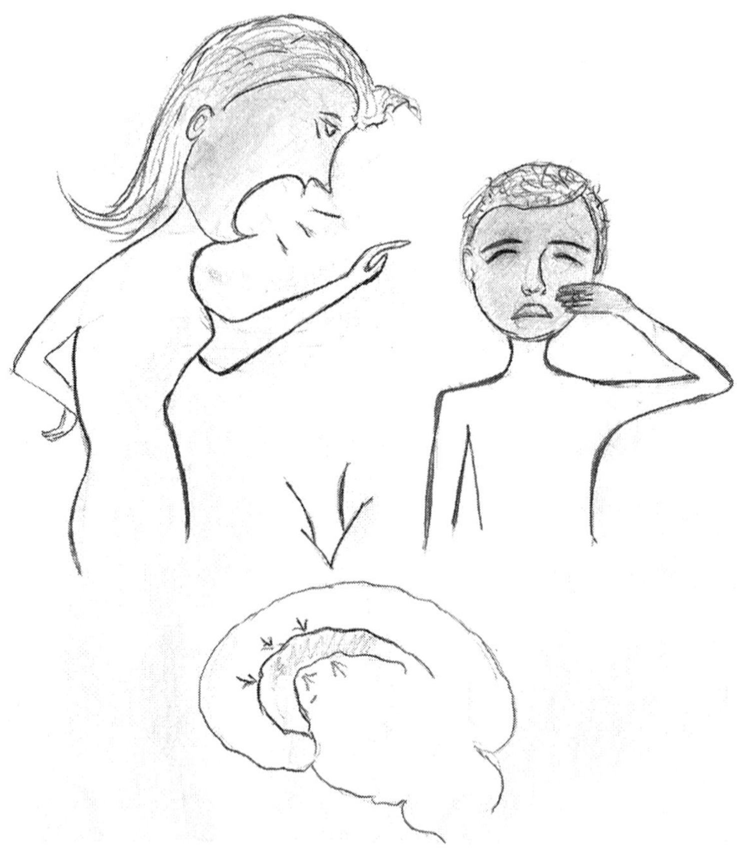

The cingulate gyrus also contributes to our consciousness in the neurological sense. It adds humane warmth and a soft friendly feeling on top of our awareness of our consciousness. When we look at ourselves in the mirror and ask who is this mysterious creature hiding behind this physical structure, the cingulate gyrus helps us to experience consciousness through the frame of warmth, empathy, humor, fun, spirituality, happiness, acceptance, and the ability to give. Therefore, consciousness would not be restricted to only how we are able to feel the sensation of this or that. Those with depression may be lacking this contribution from the cingulate gyrus, causing them to not to feel the warmth and the joy of living.

The Insula

The extension of the cingulate gyrus is the insula.

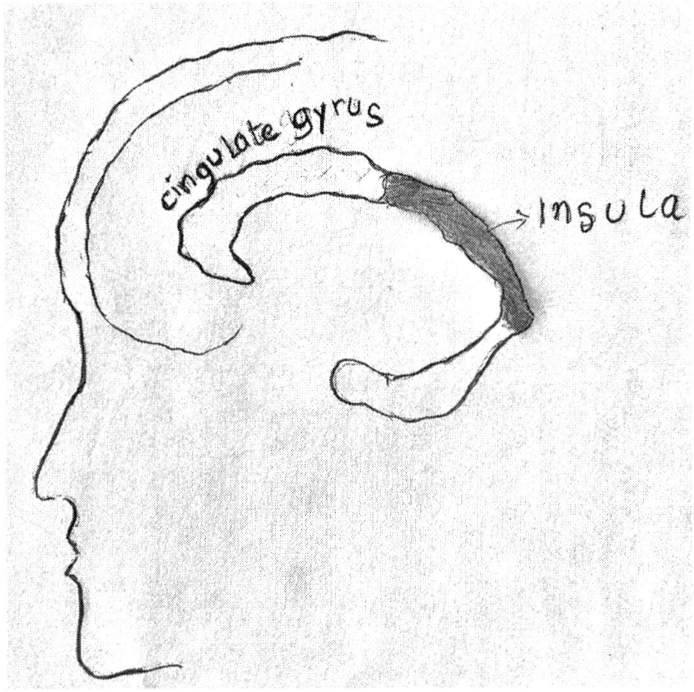

The insula is a strip of gray matter forming part of the arm of the limbic system. The insula seems to react by firing when we are faced with something disgusting like eating rotten food for example. It can also help us react to awful social situations. This will contribute to structuring our system of thought, which is related to having negative feelings. The insula helps us to react to an unacceptable act against all humans in general, such as in the case of genocide. Since it is closely connected to the cingulate gyrate, together they contribute to fine-tuning our empathy. The negative feeling that the insula allows us to have, helps build in us our mental structure as social creatures with the ability to have a vast empathy, and is a necessary element for our own survival and the survival of the people around us.

Normally when we become busy thinking of something else or get engaged in other activities, the activity of the insula will calm down so we can focus on what we are doing. The insula could contribute to depression by continuously broadcasting its negative content and overwhelming our feelings with negativity. This has a much higher chance to occur when negative environmental conditioning takes place in our lives, and when the rest of the limbic system centers are flooding the insula with sad scenes.

The Hippocampus

This stretch of gray matter forms the lower part of the limb of the limbic system. It is the center of short-term memory and the temporary storage of information, to be prepared for delivery to the temporal lobe, where the permanent memory centers exist. The hippocampus is also the center of spatial navigation, which gives us the ability to orient ourselves in the direction of our destination when moving from one place to another.

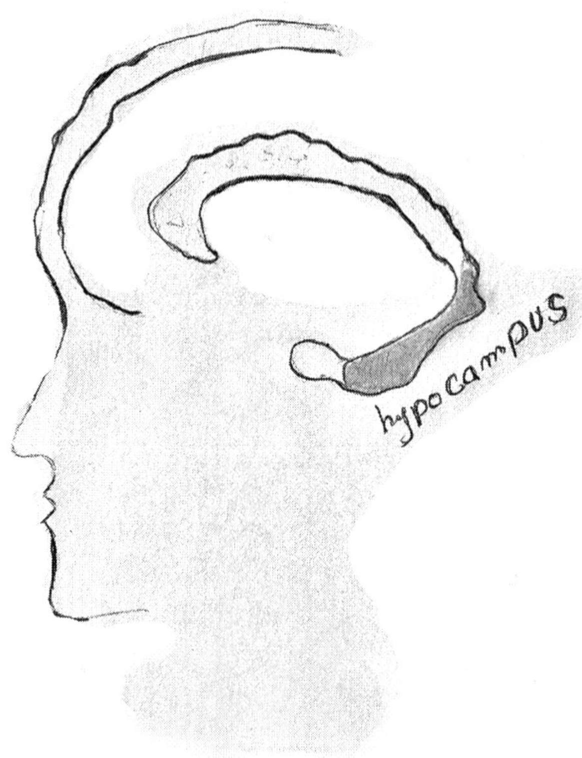

Can you imagine how busy this center is? Imagine the stimuli coming in from the eyes, ears, nose, the taste buds and the sense of touch. The hippocampus classifies these signals to be packaged into temporary files and prepared for storage.

Important social events are stored temporarily in the hippocampus and are ready for communication and feedback with other centers in the limbic system.

In consultation with the rest of these centers, the decision is made on whether a stimulus will be stored in permanent files or deleted. This decision is based on its emotional importance! The hippocampus is the closest neighbor to the amygdala, which is the general value monitor of the events in our life. It supervises the hippocampus in classifying the stimuli according to their emotional significance. How emotionally important an event or stimulus is to us will dictate how easy it is for us to memorize it for the rest of our life.

For people diagnosed with post-traumatic stress disorder (PTSD), the negative events in their life are not only kept in well-established permanent files, but these events are kept ready to pop into their background of thinking and influence their life negatively.

The hippocampus is one of the areas that shows damage in Alzheimer's disease. In this illness, we lose our ability to have short-term memory. Brain cells generally do not increase in number after birth, but the hippocampus is one of the rare areas in the brain that has stem cells. These cells are able to increase in number and then differentiate themselves into new nerve cells on demand to improve the capability of our brain to memorize and handle more information. A famous study was done on taxi drivers in the city of London, England. These drivers would not be issued a license unless they were familiar with all the roads in that city. Drivers usually go to school for about a year to learn the routes of the city and have to pass a difficult exam. While they were working, MRI scans of the brain were done on these drivers. The results showed they had enlarged hippocampi. Follow up MRI done after these drivers retired showed their hippocampi decreased in size. This study provided evidence that there are stem cells in this region of the brain, which can produce new cells on demand, defying the general concept that brain cell damage is permanent. This means that with training we can improve our memory and our ability to maneuver in two- and three-dimensional spaces.

The hippocampus is also involved in consciousness. How? The notion is that consciousness has to rely somewhat on what, when, and where an event is happening. Space and time are mandatory primitive tools for any biological organism to function and navigate the world. For that reason, good short-term memory is essential for sound consciousness. The information in the brain is similar to the information in a computer stored in files; all of these tiny files are connected in relevant ways to permit a functioning human.

The Amygdala

In front and to the side of the hippocampus, you will find the famous almond-shaped node, called the amygdala. According to all experts, the amygdala is the emotional operating center for humans and other mammalian species. It is a world by itself, meaning a brain inside of our brain. In a sense, it is the emotional brain.

The amygdala allows us to sense the fear in others and ourselves. It mediates our experience of fear and sadness, as well as happiness in ourselves. The amygdala receives sensory inputs from the world around us, interprets those sensations, and reflects to us the emotional value of each sensory input. The amygdala allows us to experience the entire spectrum of emotions, from the highest highs to the lowest lows.

The amygdala helps us decide the extent to which we react to all events. It may trigger fear from minor events as well as major distressing ones. It allows us to read the emotions of others and enables us to prepare the appropriate response. Frequently, this node is blamed for our negative behavioral responses, for example, unnecessary frustration.

Hello,
I am your Amygdala
I am a brain inside of your brain
I can see, hear, feel
and react to human
behavior, I can
Sense danger, I
have a special
Connection to your
motor System to
move you away from danger before you sense it!
I can direct you
toward pleasure,
by signaling both,
the Hypothalamus,
and your reward system,
when the social environment treats me badly,
I will condition you to have fear and anxiety, and I can contribute to Depression

The amygdala communicates smoothly with the rest of the limbic system, especially the frontal lobe, the insula, the hippocampus, and the reward system. It is extremely essential in making us behave in a socially balanced way. This balance helps prevent us from experiencing extreme mood swings during the day.

The cingulate gyrus as we discussed, allows us to mount an empathic response during our interaction with people. To be able to mount this empathic response, we must have the ability to interpret other people's reactions to what we say and do, which may not be possible without the help of a sound amygdala. This is a complicated process, which allows us to interact with others. As you see, it is all happening without our awareness.

Therefore, the amygdala responds to all situations related to emotion, negative or positive. How you ask? By firing an electrical impulse, which changes the activity in the rest of the brain. This electrical output of the amygdala is actually less complicated and easier to study than the input.

Let us take the example of the sense of hearing: this auditory input is magnificently intricate. When we hear anything, the voice is transformed by the ear to an electrical input, which includes the tone of voice and meaning of words and sentences. This falls to the amygdala reception station for interpretation. Even the skin's tactile stimulation is screened by the amygdala for emotional significance all the time. It is ready to coach us to an emotional feeling and an appropriate response. For example, when we listen to the news, we perceive sentences made up of words, which have meanings, positive, negative, silly, etc. Now, how do these meanings make their way to the amygdala? Does it have a linguistic reception center or it is relying on the neocortex to direct the message?

The amygdala will allow us to have balanced emotions in normal circumstances. But if the human, especially a child, is subjected to harsh environmental conditions such as abuse then the part of the amygdala responding to abuse will gain strength. The intracellular metabolic activity will increase and recruit more blood flow as compared to when the amygdala responds to friendly situations. In that case, the amygdala does not need to do any work at all other than to keep monitoring.

As in the rest of the brain's centers, the amygdala has two functions: one, the amygdala accurately interprets all of the events around us, and two, it sends a corresponding appropriate response. It is able to do this work by splitting itself anatomically into multiple areas. The group of cells in the lateral amygdala takes the role of the reception station of the sensory input from the outside world. From there, the information is distributed to other areas in the amygdala where they take the role of sending the appropriate response, like in triggering actions governed by sadness, aggression or hopelessness.

This lateral amygdala is the magical section of this organ. It is where the programming is taking place on an intracellular level. It is subject to what is called neuroplasticity, which is the ability of the brain to change the programming of these cells so they can play different roles. These cells become hyper vigilant to any hint of a potential threat, and through communication with other centers in the amygdala, they can send signals to other areas in the limbic system and the reward system to fixate on certain matters.

The neuroplasticity in the lateral amygdala, enabling it to change, allows us to run towards a big dog with excitement for a hug, after once fearing all dogs, or after we have been bitten by one.

The amygdala has a unique ability to perform reflex reactions. As we discussed in the prefrontal cortex chapter, it prepares very fast responses, even before we become aware of a situation. Many of us fear snakes. When the shape of a snake falls on our eyes, the signal is sent to the amygdala before it reaches the cortical area of the brain related to vision. The amygdala will order the body to act fast and move away from what looks like a snake. This happens before decision-making centers in the prefrontal cortex and neocortex are able to respond appropriately. Moreover, when we have a chance to evaluate what falls on our eyes, we may find that there is no snake at all, just a tree branch that looks like a snake. This function also allows a mouse to run and hide from what could possibly be a shadow of a larger creature, like a cat. Verification takes time.

The amygdala is connected through its medial section to the lower motor system, and it is able to start a motor response to help us escape a potential threat. As you see, it is not only able to bypass the cortical sensory system to interpret what the eye is seeing for example, it bypasses the entire motor system that is commanded by our awareness! Can you believe that? The amygdala is functioning like a brain by itself!!

Another example, but relative to our daily life, is driving. When a car swerves into our lane, we quickly divert our car away from this dangerous situation and avoid a potential collision before our conscious brain can even think. We find our hands steering the car away from a suddenly approaching car. This is a familiar scenario for all drivers. This action is associated with a sense of fear and we can feel our heart racing during that moment.

Rage and aggression are common responses facilitated by the amygdala. We can see that when the amygdala nodes are triggered artificially by an electric probe in an animal. Chronic negative stimulation of the amygdala when we are chronically abused facilitates our emotional state to become overly anxious or aggressive, and this will make it difficult for us to experience pleasure. When the abuse is overwhelming, like in the case of a prisoner who is regularly being physically and emotionally tortured with no ability to respond, the amygdala may take a passive role since any active option at that point will lead to further torture. Also, the person may stop eating as a form of objection.

After the negative situation is resolved, the person may end up with PTSD. After leaving the stressful situation, it will take lots of neuroplasticity or intracellular modification to take the person back to his/her baseline state, and that may never happen.

In summary, the amygdala has the following functions:

1. to supervise the emotional response
2. to feel fear internally, and if needed translate that fear into action by signaling the hypothalamus to prepare the body for a violent response, especially in animals
3. to express fear or remain inactive and trapped in a state of fear, setting the stage for future anxiety and depression (e.g., chronic child abuse)
4. to recognize and interpret the tone of voice, body movements, and facial expressions of others around us
5. to recognize human faces and give us the ability to recall memories associated with negative experiences which cause negative emotions (e.g., PTSD)

The amygdala also plays a role in the physical attraction response (e.g., an organism evaluating a potential mate). It allows us to evaluate the expected reward from this kind of experience by creating a continuous cycle of signals between the different parts of the limbic system and the reward system. The amygdala receives information, such as visual, auditory, and somatosensory, from other parts of the brain for appropriate evaluation in regard to receiving pleasure and it works with the reward system side by side. Removal of the amygdala from an animal will lead to the disappearance of fear or rage and cause a compulsive attendance to tactile stimulation and hyperactive sexuality.

The Thalamus

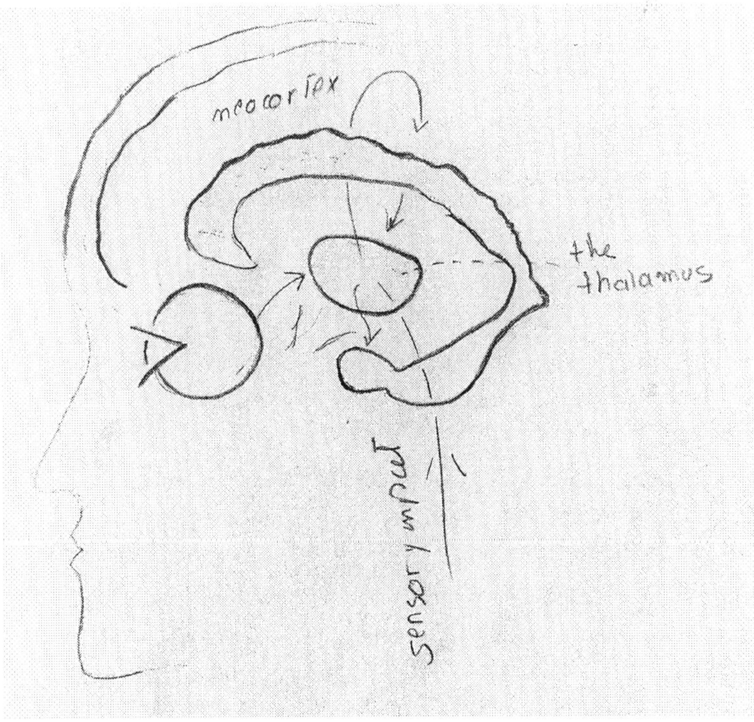

The thalamus is a midline structure, working as a switchboard center for our sensory signals. Before these signals travel to their designated parts of the cortex, they pass through the thalamus first. The thalamus is what allows the amygdala to have access to the sensory input before the rest of the sensory areas in the cortex of the brain have access to it. The location of the thalamus is in the heart of the limbic system, and this allows it to send information to the limbic system using a shorter tract than the tracts that are reaching the cortical sensory areas.

The thalamus creates short cuts for the sensory information to reach the limbic system, mainly to the amygdala. The amygdala evaluates the significance of the information, and if necessary, it will act as we just discussed.

Now when the information reaches the limbic system, it will be evaluated for its emotional significance. For example, I could be walking in a park and see a piece of paper on the floor. I may pick it up and put it in a garbage can and that's the end of the story. The emotional center has nothing to do with that. Compare that example to when we are looking at a beautiful fresh flower. This would normally trigger a sense of admiration and happiness. Our brain will take a break from thinking, and we may find ourselves in a different world for a short time. Without this emotional input from the limbic system, looking at a flower would be like looking at red oval-shaped pieces of paper put together in a certain pattern surrounding a yellow round center, and that would be the end of the story.

Does the thalamus by itself evaluate the situation then decide to inform the amygdala to mount a quick response using this very short connection to it? Does this give you a taste of the complexity of a functioning brain? Does the thalamus inform the amygdala no matter what and the amygdala decides what it should do? Is it the coordination between the two? No matter what the answer to this question is, I am trying to convince you that there is a miracle taking place beyond our conscious thinking. This miracle is trying to take advantage of the most technical sophistication in the design of these centers, which rival any computer system that we can ever dream of designing.

Above that, we get the intentionality. What do I mean by that? When we examine a computer, we find it to be composed of a combination of three things: the hardware, the software and the intentionality of the human programmer who wrote the software. When we examine the brain, we find all three of these components working together.

The Hypothalamus

The hypothalamus is able to collect information from the limbic system. For example, when there is a dangerous situation, the amygdala, the prefrontal cortex and the neocortex will contribute to evaluate the situation. The amygdala, through a direct connection, will reach the hypothalamus to inform it about the situation, and the latter will assign the task to the sympathetic or parasympathetic systems. If the situation requires a defensive response, the response will be assigned to the sympathetic system. Special hypothalamic nodes are connected to these systems enabling us to mount an appropriate response.

If you wonder why we have a fast heart rate when we are nervous, think of the hypothalamus. The hypothalamus has the most central neuronal nodes governing the famous sympathetic and parasympathetic systems, together referred to as the autonomic nervous system. When we are fearful, for example, the sympathetic system will become more active, and this will lead to a fast heart rate. We can call this ability the nervous arm of the hypothalamus.

Other hypothalamic nodes are connected to the pituitary gland, which is the main endocrine gland located below it. Through this connection the hypothalamus is able to control many endocrine functions in the body, so we are going to call this the endocrine arm of the hypothalamus. The two arms work together to prepare the body for the appropriate response.

Figure 1.10 shows the close connection between the hypothalamus and the pituitary gland, which is sitting underneath it.

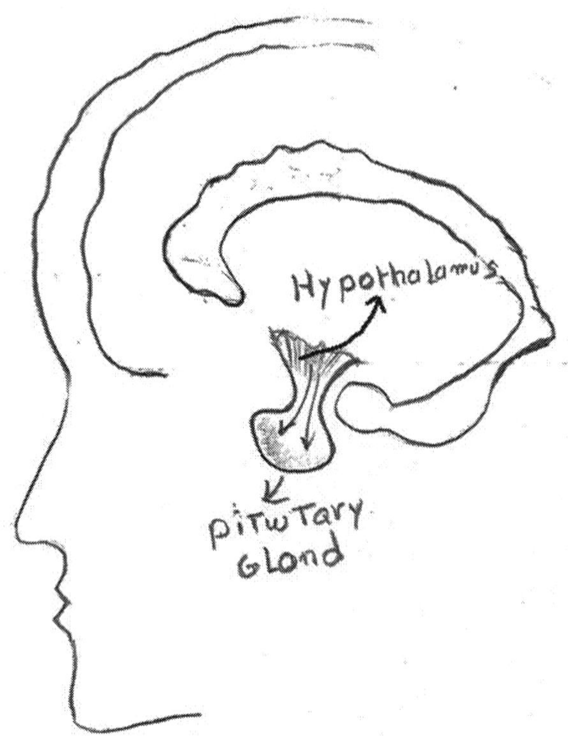

The hypothalamus is heavily involved in the endocrine function; it sits right above the main endocrine gland located in the base of the skull: the pituitary gland.

The pituitary gland controls many functions, but the main ones are the reproductive system and sex hormone production from the female ovaries and male testicles; bone growth; the adrenal gland, which secretes the stress hormone cortisol; lactation; and the thyroid gland, which secretes the hormone thyroxin. Thyroxin's main function is to control the metabolism in the body. The hypothalamus by itself produces two hormones: oxytocin and antidiuretic hormone. Both of these hormones are sent to the pituitary gland for storage, and after that, they get delivered to the bloodstream. The first hormone, oxytocin, plays a positive role in bonding and sympathetic behavior, but its main function is in delivering the baby through the birth canal and in breast-feeding. The second, antidiuretic hormone (ADH) controls the level of water in the blood, hence controlling the blood volume and maintaining along with other hormones the level of the chemicals in the blood in magically stable levels.

It is important to point out that all these hormones have a direct effect on our behavior, but abnormal levels of some of these hormones have a major role in influencing our behavior and our brain cells' activities. That is why you see psychiatrists ordering blood work on every patient, to make sure that they are not missing any hormonal disorder causing our behavioral changes.

Animal and humans react to danger by activating freeze, fight or flight responses, and one of the means to do this function is the autonomic system. Our body responds quickly to these situations by raising the heart rate. For example, the amygdala and the hypothalamus together will stain our feelings and emotions appropriately with the color of these situations. This emotional change is partially governed by the endorphin system relying on nodes in the hypothalamus that secrete endorphins, the famous natural narcotics. These chemicals have a powerful influence on our feeling of pleasure, and this is likely one of the ways that allow us to have mind body connection and to have the subjective quality of any experience, often referred to by neuroscientist as qualia.

Now you can see that the information is understood by different sections in the brain separately. The prefrontal cortex, the amygdala, the hypothalamus and the nucleus accumbens, as we will discuss later, each has to make sense of the situation. The electrical signal moves from the amygdala to the hypothalamus, which is similar to the signal that reaches the TV from the cable, creating live pictures. In the end, it is US, our spirit, or our consciousness ultimately feeling all these steps and experiencing them. This is taking place without directly feeling the amygdala, the prefrontal cortex, or the hypothalamus. What I mean by that is we do not feel them in the same manner we feel our hands and feet for example. How could these limbic system centers be able to make sense of the world we live in? These centers are able to make sense of all the scenarios in our life, and they are deciding on whether each situation is stressful, neutral or pleasurable.

Our reaction to these events varies from person to person, but sometimes these centers can make the decision on our behalf and we are just following them, or we could be watching our feelings and emotions and modifying them and controlling our response. In both cases, it is us in the end who are doing the experiencing and the feeling, and we are sending feedback to these centers to either reprogram them or let things go the old way without much change. I see no other way than appealing to the concept of a spirit or consciousness for this function to become possible! So, what is your opinion about what I just said?

Anyway, let us focus a little bit on the hypothalamus. Between its hormonal arm and nervous arm, it is able to control these functions: temperature regulation, laughing, crying, blood pressure, feeling of hunger, pleasure, initiating puberty, aggression response, sleep cycle, water balance in the blood, and regulating glucose levels.

Also, it controls sweating when the environment is very hot to prevent us from overheating and having heatstroke. Stress, love, tenderness behavior, religious feelings are also some of the hypothalamus's expertise. What about the reproductive preparation of the body? The hypothalamus is the command center of that, and mood maintenance also concerns it. The hypothalamus is a tiny area weighing about four grams. This tiny spot in the brain has all these functions, making the hypothalamus the miracle of wonders in the human anatomy. These assigned nodes in the hypothalamus are structured with nanosensors on the surface of the cells occupying these nodes. This technology enables the hypothalamus to measure the glucose level, body temperature and the inflammatory markers released to the blood from the defending cells like the white cells.

It is also spying on the gastrointestinal hormonal system to see how the fat cells are doing and prevent us from eating too much or eating too little. It is linking the autonomic nervous and other parts of the body with other parts of the brain.

René Descartes figured that the spot in the brain where the soul communicates with the brain is the pineal gland; this is a tiny gland sitting at the bottom of the brain. He had this thought based on the location of this gland and its anatomical property. But as we know now its main and only function is secreting melatonin, which is a hormone that helps us sleep.

If René knew about the function of the hypothalamus, he would have said the hypothalamus is the place where the soul is communicating with the body. I, however, am going to try to convince you that the soul is connected to all the brain cells, yet gives special attention to the hypothalamus.

STOP 2

THE NATURAL REWARD SYSTEM

I would like to start this subject off by introducing an experiment performed on a lab rat. Let us call him Hoover.

As part of trying to map the brain of Hoover, experiments consist of placing probes inside his brain and inducing an electrical activity at the end of the probe. You can see in figure 2.1, that there is a wire connecting the probe placed inside of the brain to an electric source. This enables the researcher to study each area in the brain according to how the rat responds when the areas are stimulated by the electric current.

During that mapping, when the probe was placed in the few areas in the limbic system, Hoover was in a euphoric state. The experiment goes further by leaving the probe in these areas and allowing the rat to start the electric stimulation by connecting the probe circuit to a lever. The lever is placed in the cage where the rat lives. Not surprising, Hoover figures out what to do with the lever! When he is allowed to hit the lever as many times as he can, the rat hits the lever so many times to the point of not eating or drinking. Mating is no longer important either.

Pushing the lever creates a powerful and addictive euphoric feeling that is worse than the heroin effect. Decreasing the frequency by pressing on the bar will lead to an electric firing, allowed the rat to take a break. Otherwise, if left alone, it will continue pressing the lever to death.

While observing the behavior of Hoover, we can see him experiencing euphoria by pressing the lever. This euphoria will not be sustained at the same level after a while, and signs of physical dependence will replace the euphoria. This scenario is similar to when street drugs lose their initial euphoric effects; the user has to increase the dosage of the drug to achieve the reward. Later, the addict will experience severe anxiety when missing a dose and the reward diminishes with time.

Nevertheless, the situation of our friend Hoover here could be worse. The artificial electrical stimulation by-passes many of the obstacles facing the chemically induced stimulation caused by taking street drugs. These drugs have to rely on chemical receptors and refractory states to induce their effects. Those are subjectable to changes according to the frequencies of taking the drug, and the genetic makeup of the subject.

In the case of taking drugs, the nerve cell has to have resources to be able to respond to the stimulation by the drug and induce the cascade of chemical events. Those resources are not available at the same level every second of our life. Add to that the permanent changes that occur inside the structure of the nerve cells when a drug is taken, which are going to change how the cells respond to the ongoing stimulation.

In the case of artificial stimulation by using an electric probe, the cells have to respond to the stimulation all the time. If no rest is allowed, the rat will die due to the exhaustion of numerous biological systems that need rest.

However, how do we explain what is happening to the brain in the euphoric state? The probable mechanism is related to the release of chemicals, called neurotransmitters, with proven physiological behavioral effects on our psychological function, and that is in turn connected to the design of circuits connected to the area of the stimulation.

The first famous chemical is dopamine and its ability to put us in an addictive sate anticipating the reward. This chemical is the backbone of the natural reward pathway, while the nucleus accumbens, the NA which we will discuss in detail later, is the main area that regulates this function.

The second famous class of neurotransmitters is called endorphins or natural opioids; their surge induces the high euphoric state. We need these transmitters to function, and our survival depends on their availability all the time.

In the case of our friend Hoover, the release of these chemicals is taking place out of their natural pathway, which is usually triggered by either the positive events in life, like a great meal, or as a response to severe pain from a bodily injury, followed by the release of the endorphins to ease the pain.

One way to explain what happens is that the artificial electric stimulation leads to a hypnotic state in the rat and the release of dopamine and the internal endorphins. These chemicals now are acting out of their biological order, causing effects similar to what cocaine and heroin can cause when abused. Shortly the rat will go through psychological and physical dependence on hitting the bar, and this will be followed by exhaustion, then death.

Where is the end of the electric probe? What is it stimulating? Does it really matter what the names of these areas are? Is there more than one area in the brain that could give the same result, and what makes this area in the brain different? What does the whole thing mean?

In the end, all of the brain cells have the same basic function and are very similar to each other in terms of being connected to electric circuits. What makes a certain area in the brain perform certain functions is a mystery that is unfolding slowly. Do we have more than one area in the brain that would give the same function? Are these areas in the end connected and making a unified functional node, even though they are scattered in different parts in the brain? This experiment was a mind opener for me, and this experiment was one of the reasons I wanted to write this book.

How do our brains function? Someone may say, it is a hardware design composed of nerve cells and circuits, and then the software is installed in these brain cells. It is estimated that each brain cell has a computing power of an average laptop, so just imagine that you have circuits or networks, composed of eighty billion computers. Try to connect them! Even if you do it correctly and you make them function, try to install billions of software. Which computer gets which software? How does this installation occur? Needless to say, these machines, in the end, will not have feelings as compared to how any simple living organism is able to feel, even if we correctly install the software of feeling.

To me, the brain of the human being and other organs in the body are the product of reductive nanoengineering that is guided by the function of feelings. This feeling, sometimes called qualia, is obvious when we look at human behavior and when we look at other animals.

It is more than obvious that we have no clue how we have any feelings, and the further we advance in neuroscience, the more complicated the idea of feelings becomes. The theory of consciousness, or spirit, is a metaphysically proposed solution that is more than acceptable to human reasoning to explain how these brain centers are able to work together in harmony. Qualia allows these billions of brain cells to download billions of software effortlessly. This allows us to make sense of the world when we look at it, and when we look at ourselves as creatures with feelings.

Brain researchers are approaching brain function by using both descriptive and mechanistic domains. Both will help us study the signals in the brain and try to correlate their functions with human psychology and behavior. Isolating the chemical agents that are governing the neural network allows us to make drugs that would amplify the responses of the signals. These drugs allow us to modify the human response when we are treating depression, for example. Moreover, in the future we may be able to install an electronic chip in the brain that would help us treat paralysis by replacing lost parts of the damaged circuits or even treating depression.

Trying to understand consciousness, along with how we feel and figuring out who we are, is likely to be an ever-difficult task. How we experience consciousness is a difficult problem, but why do we have consciousness is even a bigger one! Why are we making sense of the world around us? Why can this innocent sperm and egg do a construction project of building the brain for nine months? Is this project a product of trial and error of a chemical reaction?

For a practical approach, we are going to find a mechanistic theory to try to study human feelings in a very simplified way. We are going to rely on the function of internal endorphins, which will likely have a significant impact on our feelings associated with the physical and psychological experiences that we are regularly encountering. Let us suppose that the levels of endorphins, when maintained at a certain level, are in a neutral emotional state. When the levels are up, we are in a euphoric state, and when they are down, we are in a depressed and anxious state. Let us propose that a variety of brain circuits hit the endorphin production disproportionately and these circuits are different from one human to another. This theory, even though it is used by many scientists, does not offer much of an explanation, because one would argue about what had happened after the endorphins were secreted and the receptors were stimulated. Where is the ultimate reception station that would provide us with the feeling? Alternatively, the question that should be asked is where are we in this process?

If René Descartes or Aristotle were alive during our time, while neurology is making such advances, they may have helped us with this matter. Mainstream science seems to have only descriptive and mechanistic approaches to describe the functions of the human body; making the scenario of further questioning any matter related to our feelings a very unimportant task or at least a second-class destination. Living in a materialistic world obliges us to rely on what our senses can sense for our daily life to become possible. An example would be making drugs to treat illnesses. However, denying who we are in the process, creatures who have consciousness and feelings is unwise. This way of thinking carries serious consequences that scientists may not see in their labs, but physicians can see in their clinics in the form of psychiatric diseases.

The explanation of who is feeling the sensation in the end, meaning us or our consciousness, is a mandatory philosophical idea that cannot be materialized because we cannot get out of it, see it, or examine it.

How could we deal with the data coming from the sensory organs and emotional centers in the limbic system? The way I see the situation is that the closer we get to knowing the brain centers, the further we get from understanding consciousness! To propose a theory of spirit, or consciousness, is to explain a unifying mechanism that merges all of the sensations coming through our senses with the intellectual function of our minds.

This will make it possible to explain the behavior of humans and animals. It is a very appealing idea to our common sense. Of course, this theory is not scientific, but it does appeal to reason, and it makes sense for us to adopt it. The theory of spirit makes more sense than following ideas commonly mentioned in books discussing the theory of mind in our time, and some of these ideas are:

1. There is no such thing as consciousness. Consciousness is just a byproduct of chemical activity in the brain. Neuroscience is in its infancy in our time and we will know more in the future.
2. Ignore the subject completely and refer to consciousness as a function of the brain related to being awake and aware of our sensory experiences and being able to describe them. Then assign

sections of the brain that are active when we are reporting our experiences to others based on the fMRI scan.

3. It is a matter of time. When computers become more sophisticated, they will have consciousness.

I have seen these three scenarios proposed frequently by my materialistic friends, but to me and a sizeable portion of humanity, these proposals are not satisfactory. They pretend to avoid mixing science with philosophy and metaphysics, but in the process, they reduce humans to a machine that has no feelings or life. So how do we find a position in the middle? The middle is nice and friendly, but it is not popular. It is called, "I do not know!" You can adopt it if it appeals to you.

When focusing on the matter of how we feel, the theory of a spirit seems more logical than the theory that considers the brain to be just a physical entity. Sometimes, when the metaphysical proposition has a nonscientific explanation, it is better than ignoring the problem completely, or coming up with explanations that are called "scientific." In reality, they are metaphysical. We need a metaphysical argument to deny any metaphysical explanation when we cannot use a scientific experimental method to do this task.

Let us ignore the problem of qualia and consciousness. Ignoring this problem reveals a hidden desire to view the world in a materialistic frame. Therefore, both sides of the spiritual and materialist are swimming in the same metaphysical ocean, and to claim to be the scientific side is no more than sophistry and allusion.

That is not science; science has to deal with matter only, but I would argue that social science that regards humans as a material entity, has not improved our psychological life in the past two hundred years. Moreover, the consequence of this approach is the rise in psychiatric diseases in our time. If Sigmund Freud was able to see the reality of our life now, he would have written all his books in a different tone. My plea to the readers is this: when we are studying the behavior of humans, it would be wise to propose a theory that will give us some explanation of how the brain has this unified function, even though we have no idea how this entity called *spirit* work. Even though we cannot see this spirit, we can feel that it is there.

Why did the word spirit ever have access to the linguistic structure of a human being? It is not that bizarre to imagine that this word has some resonance in our minds. Realistically, it has a clear resonance in the mind of every human being, regardless of her/his opinion about the subject matter. To me, this is very strange.

After the tons of hours, I spent trying to find someone in our time who is dealing with the theory of mind, all I have found are philosophers who are assigning fancy names to theories that are essentially providing no insight into this matter. They rely on only one worldview, which is that we are only matter.

Any person walking on the street who hears this statement may have a doubtful expression. I am not sure what our rat friend, Hoover, may feel about this statement. Would he agree with us, or would he say my human friends seem to have a strange way of thinking; did your brain start to melt yet? Mine did.

Now let us go back to our subject. Where is the electrode ending in our friend Hoover? One main area is the nucleus accumbens. The NA.

The nucleus accumbens anatomically receives the signals through a bundle of fibers from the ventral tegmental area, the VTA. The ventral tegmental area is part of the arousal system. Dopamine is used in this connection, and if the electrode is placed in the connection area between the ventral tegmental area and the nucleus accumbens, the stimulation will give this hedonic addictive effect.

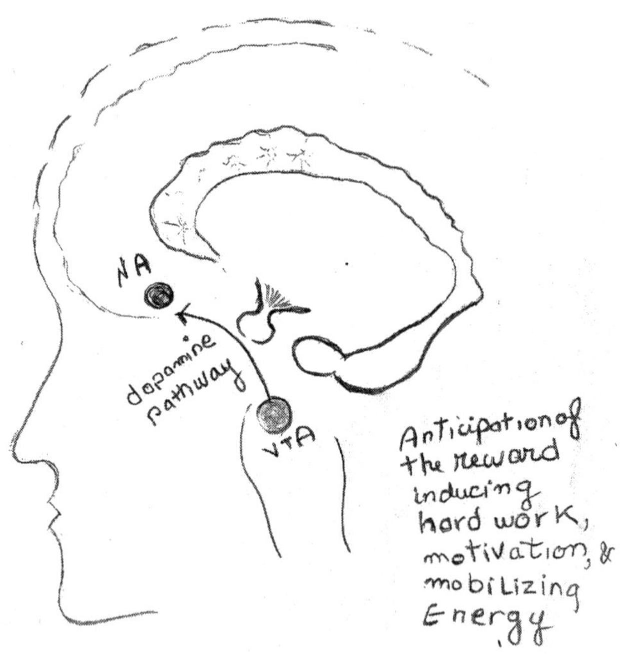

A node in the hypothalamic area could be another main area in the brain where the electrode could stimulate a similar euphoric effect. This should be of no surprise to us knowing that endorphins are secreted by the hypothalamus.

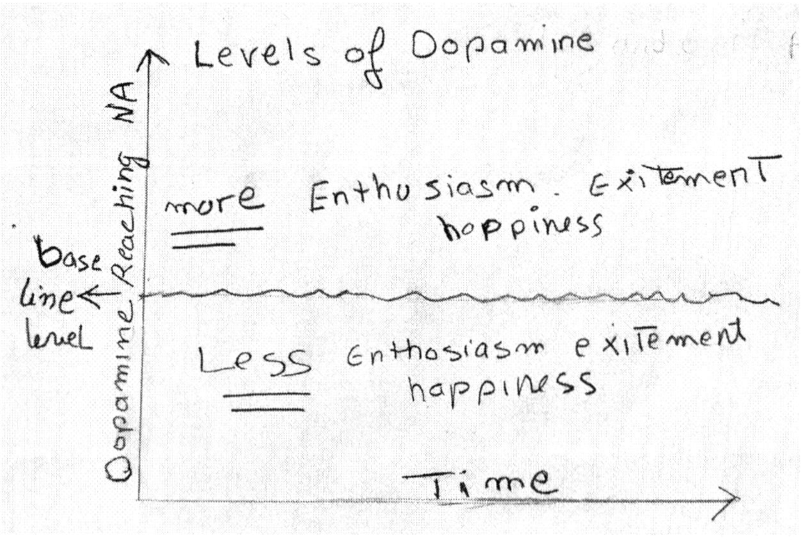

How does the reward system help us? The reward system provides us with the psychological energy and the drives that are loaded with enthusiasm to mobilize the necessary efforts to do the work, finish the task, and pursue pleasurable experiences.

After the task is achieved, the reward may or may not follow. The reward in the brain, in the end, could be mediated or translated by the release of the internal opioid, with the help of the hypothalamus, or maybe by another system that we are not familiar with at the current time. The opioid receptors are represented in many parts of the central nervous system. One of its functions is to control the pain when we experience an injury for example, and another function includes producing the euphoric feeling.

Are people with a healthy spiritual reward system able to tolerate pain more than others? Do these people ask for less pain medication when they show up in the ER after having part of their skeletal system broken? Based on the historical data this may be true, but it is impossible to verify and for that reason, I am not going to give an example. Would our understanding of a healthy reward system help us deal with the opium epidemic that we are dealing with now?

Micro Temporary Addictions

The reward system not only dictates our decision-making process when we are involved in major and complicated tasks but is also involved in the tiny small tasks that we do from second to second.

If we see a fresh cake made in our favorite way and placed in front of us, for us to stretch our hand and cut a piece, we need a functioning reward system that is going to motivate us to move our hand and mobilize the efforts to cut the cake. Then, we will put a piece in our mouth to enjoy the taste. If our reward system is damaged or cut at the nucleus accumbens level, we are not going to be motivated to move our hand. The motivation here could be described as an urge, a feeling of need, or a micro temporary addiction. This temporary period gives the urge to eat the piece of the cake. It represents a response to a temporary addictive state. The strength of it varies from one human to another. This state is needed to keep us going in life and will make doing tasks easier. This is not just coming from an imperative order dictated by the prefrontal cortex. If the prefrontal cortex tells us we have to have breakfast today, or otherwise, we may not survive for the rest of the day; we are not going to respond to this order no matter how rational or logical this order is!

Spiritualistic Dimension in the Reward System

Spirituality meanwhile adds a third dimension to our activity. A spiritual dimension may encourage us to have a humane connection to our activities. In that dimension, we experience love, harmony and rapport. Our daily activities are not just connected to filling our deep pockets with money and our stomachs with delicious food. There is a different kind of temporary addiction, especially while we are doing a task or interacting with others. We can also say that there is a feeling or presence of an idealistic warm coloring to our psychological state, which also includes our ability to observe and monitor our behavior and feelings in our minute-to-minute activities. Could the lack of this third dimension be one of the causes of depression in our time, where liability is becoming the main factor that is guiding our behavior at work? Doesn't the limbic system need to be harmonious in its functions to allow us to experience a balanced feeling and behavior? Should our activity not be guided by a good outlook on our life first, and worry about liability second?

Other Examples of the Reward System Function

The job of the reward system becomes more complicated when the reward is much delayed and requires more coordination with the limbic system. A student's life is a classic example of that. High school students may understand the reward of having an A in a class, as this may help them when applying to college, even though college may be a few years away. However, this delayed reward may not be powerful enough to mobilize the reward system and create a powerful temporary addiction to doing a task that requires years to achieve. As you see a delayed reward involves imagination, and imagination requires the involvement of the neocortex. The neocortex can provide a fancy picture in the mind about the future, showing that completing the task is going to bring the reward for sure. This idea is close to what is commonly called, conviction.

Conviction is a complicated function of the limbic system that involves the hypothalamus, which will contribute to the process by secreting endorphins in response to the entire matter. This will bring about a strong stimulation of the reward to mobilize the efforts. It is telling us that the reward will be closer than we think; some of us are well-programmed to be mobilized by the rewards that are delayed. Some of us experience agony to go through a process that may take years to achieve. Neuroscience, with time, will shed more light on the difference in the architecture of the nucleus accumbens and the hypothalamus in understanding our behavior in regard to dealing with delayed rewards.

Other Mini Rewards

If the steps toward achieving a reward are difficult and boring, like preparing for an exam for example, meditation comes to help. Meditation is a positive force in our life that helps us connect to the reality of the day, which mandates lengthy work we have to do, regardless of our enjoyment of the process. The mental institution of patience is constructed on a meditative state, which eases the frustration that is created by the repetitive physical or mental work we have to do all day long.

Conversation with Others

When we are telling a story about an event that occurred in the past, we try to make the story interesting by cutting out the boring details. We do that to grab people's attention and make the story enjoyable. We are creating traditional mini rewards of storytelling to the audience. We use this habit often, especially when we present a story to an audience with whom we do not have a very personal relationship. Movie producers and writers subconsciously follow this method.

Procrastination

Now you can see why we procrastinate in doing an important task connected to reasonable reward; it is because the chain of these mini rewards is not well-formed in our mind, or in the intracellular structure of the cells of the nucleus accumbens. There are other reasons to procrastinate other than what we just discussed. Could the brain be engaged in other activities that will be releasing a small dose of endogenous opium, like in addictions, and the suspension of these activates will lead to a withdrawal-like feeling? On the other hand, the brain may be engaged in dealing with a threatening situation, trying to mobilize the effort toward preventing what we call harm, whether real or perceived.

In the case of depression, future rewards are not worth the effort because there is no anticipation for pleasure or real reward when the task is met.

How about the arousal system? Is the activity that we are thinking about able to send signals to the arousal system to fire up the rest of the brain and give a boost of activity to move us to do the task? The arousal system has to work in harmony with both the limbic and the reward system. Just imagine that you woke up in the morning for a task to find yourself sleepy and tired and in no mood to do the task. The limbic system is able to stimulate the arousal centers in the brain stem. In this way, it is indirectly affecting the reward system to become active. The reward system is mediated by dopamine, the ventral tegmental area, (VTA), classified among the arousal system nodes in the brain stem area, sends signals to the nucleus accumbens and the rest of the brain. These signals are loaded with dopamine. You can see the location of the ventral tegmental area in the brain stem in figure 2.2.

The nucleus accumbens becomes sensitized to the point that it creates mini addictive states to mobilize the rest of the brain to do the task that we are engaged in.

The prefrontal cortex, the PFC, receives the signal from the ventral tegmental area, which in turn helps to send feedback to the nucleus accumbens telling it about the merit of the experience: is it wise and beneficial? Or there is something better than we have to attend to.

Example of a Common Reward

When you feel enthusiastic about owning a desired car, for example, this feeling could be energized by many environmental factors; your friend who shares similar interests is talking positively about the experience of owning the car, or TV ads and other media are talking positively about it.

Your neocortex always is engaged in imagination about scenarios involving the experiences that we are about to encounter. The reward system becomes sensitized to the idea, and it will work hard by creating a temporary addictive state during that period. This will keep the enthusiasm going until the goal is achieved.

When we save money to buy a car, the reward system will fire in anticipation of the reward. When the reward takes place, the dopamine surge will slow down, and the opioid secretion in the hypothalamus will go through a surge, followed by a gradual decline.

This endorphin surge will last for a period of time, the duration of which will vary according to many factors: one of them is past experiences that helped to stabilize our mood after other rewarding experiences.

The surge ultimately will calm down; the one event in the working brain cannot hijack the resources from the rest of the activities in our lives for long.

However, could buying a car be a long-lasting happy event? We have to think of this possibility, and we want to encourage it. I have met people who saved the first car they bought when they were in college and updated it, and they are old people now. Nevertheless, in a fair percentage of scenarios, one of the following occurs:

1. Your spouse thinks that the car is too expensive or that the car price is reasonable.
2. The car after all is a necessity in this century. You need a car for your daily use.
3. The newer model is better; owning this car is not exciting anymore.
4. You are having a problem with the car, such as a recall.
5. You have a new financial obligation, so the car loan has become a financial burden. When concerns are rising, the amygdala will experience negative activity and start sending negative signals to the hypothalamus.
6. Your overall financial situation is becoming much better. You are richer, and all of a sudden, you are able to buy a much nicer car. Therefore, your car is not as interesting anymore.

Via the circuits that are hard-wired in the limbic system, the amygdala starts to light up and sends signals reaching the hypothalamus, affecting the status of the opioid system and creating a sense of disinterest. We might experience a period of relative opioid decline that would decrease the emotional affinity to the subject of interest. During this period, the rest of the brain, namely the prefrontal lobe, the PFC, and the neocortex evaluate the situation and work hard to find solutions to get our feeling back to a positive state.

You can imagine now how we could easily fall into another rewarding situation to try to make a quick fix, or we could be going through a lesson in life teaching us wisdom: the wisdom of not being too attached to material objects. The prefrontal cortex is helping us find solutions to the current situation, controlling our impulses coming from other rewarding thoughts, and allowing the neocortex to find intelligent solutions.

No attachment to a material object to start with will make the experience more enjoyable without a high surge in endorphins and dopamine. We need just enough to add a tiny positivity to our overall positive feelings that we are carrying with us throughout the day. A wiser scenario would be when we are watching our emotions and are in control of them.

In summary, the reward system function is going to be affected by the following:

1. other reward experiences coming to the picture,
2. a problem with the existing current reward, like eating lots of cake increase the risk of becoming diabetic and overweight,
3. other problems in life or work we are dealing with,
4. our social networks. After all, life cannot be all about buying a car and eating cake. Our social network should be a more enjoyable part of our life than owning a piece of material. The same applies to being good parents and being humane in our jobs.
5. our spirituality. Are we spiritual at all? Do we like modesty? Is modesty appreciated in society and the media? Do the ideas of our unseen friend, God, and the benefit of piety exist in our life? Some people may say this is an imaginary idea. I would say children's imaginary friends still play a positive part in balancing children's moods.
6. our prefrontal cortex. The prefrontal cortex might not be okay with the decision to buy an expensive car in the first place, especially when this will lead to any financial risk. If the prefrontal cortex has a strong influence and has thick wiring with the rest of the limbic system, it will send signals directly to the nucleus accumbens and to the amygdala to calm the urge and influence us negatively against the idea.

As you see, many factors influence our behavior. When we have a serious addiction to buying and poor impulse control from the prefrontal cortex, the idea of the inability to buy the desired items will create a decline in internal opioids. This might make some of us, who also have tendencies for antisocial behavior, cross the line to commit illegal or immoral acts toward other humans or the environment.

Consciousness and the Nucleus Accumbens

While we are eating a piece of cake, what really happens is that the sensation comes from our eyes while we are looking at the cake and from the taste buds in our mouth while we are eating it. These stimulations reach the nucleus accumbens. The route for this sensory nucleus accumbens connection may be mediated by the amygdala, which receives the sensation first, or the nucleus accumbens could receive the sensation from the arousal system, mainly the ventral tegmental region. From the fMRI studies, we can see that the neurocircuits associated with the reward system have more blood circulation and oxygen consumption, when anticipating a reward like eating a cake.

Reasonable questions to ask are why and how is that translated into a hedonic urge or feeling? Do these neurocircuits end in the nucleus accumbens? Does the nucleus accumbens have enough neurological connection to the rest of the brain to make it work according to its liking? Why would a tiny node like the nucleus accumbens have this powerful influence on the rest of the brain and put it in a pleasure-seeking state? Is that not shocking? I see this phenomenon is screaming for an explanation.

While we are eating the cake, when our hand is reaching and doing the function of bringing the bite to our mouth, our brain is exerting a tremendous amount of coordination with billions of brain cells in many centers to make this function possible. A few areas contributing to this coordination include the motor centers in the cortical areas, the balance centers of the cerebellum and the basal ganglia, the sensory system of sensation, and many other functions. The question that I like to ask is why this action is taking place. Why would the excitement of the nucleus accumbens lead to this series of actions?

Why and how is the brain able to be commanded by this command center? How could that small nerve node have this influence on us? It is able to give us enthusiasm and psychological energy. Why and how is this one tiny node able to take over all the functions of the brain in terms of the psychological feeling and observable corresponding behavior?

Is the nucleus accumbens connected directly to relay centers distributing the signals from that point to the rest of the brain? Is the interaction between the nucleus accumbens, the hypothalamus, and the rest of the limbic system enough to shed some light on this function? Is the hypothalamus the endpoint of all our feelings? I hope I am able to relay to you the picture in my mind about how complex it is to have a functioning brain, and how difficult it is to assemble a brain model with hedonic feelings. Is the response to the hedonic feelings just a domino effect starting from the eye that is looking at the cake and ending with finishing eating the cake? Is the process that involves several billion synaptic steps put together by chaotic materialistic events through the mechanism of trial and error? What makes the situation a million times worse is that we do not see this domino effect on the materialistic level when we look at the brain. What a miracle story we have been told by our materialistic friends to describe how the brain is formed. The seamless occurrence of this mechanism is essential to our ability to live. How many trial and error attempts do we have, using chance alone to construct this system? Be advised that this system has been constructed correctly every time we see a newborn baby.

I am trying to convince you that the theory of spirit makes more sense, for it is the real command and communication center in the brain. This spirit has continuous reciprocal interaction with all neurological nodes. Each brain cell with a variable degree of interaction with our spirit is depending on the current psychological state. This spirit is trying to be a command center, but the rest of the centers in the brain function according to their anatomical, histological design and many genetic factors. These materialistic centers are not just passive wax sitting under the mercy of consciousness. We are the product of the interaction between the two! The materialistic world contributes to our behavior and feelings along with who we are.

Social Models Influencing the Reward System

The reward system has been programmed during our childhood, initially. It is very primitive but powerful. It will let us cry and scream when we are hungry, and we have no hesitancy in nursing till we are full or to the point of throwing up, a phenomenon I see in the office every day. We are looking actively to other social experiences by looking for sympathetic happy faces, we cry to be held, and we are ready to scream at the slightest hint that our needs are not fully met, or when we experience any discomfort.

At the same time, we are very careful in screening the environment for any activity passing by us that would stimulate the reward system. During the first few years of our life, the reward system will be influenced by what we are seeing and hearing, as well as by our social environment. The stories from friends and relatives have a great, unquestionable influence on us. Our materialistic connection is primitive at that stage. A small toy car is enough for a while, and then in a few years, that is no longer the case. We start comparing ourselves to the rest of the adults around us, especially if there are elements of a power struggle in our social surroundings. During that time, the environment takes full advantage of the easy neuroplasticity of both the intracellular programming and the mode of wiring between the nerve cells, which go under heavy construction during our childhood.

We are sitting under the mercy of our genetic make-up and the environment, and we are experiencing the pleasure and pain coming from their interactions.

STOP 3

DEPRESSION

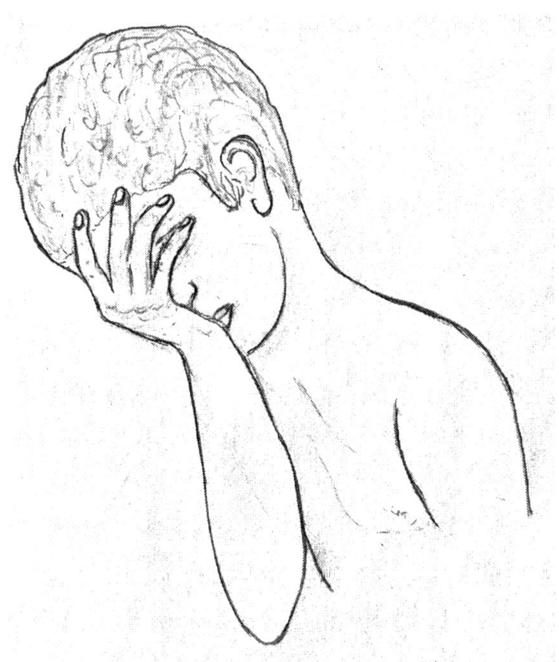

Depression is a painful mental illness which makes living a very difficult and miserable experience. It is extreme sadness associated with sleep disorder and decreased mental ability to perform tasks and often is associated with feelings of guilt, hopelessness and helplessness, and sets the mind on low energy drive or agitation.

When it escalates, we will prefer dying over living to resolve the pain and the agony in our life.

We are going to start our discussion of this topic by studying our generous rat friend, Hoover. We are going to put him in an imaginary situation, but not too far from reality, then try to study his feelings.

Let us put Hoover in an isolated cage, with no other rats around, no toys to play with, and no opportunity to do any other activities. We are going to leave him in this state for a long time. While he is discovering his new place, he starts to look for food. Quickly, he will find it. Our friend sits in one corner in the cage and the food is replenished daily. He has no desire to look or hunt for food or to do other activities. we try to help him by placing many toys in the cage, some of them are electronic.

After a while, we are going to put Hoover into a much bigger cage, and we are now going to add other rats to the cage. Our rat now is initially doing better; he is interacting with other rats. He has a supervisory role over them, due to his physical strength. Also, because he has seniority in the cage, he can choose his female companion. His food continues to be replenished daily with a variety of food. Day after day, he remains in the same cage, and the temperature in the cage is well-monitored to keep everybody comfortable.

Is Hoover in a better or worse condition for acquiring depression? He is experiencing no hunger, he has no difficulties in life, his home is secured, but he has no idea how he secured this home. He is controlling the rest of the rats around him, he is eating frequently, and he experiences no sweating. Occasionally, he is transferred tenderly to a new cage for cleaning by the workers of the lab.

Sometimes he is transferred to another lab with even better conditions. But he cannot leave the cage. He has no spiritual life. Although he seems to be a master, at the same time, he is a slave. Hoover is feeling this dual role in his life. Other rats around him are telling him that he is of much higher status. When he expresses a desire to leave the cage, they ask him, why do you want to go outside this cage? Why do you want to experience the risks of life and its agony? The outside world is full of hard work, dangerous interactions, and the food is not as good. Hoover has no choice but to obey his new social order. He has to stay cool and happy in front of the rest of the rats in the cage, so he can maintain his leadership. Somedays he plays this role well and somedays his frustration is obvious.

It seems that Hoover's life is not much different from the life of any king or queen or a mighty person of our time, who isolated himself from the normal interactions in life. Now you can understand why some of the very rich people or state presidents are making horrible decisions on behalf of their people and the planet Earth.

There are many other scenarios that this rat may encounter, but in regard to the subject of depression, one other main scenario would be of interest to us: imagine that Hoover happens to be a small and weak rat living among aggressive abusive stronger ones in that cage. In this scenario he endures living in a harsh and miserable condition in the cage. Between the elements of these two scenarios, you will find some of the root causes of the environmental factors of depression.

The State of Depression

The state of our mood is often the focus of our mental life. Our emotions fluctuate above and below a neutral line, creating our state of happiness or sadness.

Depression is the cornerstone of my practice, unfortunately. When I was in medical school, I never imagined that this is what I would be dealing with, especially in pediatrics. The implication of this harsh reality on medical practices has been progressively worsening each year, for the past ten years.

Child and adult abuse, eating disorders, drug abuse/overdose, divorce, isolation, and criminal activity performed by adults around the child, are often associated with this pathology.

Many factors work together to establish the *habit* of depression. Consider the variety of life events and their ability to influence our mood. We will briefly discuss possible theories to describe the depression state.

The Theory of the Vicious Cycles of Depression

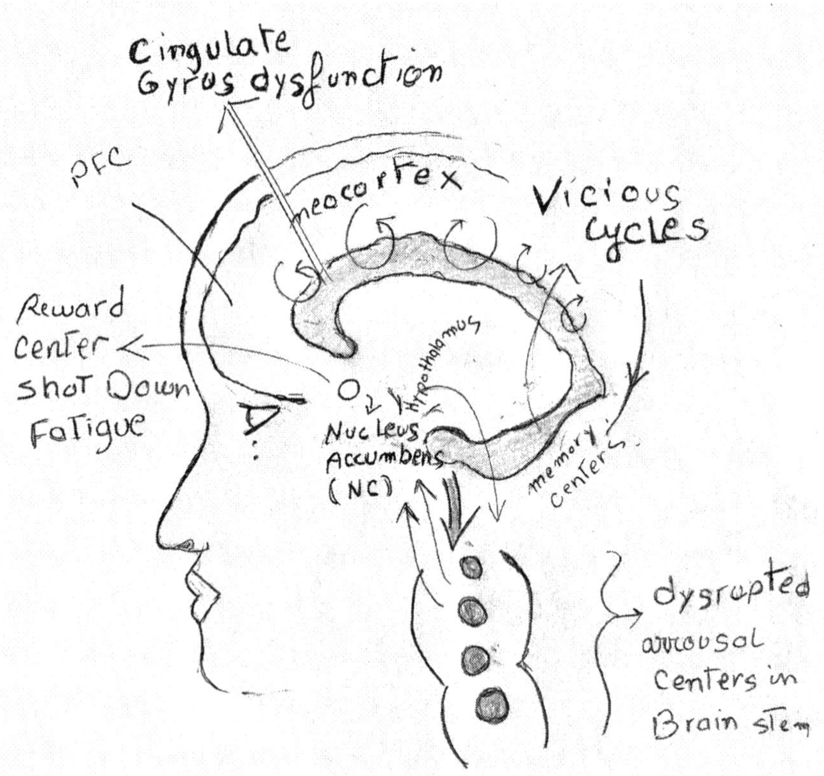

Based on the knowledge that we have about the social centers in the brain and their function, we can imagine the role of these centers in contributing to depression. The neocortex assists in supplying the limbic system with a variety of negative scenarios that could be imaginary or based on memories of sad events. These scenarios may become the basis for our future outlook on life in general. The limbic system, especially the insula and the cingulate gyrus, shuttle these past events back to the neocortex and the memory centers for reinforcement, creating a vicious cycle that is hard to break.

When depression becomes well established, it is translated into new neurologic circuits. The prefrontal cortex is unable to intervene to disrupt these circuits and the arousal centers are unable to regulate the higher limbic centers. When the reward system becomes disabled, this leads to hypothalamic dysfunction causing sad feelings, disruption of eating, sleeping, reproduction, and endocrine function. It can lead to elevated stress hormone levels being secreted by the adrenal gland located above the kidneys.

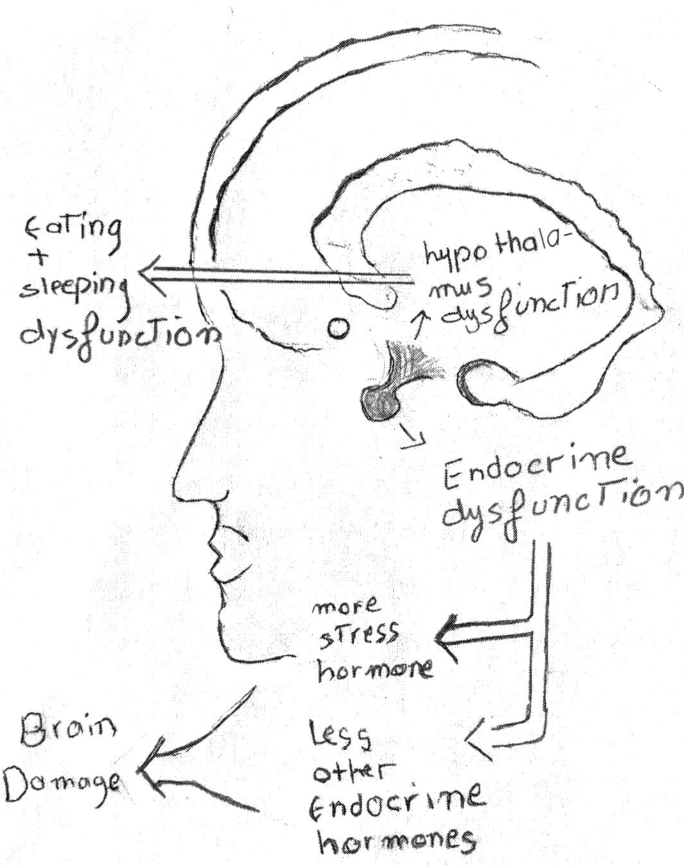

The Disruption in the Arousal Centers

These centers are trying to keep us awake in a functional way, so when we are awake, our eyes are open and our neocortex is working on solving problems. Our motor function enables us to move and our sensory system registers data from all our senses. Also, our social brain is working. You can see that there is an obvious level of coordination among these many centers to make us awake and functioning fully as perfect humans.

The limbic system is responsible for solving our social-emotional problems, and the rest of the systems are doing their function. The arousal system that we have has to wake up our social brain enough to put a positive tag on how we perceive the social environment around us. But this social world has to first be worthy of our attention.

A key part of the arousal system that plays a role in depression is the serotonin system. The disruption in this system often blamed as a cause of depression, and this area is a main target of medications like serotonin reuptake inhibitors. A healthy serotonin system plays a role in enabling us to be receptive to and interact with the positive social cues in our environment, and in allowing us to experience emotional social feelings related to optimism and happiness.

Another key part of the arousal system is the dopamine system, which fuels the reward centers, mainly the nucleus accumbens. The dysfunction in this area will cause a lack of enthusiasm as we discussed in the chapter of the reward system.

Genetic and Environmental Factors

It is reasonable to think that human behavior overall is influenced by the expression of our genes. Genes express themselves by making proteins that ultimately maintain or change the intracellular structure of the brain cells, and prime the interaction between different areas in this organ.

Biologically, changing the genetic expression could happen by turning genes on and off, or by modifying the strength of their expression. The physical environment plays a huge role in the health of the nerve cells. Examples of negative factors are starvation, exposure to extreme weather or toxins, and experiencing a direct physical injury to the brain. But in normal circumstances, our nerve cell activity is mainly influenced by our social environment.

But what exactly is our social environment? Our social environment is made up of what we hear and what we see. We transform thoughts among each other into reality through language. The pitch and frequency of the tone of the language we use and its emotional load are internalized and understood, allowing us to communicate and listen to each other. Consider facial expressions and body language; they are created by the movements of every single muscle of the face and the body. This language can tell us a lot about the psychology of the people we meet. This creates motion pictures we can derive conclusions from. We, humans, and many animals share this universal language. We are trying to tune into the feeling of every human we encounter, even when we do not speak the language that she/he is using or when that person does not want to say anything.

During childhood, we are exposed to a variety of social circumstances. Consider the existence of loving parents, supportive relatives and friends, who have a sense of optimism and humor that trigger joy and laughter. Also, consider the significance of values expressed in the normal conversations at home as adding significant elements to our social environment in general. The use of words, such as honesty, integrity, benevolence, forgiveness, and altruism put optimism in our hearts. When these values are offered through a spiritual dimension within the family life, the social brain takes note of that.

Do the concept and practice of meditation exist in our life? Are children raised to believe in a loving universe? Are children given the chance to explore the belief of eternal life or life after death? Is the concept of a loving and merciful God presented to them? Can faith and reason coexist so the child may navigate life with a secure state? Is living a morally ethical life taught to be rewarding? Do we hear that ethics is essential to the existence of society?

The existence of these words and concepts in a child's life in an honest way is going to influence and shape the social brain of the child and subsequently her/his future behavior. The influence of these words is profound when they are backed up by actual translation to meaningful, visible behavior and actions from the people around us. When the media support these concepts, our adoption of them becomes easier.

The child's social environment is also shaped by other concepts such as chasing money and prestige in order to acquire a state of elegance, beauty, self-worth, and respect. The child learns to equate physical materials with happiness.

When the spiritual dimension disappears and life is defined by physical materials, we belittle the many miracles which make up our experiences. When we dismiss these miracles and our language only focuses on the physical world, our reality changes. This dead materialistic language has a lasting influence on the child's behavior. The influence of words is not limited to children's psychology; we are receptive to this influence throughout our entire lives.

While we are aging, we tend to rest our views in a psychological shelter. We feel unease about adopting new ideas since our views have become linked to who we are to some extent.

When we go through tough life events or dips in our psyche, we find refuge in words heard or spoken by us. Words can be a quick fix. They enhance our broken reward system and self-image, and they create hope. Friendly words inspire positive behavior and encouragement to get us out of the stagnant negative psychological atmosphere felt by some of us as depression.

No doubt that life circumstances and negative events are digested differently by different people. What may be considered stressful and traumatic for some, may not be as difficult to others.

Regardless, we as human beings are vulnerable in one way or another to the mechanics of our social environment. Surely many of us are resilient to the effects of difficulties in life, and we grow to be successful despite going through harshness, but not all of us. There is a portion of our society that has lost themselves to this harshness; many turn to drug addiction, suicide or to selling themselves on the street. Or they may lose their mind and get involved in senseless criminal acts like school shootings. These humans are weak and vulnerable; they are not resilient.

Can the outside world change gene expression? Does it mutate our genes? Can external factors turn on and off some genes? Many psychologists would agree with that theory.

The science of epigenetics is an old horizon in biology. It is concerned with the mechanism of how the environment can change the genetic make-up of a living organism. This was clearly demonstrated in the case of drug use during our teenage years to cause permanent changes in our genes related to addictive behavior. I have to mention here that evidence suggests that environmental factors are not able to change the genomic makeup of human sperms or eggs.

The genetic makeup of these reproductive cells stays the same no matter what happens to genes in the nervous system cells unless we are affecting them directly with radiation or by using medication to inflict direct damage on them. That means our children's genetic makeup has a fresh start in life, unaffected by the genetic changes that happened to us as parents.

Medications given for depression and other psychiatric diseases ideally should turn our genes on and off, in favor of treating this condition.

The industrial revolution has led to complicated intense advertisements, beyond what humanity used to in the past. Among other things, for the past several decades the media has been infiltrating our lives with numerous nonessential necessities in our life and has been bombarding our senses with unachievable goals.

This new focus displaces other brain activities. Coupled with social harshness and the lack of a warm, supportive social environment, this focus can create a negative cycle. This cycle is becoming vicious and strong with time, creating a good recipe for the increased incidence of depression.

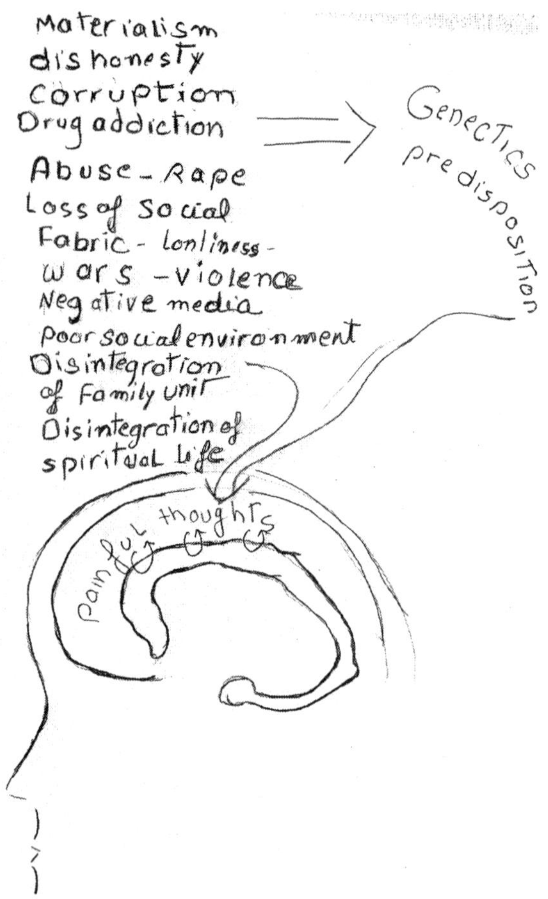

These days, when I see an adolescent in my clinic, I tell myself to look for signs of depression. Sometimes the facial expressions of my patients are enough to tell me I have to bring up this subject. Furthermore, health insurance companies are now requiring physicians to administer a short written psychological test, composed of questions the patient needs to answer. I then score their answers using a standardized scale which offers a final numerical score. That judges the mental state of the patient in regard to depression.

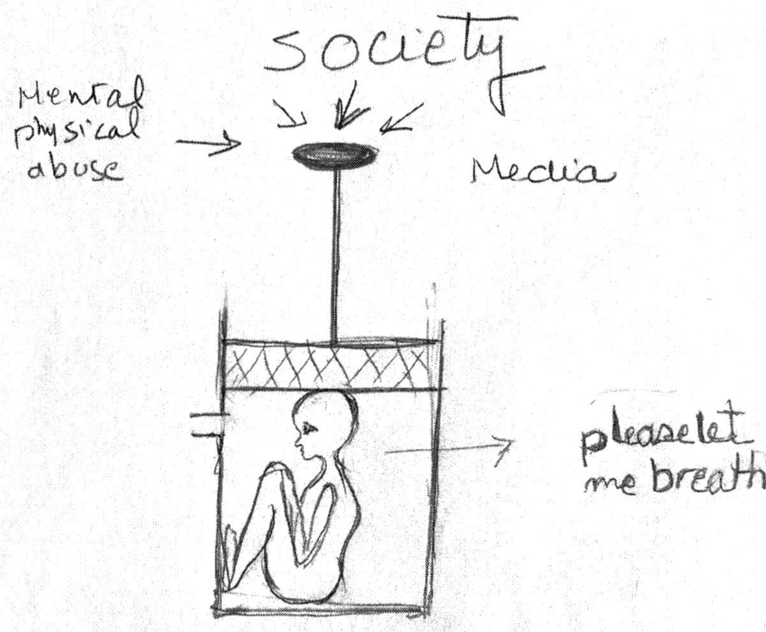

Why is this happening in the age of enlightenment and advanced social and material science? Scientists are at every corner in every university, doing research aimed at understanding human behavior. Why is the rate of depression reaching twenty-five percent of the population and starting earlier and earlier down to less than ten years of age? Please do not blame that on genetic changes and natural selection; we did not have enough time for that to happen. This change is happening before our eyes for the past two generations.

Why is the number of women living at or below the poverty line growing in the western and advanced free part of the world? Why is the land of opportunity not giving the opportunity to the overwhelming number of single mothers, who are lacking high education, finding mainly low paying jobs, and fueling the line of human misery?

Is it the responsibility of the social science and the psychiatry departments in the universities to take a look at what is happening? What about the rest of the scientists in other branches at these universities?

Is this just an issue in the poorer segment of society? Has depression entered the homes of our scientists yet? Have we had a firsthand experience of the problem?

Is it a coincidence or cause and effect? Is the state of depression an expected response to the current social environment with its new mechanics? No one predicted this was going to happen. Advanced science should go hand in hand with improvements in economic standards and overall quality of life. Why are we failing in that?

Depression Triggers

Many biologists, geneticists, and psychologists are teaching us that there is a genetic component to depression, and all also agree that there are environmental factors. We will leave figuring out the genetics to the researchers and concern ourselves with the environmental factors.

Environmental factors have to be available to trigger the genetic predisposition, but what are the environmental factors?

Obvious Triggers

An obvious trigger is the death or sickness of a beloved relative or friend. In my practice, I see many of these cases. After the death of a grandfather or mother. The child may become depressed for a long period of time, maybe even months, depending on the degree of connection to the grandparents.

Physical accidents and illnesses also take a toll on our emotions. Impacts caused by accidents usually decline after one year. But in patients who are predisposed to depression, this may not be the case.

You can see that the above factor is related to bad luck. There is no one to blame for these events. We all accept that all of us at one point in our life, will experience sickness or death of someone we love.

There are events in our life that we tend not to accept as universal common events. We tend to feel that we are picked on to experience these incidents. These events are triggered by another human being because of senseless selfishness and lack of consideration. Preventing these events would cause no harm or may be beneficial to all sides. Imagine someone losing a parent to a criminal act, act of war, or a car accident related to driving under the influence of alcohol. Here the situation is connected to the fault of another human, which will leave different marks on a child's psyche. It promotes a sense of distrust of the social structure around us.

Neglect and abuse, especially during childhood are major triggers. For example, living with parents who are continually fighting and yelling, or experiencing a separation from parents. Obvious separation is seen commonly when a child does not see one of her/his parents for a period of time. But psychological separation is caused when parents are separated from their role in a clear manner. Examples of this include an alcoholic father or a drug-addicted mother.

Subtle separation may manifest itself when the parents are living in their own world, without giving the children the necessary attention and interaction they need to feel secure. This may also be seen when parental interaction with the child takes a formal role. This interaction lacks the necessary warmth and tenderness that should accompany the touch, the look, and the tone of voice.

Physical separation from one parent is very common in our day. Many patients of mine are rotating homes, staying with one parent for a few days while the other parent is playing the role of a part-time parent who is looking for a new love experience. This situation gives the child signals that she/he is not worthy of their time and emotion.

Rough siblings, relatives and neighbors, interacting with these children continue to deprive them of experiencing friendship and warm relationships with others.

Frequent encounters with narcissistic, harsh, abusive people in school and at work, create a negative, senseless experience. The bullying that takes place in schools and social media may leave permanent scars in the psyche of vulnerable children.

Peer pressure often follows the negative model set by movies and TV series, which emphasize the false necessity of materialism and many other dysfunctional social elements in our lives. I am going to leave it to your rich imagination to come up with more scenarios, provided that this path of thinking makes sense to you.

Subtle Causes

Now I would like to discuss other reasons for depression; let us call them *subtle causes.* I will start with this scenario: a person is standing at a bus stop on a cold, rainy day and sees an expensive car passing by. Let us suppose that this person has pessimistic views about their financial future and feels it is almost impossible for them to have a car like that.

Many days go by and the situation does not get better. The person becomes obsessed with the thought of being deprived of money. You may want to describe this person as having low self-confidence, or you may choose another description.

Now I would like to ask you to be the person standing at the bus stop on the cold, rainy day. Try to imagine that you are experiencing this scenario. Would you have negative feelings about seeing an expensive car passing by you on a cold day with the thought of never being able to afford any car in your life?

Many of us are very resilient when facing negative circumstances in life. For example, some people may not have negative feelings about being bullied or losing lots of money in a deal. But some of us may indeed have some negative feelings about this experience. I would like to put these examples in this category, subtle causes of depression, because these factors have both intrinsic and extrinsic elements, combined with various degrees of interaction.

Not being affected by seeing a car passing you while you are standing at the bus station in the cold, would mean a few possible things: you are educated and informed enough about wisdom and happiness, and you know that materials, in the end, will not make you happy.

Or maybe you can control your desires and you understand that your desire for materials is the reason for misery. Or perhaps you are a truly spiritual person living a modest life and know all you really need to handle the cold day is to dress warm and wait for the bus to arrive. You like your lifestyle, and you appreciate your life's circumstances. Waiting for the bus does not have to be a difficult experience. On the contrary, it could be enjoyable.

Some may think that a beautiful car passing by is just something nice to look at and that is the end of the story. They stay in their own happy thoughts about what they are going to do for the rest of the day. Some may see the car as an inspiration to work hard and buy one like it. Others may get fascinated by the design, and this could influence them to become a car designer and work for an automotive company.

As you see, internal factors are causing us to have different psychological reactions and judgments about any phenomenon. These internal factors cannot simply be put into a genetic frame, meaning they cannot be traced back to this gene or that gene. The process that will make us assume a certain position in life is very complicated and may be contingent upon our experience. The way we interact with the outside world and make conclusions to settle any matter may vary from one person to another. Needless to say, our emotions shine through every single step of this process.

I chose the example of seeing the fancy car and its relationship to depression to show the effect media can have on our life. By media, I mean the traditional media like TV, internet, etc. as well as what we see and hear from our relatives and friends.

The media is capable of creating an endless list of needs in vulnerable people, by placing endless advertisements showing us what we are missing in our lives, and what we have to do to fix it. We need a vacation, a dream home with a special kitchen, clothes with certain brand names. Also, we need a nice car and a nice looking or perfect partner designed to fulfill all our psychological needs.

The media, on the other hand, can also have a positive effect on our life. It can endorse values, ethics, and spirituality by emphasizing the importance of empathy and compassion to other humans. The media does a very good job overall in showing the real beauty of nature, the hidden world of plants and animals, that inspired many of us to be happy, vigorous members of society. I have no idea why the media is declining to play a more positive role in the life of citizens of every country.

Going Back Home

Now let us go back to the persons who felt defeated when they saw the expensive car passing by. Let us suppose they go back home and find their social company to be very supportive. this person may have great brothers and sisters and comes home to a warm atmosphere. His/her siblings are joking all the time, and everyone is sharing many laughs. They are connected by the spiritual positive elements in their house and are supporting and helping each other. Our friend is used to hearing inspiring words like wisdom, trustworthiness, honesty, and virtuosity. Let us imagine a child brought up in a house with these words as part of the language fabric she/he is hearing, along with regular use of humor.

So, what will happen to the effect of the negative experience he had that day? Our intuition tells us the effect will be diminished, even if the person is psychologically vulnerable to have depression.

The environment also has effects on other mental activities in our life. Consider a young girl with a genetic mental challenge who has an awesome and supportive parents and teachers. Would she have a fair chance to succeed in school despite her mental challenge? Do you think this is realistic? I can assure you it is! good parents and teachers bring the student tons of emotional building blocks to boost her mental faculty, and this subsequently will benefit her future. This is just a small example of what society could do in regard to influencing the state of its members.

We must become conscious of these issues, otherwise, we will continue living in a subconscious state, and we will continue to see the alarming increase in childhood depression.

You may consider depression as an artificial social disease. The causes often emanate from the outside world. Think of having negative experiences with your neighbors or witnessing a difficult relationship between parents. Think of peer pressure to behave outside of your comfort zone, viewing violent movies, or watching your grandparents succumbing to their addiction to gambling. Every negative experience is feeding into the depression cascade.

In a society that values the physical appearance to a great extent, let us think of all these teenage females subjected to the pressures to look like movie stars and models with the "ideal" look. Many of these images, idolized by young girls, are photo-shopped and technologically manipulated images of other females, leaving many young girls feeling less beautiful or not as thin. Vulnerable patients may feel unworthy in the materialistic eye of society. We just do not view these scenes and images without psychological interaction. These interactions are similar to software downloaded on a computer. We are left to deal with inevitable changes in our emotional state.

The Complexity of the Economic Time

Our complicated economic environment affords everyone a chance to choose a path to what society calls "success." Therefore, the individual has many decisions to make and responsibilities to take. Often, we feel the social pressure that is watching our performance on the stage. A bad choice or failure on a project could be interpreted by the vulnerable individual as an ultimate failure. This ultimate failure perceived by the person could lead to self-blaming and suffering. Some of us will have difficulty in accepting failure but still can use the experience to learn from and move on. But others may get stuck in this stage. This is especially true in psychologically vulnerable individuals who may fall victim to depression. A witness for this is the rise of suicide starting in the seventeenth century which brings fundamental economic changes, moving on to our current time.

With options in life that are wide open, choosing a path different from the path of our parents and close relatives becomes more common. The new situation may require us to leave town. With that, we become physically distant from the direct interaction with our social networks. This will bring with it the slow disintegration of our social fabric. An example of that is shown by the rise of the industrial revolution in Europe which was associated with the weakness of the social fabric. This in turn contributed (among other elements) to a decline in the role of religion in maintaining this social fabric, starting in the seventeenth century to our time.

Religious institutions simply could not adapt to the new environment. The inability of these institutions to preserve their role has no one to blame but themselves. No one is preventing these institutions from playing a major role in our lives. So, can they add happiness to our lives? They can set the rule of declaring honesty as an important tool in human interaction and can be leaders in showing the necessity of ethics in our lives. They can give psychological support to people with difficult situations and insist on keeping spirituality as an important element in our lives. They can shed light on how the rise of materialism with its promises of utopia and happiness is no more than an illusion and does not carry in it the promised happiness, even when we succeed. Religious institutions can work on maintaining the family structure in society. They can prove to be uninterested in taking people's money or abusing their power. They should make genuine efforts to teach the young generation wisdom in life since schools do not want to play this part. Also, these institutions must distant themselves from the political machine. They can distance themselves from building luxurious buildings; after all, sophisticated designs are not going to touch the heart of the youth. After they clean up their act, these institutions may become more convincing to the public.

Another element that influences our life negatively is divorce. Divorce is a byproduct of the massive social changes of the past three hundred years worldwide. For an adult going through a divorce, this could be a major problem. But for a child, it is for sure a major problem; it hits the center of existence and essence of his/her life. It basically means that the child is starting life with failure in maintaining this basic life structure, the social home. How could this new creature come to life and handle the disintegration of this basic life support and not react negatively? How long is a child going to be stuck in that stage of failure before she/he can digest it and move on in life? That may never happen.

The institution of divorce leads to the rise of single parenthood. The latter is trying to define itself, but with major difficulties. On one hand, it is built on the ruins of the structure of the marriage. On the other hand, it is interacting with three other social mechanics: the rise of sexual freedom, the demise of religion as a social and spiritual institution, and the rise of depression. The last one, the rise of depression, is screaming for recognition today. But the minds of our universities are busy doing something else. They are looking through the physical ruins of the past, as we picture the human being, as an anthropological, archeological and biological entity, we call it Homo sapien.

Potential Positive Effect of Spirituality in Our Life

Adopting spiritual experiences as a conscious intended approach to life is a very wise choice, as compared to engaging with the world as only a physical entity. Many of us acknowledge this comparison. For example, the human relationship between men and women, a relationship based only on physical attachment, without spiritual-religious back-up has proved in our time over and over again to have limitations in maintaining a long-lasting bond.

Relationships based essentially on physical and psychological attraction, without social and spiritual dimensions will leave this relationship resting on the mercy of the reward system. Often, we are left in despair trying to make sense of our changed feelings toward the opposite sex.

When love is taught to be unconditional and is not based on self-centered gain involving the reward center, loving each other in our homes and loving our relatives and neighbors become easy. We will benefit tremendously from having a spiritual dimension in our life. With Earth, it's becoming a small village, and loving all humanity becomes easier.

Take another example: the dilemma that we have in the workplace, facing the West these days, with negative interaction between the employees and the management. Having spiritual dimensions on both sides will solve lots of these problems. Many philosophers and economical theorists in the sixteenth century envisioned a political system that has no spirit, dry and cold. It may be successful temporarily, then inevitably this will lead to a dysfunctional situation. The employers want the job done with the least cost and least involvement in the life of their employees, and the employees want their paychecks with the least involvement of honest hard work, complaining about the working conditions. Both sides of the relationship have paved the path for job migration from the West to overseas, creating a dysfunctional and unrealistic situation.

Spiritual experiences should never hurt the individual or the society; on the contrary, its benefit is more than obvious. When adopted in the workplace, management will have a merciful approach in dealing with the employees, which will improve their satisfaction and their productivity. Meanwhile, God-fearing employees will be worried about wasting the resources of their employers and will improve their efficiency and productivity.

Religion plays a great role in dealing with anxiety and depression. The statistics available to the public show a decrease in the rate of depression and increased happiness in religious communities. Meanwhile, I am going to agree with you that the people in charge of the religious institutions are essentially corrupt.

Authentic Happiness, a web site connected to the University of Pennsylvania, focuses on modern observations of the relationship between having faith or being religious, and how people rate themselves on the scale of happiness. The data are available to the public on their website and in their book by the same name.

When the story of our life ends with death, it will make the beginning of the story also not cheerful at all. What kind of life did we live? After all this running and struggling, the end of it is death! After the age of fifty, most of us come to an acceptance of this reality under the pressure of social programming over the years of our life. But how are you going to convince the ten- to sixteen-year-old patients, that at the dawn of their life, they have to accept death as the end of their story? Accepting death, the ultimate evil. How would you suggest to a sixteen-year-old human that his/her guaranteed fate waiting for him is illness, pain, mental and body disintegration? Then he/she is going to be turned into dust by using various techniques or buried in the ground. It is not surprising for me to see depression blooming in a social environment that denies life after death.

The Effect of Movies on Our Emotions

The average human being might see a movie a week. During this one to two hour spent watching a movie, we can see a whole drama downloaded into our brains. Many faces with fake facial expressions and fake emotions are interacting with our emotions. We are brought up from the time when we are babies to consider movies as an essential source of entertainment. Not frequently, the content of these movies may have considerable depth below the shallow act.

At a very early age, we start seeing people in movies with obvious signs of depression. It is common to see faces with despair and sadness, hear voices tinted with negative tones or even vulgarity. We observe conversations loaded with negative inner brain dialogues.

Action movies with ample violence are considered popular. Meanwhile, our brain is incapacitated from asking the question, why is this action taking place? Is it human nature to behave this way? But why? At the same time, our emotions are struggling to understand the fact that it is only a movie. Movies can give us the opportunity to experience depression even before we have experienced a realistic, negative situation in life that potentially makes us sad. We are mentally engaged with the characters of the movie: our social brain, the limbic system, the prefrontal cortex and the hypothalamus are trying to synchronize with the characters of the movie. We naturally try to react to their experience, and we try to give a hand to help the person out of their difficult situation. But we cannot do anything to help the person in trouble in the movie. We cannot jump into the screen.

The plot of the movie has to include difficult situations and humans experiencing agony and despair. The difficult situation that actors may endure could be the result of natural disasters, but in many movies, these horrible scenarios are created by other humans. This is going to establish the role of negative human interaction in our life. Often the movie has to bring on a character with unusual abilities to solve the situation, the hero of the movie. This is going to show our inability as a collective to solve this situation with negotiation and cooperation. A movie that is going to show humans as rational, empathic creatures dealing with the reality of life using common sense would be boring. We have to have a strong will to make movies that use real human skills to solve our problems.

The effect of movies on adults has already been studied by many psychology departments. They measure the subject's blood pressure and heart rate, take blood samples to measure stress hormones, and administer psych testing after the movie is finished. Meanwhile, we should remember that those adults have watched many movies in the past, and they might have had similar experiences in their own life, which is a buffering mechanism that ameliorates the effects of the movie on their emotions. But the effect of movies is way more profound in children who synchronize with the characters of the movies easily.

What applies to depression, also applies to fear and anxiety. Movies are telling us what a fearful situation is all about. This will prime a fear circuit in our brain even before we have a realistic experience with fear. Our facial expression will tune into those of the actors, and our emotions will go for the ride.

So why do we watch movies? Simply because we have a deep longing to meet others, and to be with other humans, even at home. We love to be surrounded by many supportive friends and relatives. We love to a have secure relationship with others. Our minds crave full synchronization with other's minds. Consider what a mother goes through to have a baby. She is willing to go through the process of pregnancy and delivery, so she can have a real secured friend for a long future.

Through the new media, human brains for the past one hundred years have been presented with extensive drama in extremely unusual ways as compared to the people who lived before the invention of the TV. In the past, fair portions of their thinking and feeling were extracted from their life events. Their minuscule media were formed by the people around them and they were missing the huge drama that we are surrounded by with the new media. They were missing the ability to walk a few steps and turn on the TV. Also, they were missing a huge amount of artificial light emanating from the advertisement adds when watching TV.

During Our Modern Time

The family unit is getting smaller, brothers and sisters live in different cities, old relatives are in nursing homes, and friendships are not fostered enough by society to be optimum. Materialism is taught in schools and more in universities. The materialistic views of the world are extending not only to our social environment but also to us as individuals. Colleges are siding with one metaphysical view which states that we are sacks of chemicals, not realizing that they are diving much deeper in the metaphysical world, like any religious institution. Other views endorsing the spiritual part of humanity is something of the past; it is not scientific. Even though we may agree superficially with this metaphysical concept, our inner feeling and dialogue are telling us that we are emotional spiritual beings and not bags of chemicals.

What is going to worsen the scenario of depression is when we try to fix the problem of the sad feeling by engaging in dysfunctional activities. For example, addictions to street drugs, alcohol, overeating or playing video games give us temporary relief, but these activities have serious consequences.

Living in modern times exposes us to endless possibilities of what we can do in life. Often, we are living an individualistic life, it is upon us to examine the world and our role in it. We try to make the right choices, socially and economically; success or failure is on us. When we are coached by our parents to do this or do that, or by the school, we may tend to see that as interference with our ability to choose for ourselves. But why do we feel that? Simply because software, you can call it "our possibilities and choices," was installed very early in our life, and our social and economic atmosphere has endorsed it. In this reality, when we are faced with failure, it is very hard for us to find help and support from our social surroundings. The economic prosperity of our time depends on individuals being able to invent, create and burn themselves out in hard work to make the change necessary for prosperity, which sounds okay. But it is way worse when we try to become rich quickly, by being clever, without putting the necessary efforts and by adopting less than idealistic means to acquire the wealth.

The necessity of prosperity on the overall human psychic might imply that having a job that would give shelter, food and basic transportation is not valuable enough, and it is unable to induce happiness and satisfaction.

Compare that to life before the industrial revolution, where our choices were limited and our family and the environment mandated societal rules. But these rules, we did not feel them as rules and nobody called them rules. When we live close to our relatives and friends, the sense of community gives us ease and comfort. The strong social fabric is capable of netting our arousal and reward systems one stitch at a time, using the needle of supportive human contact.

Despite the fact religious institutions have relied on corrupt people, religion is still a strong factor in forming a sense of community. It creates a heart for human values and psychological inspiration, as well as a resting station for our mind when needed. Émile Durkheim was a French sociologist who wrote the book *Suicide* exactly discussing this matter. In Émile's opinion, the disruption of the social fabric was the cause of the increased suicide rate. This disruption is the birthplace of depression, bipolar disorder and delinquent behavior. We don't have to invest billions of dollars in university research to look very hard for a genetic cause for depression and drug abuse. We do not need to dissect the brain and subject it to sophisticated studies for a problem that is clear to us like the sun in midday.

The wonderful productivity of the industrial revolution that is promising to rid humanity of its ailments of hunger, diseases, difficult manual work, and high cost of owning a shelter, brought with it the unintended concept of social liberation. But is there really such a thing as social liberation? Is a human being ever able to become free of all his/her social and environmental ties? Could we really find a nation where all of its citizens are philosophers and spiritual teachers immune are from the effect of society, or it is a new system replacing old ones?

Did the negative effects of the religious wars in the West lead religion to this inevitable destiny? Did treating humans who committed small or big crimes with extreme harshness, as following some religious custom, have led religion to this destiny? Voltaire, who lived right before the French Revolution, understood the importance of religion as the main fabric in any human society, but he was shocked at the inhumane practices of the judicial system in the name of God. The seemingly endless religious wars also fueled his writing to find a rational solution to save the social religious structure in Europe. He feared that the demise of religion would bring with it endless negative consequences like creating a society that has no center.

Elegantly, the modern philosophers of our time are trying hard to rely on other elements from our life, to find alternatives to the preindustrial social and religious structures, by introducing new elements like culture, art, sports, science and a sense of belonging to a nation. The latter may work during a time of war, but it cannot sustain itself during peace. They throw these factors on us as proposed working alternatives since going back to the preindustrial societal structure is close to impossible. But do they work?

We are left to individualistic choices, but is that by choice? How much of a choice do we have? The word choice sounds beautiful and humane, but how real is it? Maybe it should be replaced with mandatory options. How much of a choice do you have? If you are a child born in this age with very limited social resources and video games are around you as the main outlet for your social need, how much of a choice do you have in becoming addicted to these games?

Compare this scenario to the hunter-gatherer and small farming community, where life requires humans to do ample physical activity and seek help from close family and friends. And when we are facing difficulties during the day, the people around us are readily responsive to our needs and happy to give us help. The strong sense of community and the simplicity of living makes life easier. The day is spent on learning skills to deal with present life and not worrying about the future. Current observation says hunter-gatherers have the lowest percentage of depression.

Antidepressants to Replace the Role of a Sound Society

Friendships and connections with others help maintain a balance of serotonin, norepinephrine and dopamine production from the arousal center in the brain stem to numerous targets in the brain. Depression chemically seems to be connected to lack of healthy neurotransmitters levels in these target areas, caused by the lack of human support, and a miserable social environment.

The medications for depression, we call them SSRIs (serotonin selective reuptake inhibitors) and SNRIs (serotonin and norepinephrine reuptake inhibitors) are trying artificially to do what the environment has not done to the individuals. They are trying to increase the level of serotonin in the target area to a healthy level. The healthy level of these neurotransmitters should have been triggered by an interesting friendly social environment. Why should we be aroused chemically by medications to face an unfriendly world? Physicians feel great when these medications are helping patients by restoring their positive feelings and decreasing the impact of depression. But these medications often do not work at all or may not work better than a placebo.

The Role of Sedentary Lifestyle on Our Mood

Reasonable physical activity during work is less than what it used to be. Most neuroscientists consider physical activity during work an important factor in maintaining psychological as well as physical health. Meanwhile, many ads in the media are telling us that you should be sitting down in the casino playing with money or sitting down in a yacht where other people are serving us alcohol. If we are not doing that, we are missing a lot of fun. This concept is wrong, as proved by modern neuroscience. What makes us physically happy is engagement in social and physical activities, which boost the levels of dopamine, serotonin, endorphin and others in their main targets. Yes, you could be living a much simpler life, and be way happier than a rich person spending her/his days on a yacht.

Physical activity and manual work every day as part of the individual daily activities are a very healthy way of living, as long as it is not too harsh to the point of destroying our bodies. Jobs that require heavy weightlifting should employ ways to prevent back and joint injury by providing the necessary tools to the workers to help avoid these kinds of problems. Anyone who has a job requiring some physical activity should consider oneself lucky to have this opportunity, provided they love what they are doing. We should have enough rest after work and not resort to excessive eating or consumption of alcohol to console our tortured ego because we are not rich.

During work, we have the opportunity to make decisions and act. When we have a built-in desire to be wise in every little step we take, we will have a sense of satisfaction, and a little boost to the reward system. It is healthy to take tiny mental breaks during work. This gives us a chance to choose a wiser option before taking the next step and will improve the quality of our work as well as give us a sense of satisfaction. Our ability to offer ourselves the idea of choosing the wise and ethical next step at work will induce enthusiasm and happiness. Work by itself becomes a form of meditation. Humans need to be conditioned the right way from the time they are young to love and respect manual work and physical activity. It is not healthy for us to go to work and wish that we are somewhere else; neither is it healthy to limit our physical activity to sport participation.

Many of us feel the reward of physical activity on our psychology by going to work-out places, especially when we have jobs that do not give us the necessary level of activity we need. And this is a good way to supplement our life with a healthy dose of activity.

But Why Does Exercise Have This Effect on Us?

It is connected to the arousal system. Physical activity simply requires the arousal system to be firing aggressively from the brain stem to boost the production of dopamine, serotonin, norepinephrine, acetylcholine and others. The hypothalamus becomes engaged in regulating the temperature of the body, the glucose, and the blood pressure, instead of responding to sadness and depression signals that are coming from the malfunctioning limbic system.

The hippocampus is working on telling us how to move and navigate, the neocortex is working on solving mechanical problems, not trying to figure out our social problems. The autonomous nervous system is working with the hypothalamus on helping our muscles by working, regulating sweating and body temperature, and adjusting the heart rate. This is much better than having an elevated heart rate and blood pressure from anxiety.

I try to explain this concept to my patients. I ask them to clean the house with their parents, help with physical work around the house and engage with moderate sport activity for fun, not for secondary goals like becoming a millionaire.

Exercise is not limited to physical exercise; mental exercise is an essential element in dealing with depression. I would suggest trying to memorize one page every single day by heart. Pick a favorite book or topic, read one page one time, then try to recite it with your eyes closed. The effect of that is similar to an antidepressant pill but without the side effect. Mental and physical exercise can include other activities like, art, crafts, gardening and farming.

Helping others with their difficulties in life is a good way to help ourselves. Community service and volunteering are very good ways to connect with others and help them. This will bring great psychological rewards to people who are involved in them.

The Sunflower Seed

Did you eat sunflower seeds in the past? What does that have to do with this subject? It is a little different in this leisure activity between the past and the present. Today, sunflower seeds are available, peeled, and ready to be eaten. In the past, you had to spend a little bit of time and effort to open the shell and eat the core. This little bit of effort is important for two reasons: first, it regulates our eating, so we do not consume a lot within a brief time. Second, it regulates the effort and the reward. The idea of the effort first then the reward to follow, is an essential building block for integrated systems that will consider the brain as a whole. Work then reward is much better than an easy reward. The latter will not prime the brain to receive the reward.

When survival needs work and effort, it means that survival is precious. It is something we strive for and we happily put the necessary efforts to provide for ourselves. The structures of society have to offer children these ideas from the early phase of their ability to make sense of the world around them.

STOP 4

ANXIETY

Anxiety in its medical meaning is an uncomfortable feeling that comes from thinking about events that will happen or might happen in the future, and when this feeling becomes excessive while trying to contain a large area of human thinking it becomes GED or generalized anxiety disorder.

Many philosophers examined the concept of anxiety for ages, and many consider some degree of fear and anxiety to be a normal human condition, a behavior necessary for life to move on, and for people to go to work and function.

Minor degree of anxiety may be the engine for mechanical life. It has a purpose for all ages. The fear that the child has about their mother finding out that they did something wrong may prevent them from engaging in unapproved behavior. Another example of healthy fear is slowing down for a pedestrian crossing the road to create a safer passage for them, even though the drivers could be driving at a safe distance from the pedestrian and knowing they do not have to slow down.

Fear is a word that is hard to define without using a whole bunch of other words! However, we understand what fear means and its impact on our lives.

We learn from experience when we are very young not to touch a hot teacup until it is cool enough, and when we face a more serious situation in the future, like being in a burning house, our conditioning will order us to leave the house as soon as possible. We make many decisions based on being rational agents, who learn from experience and understand the consequences of not avoiding dangerous situations. When harmful scenarios are threatening our life, the process of our mental assessment will merge with the feeling of fear and we become shaken by the situation. The feeling of fear and anxiety may mix with or replace the rational decision-making process. Our movements become fast and reactionary. We will have tremendous amounts of energy that will give us the necessary speed to try to save ourselves and possibly save others trapped in a burning house. In most hectic situations, we find ourselves using both of these mental structures: the higher or rational mental structure and the lower or reactionary mental structure.

The higher mental structure requires us to be rational and calculating while the lower mental structure is reactionary, requiring us to react quickly. Both states help us achieve safer outcomes. As you can see, we need a balance between the two. When the situation is not urgent, there is no benefit from being reactionary, as our actions will lack prudence and accuracy, and we will be living in a chaotic state for no reason. You can see that the decision of which mental structure we take at one point, is based on our feeling. This is how anxiety and unnecessary fear are able influence our lives to the point of making it dysfunctional.

In the ideal situation, while we are going to work in the morning and engaging in our daily tasks, the overall experience should be enriching. It should involve encountering new situations to learn from and engaging in activities that keep our minds fresh, and we should end the day with a pleasant feeling overall.

Our daily tasks often include providing services to others, which is one of the many drives that keep us advancing in life. However, unfortunate accidents and human error can happen, which will disrupt the heavenly ideal environment that we strive to create. When faced with serious problems leading to bad outcomes, we struggle to make sense of our functions and existence in society and life in general. We try to reach our cognition for help, but often we do not get satisfying answers. A vulnerable segment of humanity that is not able to reconcile with the flow of life along with its difficulties and mishaps becomes victims of anxiety.

Children often learn about difficult life circumstances and bad outcomes from observing their immediate family members and relatives. When a negative environment persists, it will increase their chances of having a negative outlook in general. When parents demonstrate to their children that difficulties in life are a common phenomenon, and a resolution to the problem will inevitably occur, they will have a better understanding of how life works and will have a more positive outlook on life.

Some of us who have anxiety as we age and acquire experience will start to adopt better mental tools to deal with our painful feelings. Negative events in life become less serious, and slowly we find ourselves mastering our feelings and worries and accepting living a life that is essentially not ideal. Slowly our skills in controlling our anxiety will sharpen, and we find ourselves living in peace. This scenario applies to a large portion of humanity.

In neuroscience, anxiety has been extensively studied in animals and humans. The basic idea of studying fear in an animal is through conditioning. Since mice are incapable of volunteering and telling us about their worries, we condition them, such as allowing a stimulus, like a sound, followed by a mild electric shock, which I hope is mild and not painful. Then we study their behavior when they are exposed to this stimulus in the future.

As we are conditioning these animals by an external simple obvious stimulus, they respond to the pain, which becomes a feared expectation. Humans are conditioned in the same way to acquire fear and anxiety! So, what is the difference between us and other animals? If you want to take the example I just mentioned, you would see no difference. Animals and humans can be conditioned in the same way. Nevertheless, what separates us is the presence of our large neocortex, which is a massive machine that can create extensive thinking, imagination, and prediction. This will influence us to live for a future, which will make us worry about its possibilities. This massive machine can take us into imaginary scenarios and bring to our attention stories and events that could have negative outcomes in our life. Unfortunately a few negative events, occurring early in life in vulnerable humans, may prime this path to be paved and strengthened. This conditioning is going to be worse when the occurrence of these negative events becomes frequent.

The limbic system will dive into those scenarios influenced by the power of imagination. When we focus on examining these potential negative events, a state of worry and negative expectations is created.

We may have genes in our genetic systems that prime us to become anxious and worry about future events that could be unpleasant. This may lead us to prepare a plan to deal with those events to turn the outcome to a safer one. This seems to be a reasonable approach to life. However, trying to tweak every event to produce a safe outcome is not always in our control, no matter how calculating we may try to be. This will make us shy away from taking chances in life and adopt a conservative approach to dealing with our choices. The latter will affect our potentials negatively and may create sad feelings.

Life events and circumstances tend to activate anxiety genes, and negative events specify what we fear. Excessive occurrences of negative circumstances and their gradual domination of these thoughts often lead to GAD, or generalized anxiety disorder, which will turn life into a constant worry.

The new social structure that we live in provides endless choices for every step in life, pushing our neocortex into a thinking frenzy if we consider two things: choice and outcome.

Anxiety is not much different from depression, in regard to the environmental contribution to these entities. However, the human reaction to these environmental events is different, whether we are going to have anxiety, depression, both, or none. Figure 4.2 is an attempt to summarize the environmental factors that would prime us for anxiety.

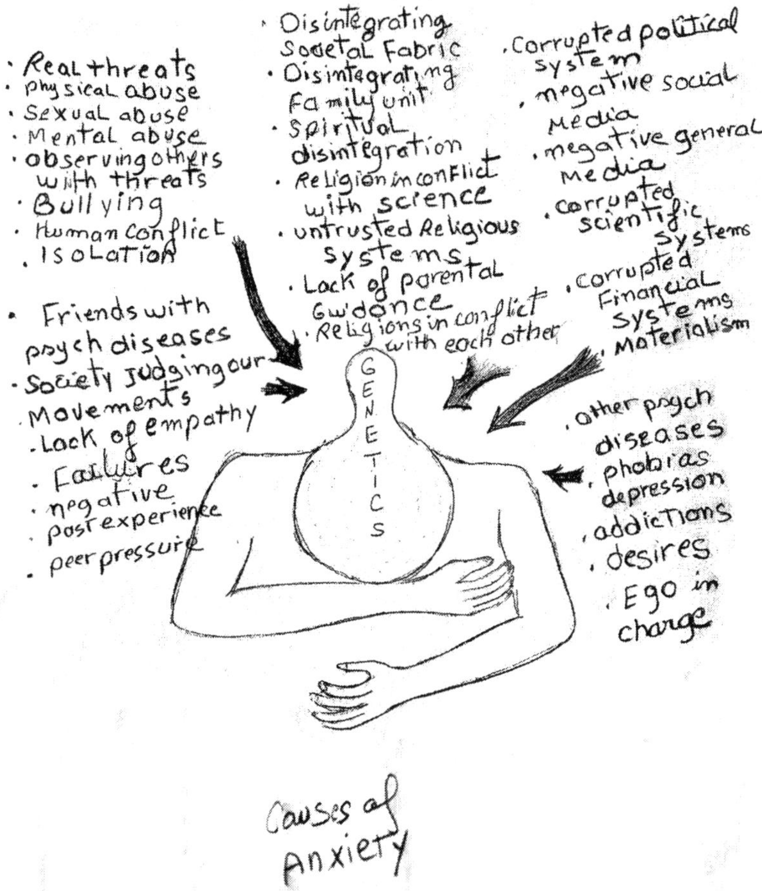

Anxiety in a Hunter-Gatherer Society

Difficulties and suffering are an expected part of life no matter how ideal the social environment is and these often are called stressors. Trying to shield children and ourselves from those stressors is impossible. Let us look at people living a hunter-gatherer life in the jungles. From our viewpoint, and the viewpoint of people living in larger cities in developed or developing countries, life is full of many reasons to be anxious, fearful, and worried about our safety. We are living in a developed world with all of its materialistic facilities and safe environments, but the reality is that the people living in a hunter-gatherer community have a much lower level of anxiety. Look at their facial expressions while they are hunting, as we can see in numerous TV documentaries, and try to interpret their moods and feelings. Amazingly, they are relaxed. So why is that?

The stress of living in the jungle is mitigated again, as we discussed in depression, by the stable social connections that they have. The stability in the social structure, composed of their immediate and extended family, as well as their friends, plays a major factor in adopting this relaxed mental state. They lack numerous complicated social contradictions in their daily activities, like going to school to seek learning only to find yourself being bullied, as an example. So, the real stressors in life are mainly related to humans interacting with each other. This fact will bring us good news and bad news: good news because we can do something about it and bad news because we have not figured out how to do that yet. Why are we so slow? As humans, and with a variety of cultures, why are we not waking up to this fact?

In primitive cultures, people spend the day working to gather food, fix their shelter, take care of the sick, and may have some time for entertainment or ritualistic activities. These functions make simple sense. This lifestyle not only gives an advantage for the people of these cultures concerning psychological health but also for their physical health.

They have feelings that are part of nature; they are not living in some social and mental artificial structures as we do in our time. I look at the children's faces when I see them in my clinic, and I can imagine what is going on in the child's mind. The child is asking questions. For example, is my family stable or not? Am I spending next weekend with my mother or my father? Am I going to see my relatives or not? Why did my friend commit suicide? Why are the people around me fighting all the time? Are we heading toward destructive global warming?

Similar questions cross the mind of adults, such as are the politicians we are electing honest or not? Is the car I am buying in good condition? Is my choice for college a good decision? What neighborhood should I be living in? Is my job stable? What school should my children attend? Am I making enough money to save for my retirement? Should I file for divorce? For us, to adopt to this thinking, it is produced mainly from living in an environment that is soaked in these ideas.

Movies Influence the Fear Circuits in Our Brains

Now let us suppose that we come to a primitive tribe in the Amazon of South America and ask them to put a TV in their main staying area showing movies filled with horror and violence, and have them watch these on a regular basis. Imagine the tiny, slow impact of the horror movies over months and years on the new generation growing in that village or tribe. As we discussed in the section on depression, the viewer's emotions will be synchronized with the character's emotions and feelings as expressed by facial expressions and body language.

This artificial fear activates no useful reasons other than grabbing the viewer's attention to spur emotions. For vulnerable young patients, the frequent watching of movies with hectic situations, horror scenes, and gruesome outcomes will establish circuits for fear and anxiety.

Crimes of many varieties are clogging the TV stations and the movie industry. The majority are showing human beings behaving for one purpose in life; it is to act on their bizarre impulses! They are willing to lie, steal, and kill, almost like unconscious zombies with contagious traits. They are trying to spread these traits across the screen to viewers without physically biting them.

Factors Contributing to Anxiety

We can mention many factors that contribute to anxiety. Some examples range from frequent events in life with a poor outcome, a critical social environment, bullying, poor social connections, abusive parents and relatives, unrealistic school demands, watching others with difficult experiences and poor outcomes, having friends with anxiety and depression, living in a single-parent home with difficult finances, political conflict, and negative peer pressure. The examples provided are just a few reasons people may have anxiety.

A materialistic dominant view with incoherent social structures could prime its members for the confusion. This confusion is created by dual views that we find ourselves born in. On one hand, we have spiritual and social needs that are unable to be met because of corrupt religious institutions and broken family structures, while on the other hand, we are told that we are just matter, just another form of primates.

The Outcome of Those Factors

The state of hypervigilance and hypersensitivity to potential threats will prime us to interpret regular events as harmful. This will affect our adaptation to changes and keep us worrying about the negative outcomes. We feel more comfortable in adopting defensive behavior; meanwhile, our actions will lack the skills to deal with difficulties and real problems when they arrive. Our blunted empathy is a result of poor interactions with other humans. This will make it difficult to attract supportive social surroundings. When our worries are numerous and intruding into the majority of our activities, the diagnosis of generalized anxiety or GAD will apply.

Based on this shaken foundation, our neocortex tries to build a mental construction, describing many life events as potentially threatening. With time, the number of these events becomes larger. This construction will result in creating more feelings that are painful, meaning we will avoid engaging in a variety of life activities and isolation becomes comforting.

Avoiding triggering situations when the phobia is limited, not generalized, is a very common strategy that we take. We try to avoid situations that trigger our fears. For example, people with social phobia may not want to go to school and want to be homeschooled instead.

Sometimes these phobias cannot be avoided, and we find ourselves forced to face threatening situations, which can be the way to a break out of this mental stagnation and have a different approach to dealing with life. This is also a therapeutic technique used by psychotherapists. However, in severe but less common cases, we find ourselves unable to do anything other than endure the same suffering and painful feelings. The amount of wise social support we have from our immediate social network, and empathic attitude from the overall society, might help us mature out of this state of persisting anxiety. Unfortunately, good supportive homes are a rarity these days—how saddening.

What is going on inside the brain? as we discussed in other chapters, the amygdala, which is the first emotional station in the brain, is scanning every single input for any significance. It has been programmed from the time of our infancy. When negative life events bombard our life without being neutralized by wise parents and supportive friends and relatives, these events are going to enter the world of the amygdala and try to do the following:

1. Sharpen our senses to do a further examination of our environment to gather more clues about the threatening situation,
2. Send signals to the cortex, mainly the frontal cortex, along with the executive center of the brain, asking for a further focus on the problems related to anxiety, which will draw further resources from the neighboring centers into neurocircuits dealing with anxiety. The prefrontal cortex, after consulting with the neocortex and the rest of the limbic system, will try to control the amygdala and reprogram it. The result of this power struggle will shape the degree of anxiety.
3. The amygdala becomes resistant to the down regulations coming from the prefrontal cortex, and this paralyzes our ability to have a really wise view of our life, which will help us experience pleasure and relieve us from stress.
4. The amygdala will have other parts of the limbic system working with it; the hippocampus will register memories that are related to the negative events instead of serving the brain with short-term memory and mapping the environment. In addition, it will push the cingulate gyrate, the insula and the stria terminalis, or the

extended amygdala, to work with the amygdala in evaluating the threats so that we become socially disengaged, our empathy may decline, and we become introverted in a malfunctioning way.

5. The amygdala influences the autonomic nervous system via connection with sympathetic centers in the hypothalamus, triggering somatic symptoms like a fast heart rate, sweating, near syncopal events, and panic attacks.
6. The amygdala connects the endocrine-controlling nodes in the hypothalamus allowing the release of the adrenocorticotropic hormone (ACTH), which increases the release of cortisol, the stress hormone, from the adrenal gland. In severe cases of anxiety, the entire organism to face this hormonal stress, leading to negative medical consequences.

Figure 4.4 is an attempt to describe the malfunction that involves the prefrontal cortex, the anterior cingulate gyrate and the insula. This figure shows the normal function of these centers, and the change that occurs when anxiety is established. You can see the normal function of these centers before the arrows, then the pathologic function after the arrows.

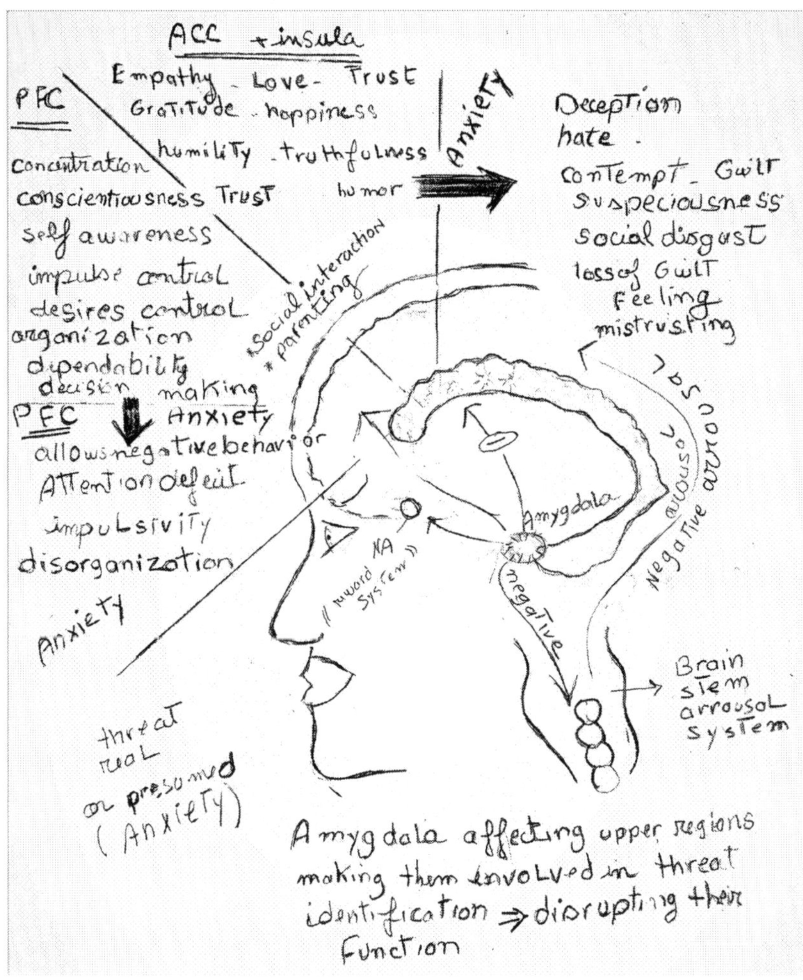

Why is the amygdala able to process this threatening information as a threatening situation? Why is the amygdala functioning as a brain by itself? How is the amygdala assisting in the fight or flight response when we are faced with a threat? Modern views seem to rely on the idea that neuroscience is in its infancy now, and the future is going to tell us how, yet I feel that this is only wishful thinking!

We feel the amygdala's function, when fear storms our minds when we see a child crossing the street and a fast moving car is approaching him/her. We should ask ourselves the question: How are we feeling this function of the amygdala? Why would the chemical function taking place inside the cells in the amygdala be translated to feelings? How is this small almond-shaped collections of nodes able to have the memory over the years of our life concerning the emotional importance of the events in our life, and the thoughts of our neocortex?

This gives an idea about the computing power inside the cells of this center, which is tremendously vast and also gives an idea about the coordination between these cells. Could our mind imagine this coordination to be just a simple domino chemical reaction that constructed itself through trials and errors? Even if we believe that this amazing miracle took place, this is not going to solve the problem of who is experiencing the feeling.

The word consciousness, in reality, is a mental construct and an abstract concept created to replace the word I. So when philosophers working on the theory of mind say there is no such thing as consciousness, they are really politely stating that there is no such thing as me or you.

If you'd like to take the materialistic view that the entire brain function is based on matter, you have my guaranteed respect and acceptance of your position. I see the rationale behind your views and where you come from, and I want to ask you to do the same: see my rationale in taking a different position.

Why are the cells of the amygdala doing this function and not those cells in another part of the brain? As neuroscience tells us, the brain networks are all interconnected. Maybe the amygdala has a unique connection with the hypothalamus where many of the feelings are cooking. This again shows the importance of the hypothalamus as the center of our psychological function, and the end of many neurological signals coming from the limbic system.

Dealing with the Problem of Anxiety

Modern psychotherapy offers different techniques to deal with these problems. You can read many psychology books talking about these techniques, but unfortunately, every time I send a patient to a psychiatric clinic, she/he comes back with a prescription of medication for anxiety and depression. It is very frustrating to see that behavioral psychotherapy to be extremely underutilized. However, the newest techniques comprise psychotherapy in conjunction with a very short course of medication to disrupt the memory of the negative events of our past, while these memories are due for updating. When the event is retrieved during the psychotherapy session, a burst of medication is administered. This will cause this event to lose its emotional impact on the patient when it is recalled in the future. This is promising, especially in patients with post-traumatic stress disorder (PTSD).

Many scientific papers published by neuroscientists from major universities in the United States describe successful studies in dealing with anxiety and PTSD that have no real application in the world of medicine. Maybe this is happening because there are not enough qualified therapists and psychiatrists. Their number is no match compared to the growing number of patients with psychiatric illnesses, and psychotherapy becomes impossible to be used.

From what I see, psychotherapists are working as psychiatrist's assistants. They are collecting information when interviewing the patients, then presenting them to the psychiatrists to secure a diagnosis. After that, treatment with a pharmacological agent is started.

While dealing with anxiety and depression, it makes sense to apply what psychologists call cognitive therapy when the situations are appropriate, and the patient has an interest in understanding the mechanics of anxiety. It might be helpful for some patients to explain how psychological and environmental factors play a role in priming us to become anxious. Some patients may benefit from understanding the basic brain functions related to anxiety. Having the patients read books related to the subjects may enable them to take a different approach to view the big picture of their emotional state and have a bird's eye view of the self.

Creative imaginations, for very motivated patients, are a form of self-psychotherapy. Patients who have no access to modern psychotherapy are directed and guided by their physicians to use this creative imagination. In addition, it could be helpful in patients who do not respond to medication or simply have side effects to medications.

Imagine the conditioning situations arriving and reenact the reaction as if you are encountering the real situation. In this case, the reaction is taking place in a conscious state; it is starting in the neocortex and prefrontal cortex instead of the emotional semi-subconscious state of the amygdala. With dedicated training, the patients can create a different imaginary scenario to how they are responding to what is considered an anxiety-triggering situation. With time and persistence, the training would allow the prefrontal cortex to administer down regulatory effects on the amygdala, where the anxiety feelings are starting.

Neuroplasticity can change the programming of the cells of the amygdala. An example would be a patient with agoraphobia who has a problem with being in a crowd can imagine that she/he is in a crowded place with no escape in sight, and then the patient can imagine that she/he feels very calm and is actually calming others who are trapped! If the heart starts beating fast with this exercise, they need to accept that reaction to be just fine and normal. Acceptance is a tool, which is finding its way to mainstream medicine, to improve the outcome for patients with chronic medical and psychiatric illnesses.

Moreover, for students who are subject to bullying in school, with the help of parents, gradual rehearsal of the situation at home over several weeks with a gentle gradual decline in the anxiety response to bullying, would strengthen this skill and lead to a tolerance to bullying. This should be done in conjunction with counseling the child on how he/she can better their communication and social skills. After all, the bully is a tortured soul living in agony and his/her society was not able to help him/her. This can only be done with older students and motivated parents, who agree that this approach is reasonable.

A spiritual approach to psychotherapy can develop patience and tolerance of the difficulties that we face in life while trying not to make a big deal out of them. Looking at the self as a spirit, all other situations, whether they are thoughts in the mind or materials for the senses, are in absolute transient nature and none of that is lasting. This will allow us to take things with lightheartedness, no matter how big or small they are. This will help in changing the entire social center in the brain even when the environment does not change.

We can only dream that the world is changing by everyone becoming friendly. We are treating each other with forgiveness, patience, and tolerance. We can hope that society has something else to worship other than money, power, and prestige. Could the media realize the error that was done in the past decades and take serious steps to fix the problem? Solutions are not going to come from friendly promises, such as when Hollywood responded to President Clinton, after one school shooting, to decrease the violence in their movies. In addition, of course, you can always pray for the religious figures in the world to do their main job in society, which is to counsel the rest of us with our life difficulties, promote the highest ethical standards in our behavior, like charity, empathy, modesty, spirituality, and encourage prayer and meditation. Why can they not be a living example of tolerating the differences between religions and focus on the common parts, which is the essence of every religion? Moreover, we can hope that religious institutions end their competition with politicians for power and fat bank accounts. Why can they not take their hands out of people's pockets? In addition, we wish that they distance themselves from all philosophical controversies.

STOP 5

PEER INTERACTION

The modes of creating bonds with other human beings are immensely vast when compared to other species. We not only make lasting friendships with other humans in our surroundings but also with humans who live in other parts of the world. We can appreciate friendship among animals in a very vast spectrum. The interaction between ants represents an amazing miraculous survival skill, which will assign very delicate functional roles to each member, and without it their existence becomes impossible. In a colony of birds, despite the quarrel and the competition for resources, these birds would not think about leaving their colony and nest somewhere else, because they know that is not in their best interest. But an eagle does not have to do this and may be content living a solitary life. A female deer finds security and comfort in living among a group of females, and males do the same. They live in groups, showing obvious traits of friendship, which help them find food and shelter. This situation will change during the mating season. Fighting for the right to mate with all the females becomes the main mode of interaction between males until the mating season is over. It is the system that will assure the survival of the species. In wolves a lone wolf is a dead one; this motivates wolves to live in extended families.

During childhood and teenage years, we strive for acceptance from our peers and share the same activities, values, and thoughts. We have an innate desire to gain acceptance from the social surrounding that we belong to or the social environment that we desire to belong to.

This need is way more powerful during this stage of our life and it manifests itself through hard-wired brain circuits connected to the reward system, pulling us towards the world of social life.

Positive interactions with other humans foster this desire. Fitting into groups, especially with our peers, seems to be a reasonable approach to this interaction during our childhood, as we are still exploring the world around us and trying to mature.

Successful interactions with others promise to fulfill another natural emotion, which is becoming independent from our parents for our survival. As we can see, their support of us is going to end at some point in the future. Recognizing the importance of our parents in our life, we give them special status in our wide social circle of relatives and friends.

Belonging gives us a sense of security and assurance about our ability to have the necessary qualifications, to be able to fit into our social surroundings. Interactions with others in some situations may put pressure on us to change our behavior to imitate the behavior of our friends. This phenomenon is called peer pressure.

The desire to have friends extends its influence into the rest of our life, but the root of this desire grows during childhood. We are always looking for groups of humans outside our home and immediate family environment to interact with and form social bonds. This is a necessary state for us as children to give assurance that we are going to be all right when we are maturing and becoming adults and will be able to make social decisions on our own. Our friends, initially, are other children whom we meet first; they are usually relatives or neighbors. We accept them as they are, considering the simplicity of emotional life during this stage. These successful interactions leave a lasting impression on our memory.

When we are older with wider experiences and interactions with others, we learn from our past experiences, especially the negative ones if we have any, and we become more careful in choosing friends and adopting other people's views and ideas. As we age and screen people carefully, we become more or less forgiving of other people's mistakes and mishaps compared to how we acted when we were children. The fine-tuning of this matter could be an individualistic result of how the limbic system is maturing.

Interaction with peers brings synchronization between different brains and this induces pleasure. This leads to a strong desire to have a social life. The synchronization in children with their peers allows them to experiment with a smaller version of adult life. Meeting other children allows us to talk about our current daily affairs and our dreams, and to test our abilities to function in variable social situations. These experiences allow us to break away from our parents and close relatives temporarily, and experience our social life independently. This process is usually smooth and simple and does not challenge any of our innate normativity, but sometimes it is not, and in that case, it becomes a pressure.

Is it innate for some of us to deny our parents' path to our mind and give a free pass to our friends to download whatever ideas they have into our mind? Does social programming have some say as to what extent we should listen to our friends versus our older relatives? The structure of our social environment plays a role in the outcome of this interaction. Dysfunctional interaction with our parents may tilt the scale toward the following advice from the world outside our homes. For example, when parents are harsh in dealing with their children, when a mother has depression, anxiety or drug addiction, or a father has narcissistic personality disorder with anger problems. These negative elements in our social environment are going to influence our limbic system and steer our emotions toward relying on other humans for psychological support.

When we feel we have to change something in us to fit in, often we are willing to make the change happily especially when it is easy and acceptable to our normativity. But when there are barriers in the face of this change, we might become distressed. In modern societies parents often give in to their children's requests when they are related to peer pressure because, naturally, parents want to relieve their children's distress. Examples include buying only certain brands of clothes, even though parents think that this request is not rational. But they do that knowing that the child is going through a stage and she/he is going to grow out of it.

The Idea of Friendship

We have a powerful desire which occupies the limbic system in regard to interacting with others. This desire is hard-wired in most of us. We enjoy being surrounded and accepted by other people. Forming friendships goes beyond the simple pleasure coming from synchronization with other humans. This connection with our peers must form a strong, lasting bond, resulting in being able to give reliable support to each other.

Figure 5.2 is an attempt to describe the need for synchronization between our social centers in the limbic system and other people's social centers.

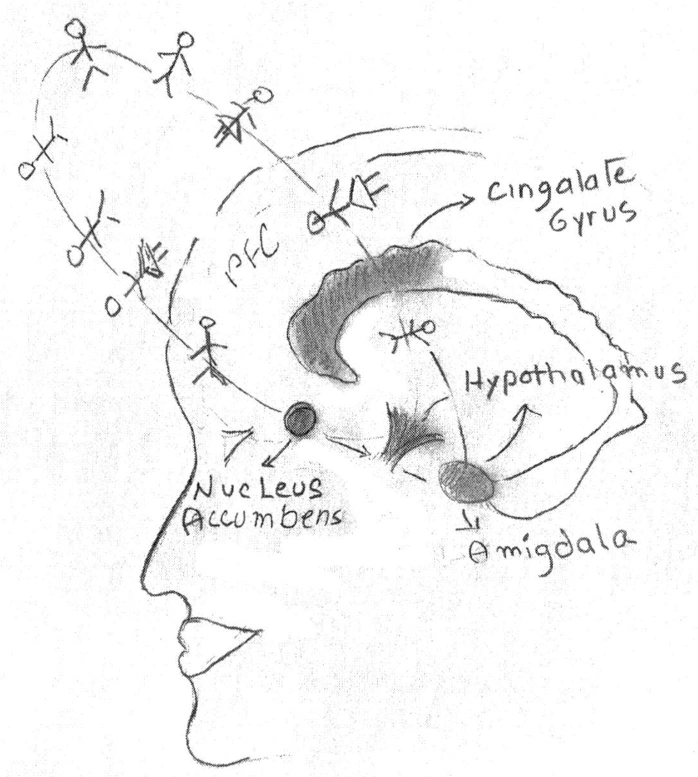

This desire for social acceptance becomes too powerful to the point of almost becoming an addiction, which will lead us to the point of anxiety when we are deprived of it. This acceptance also might give us the idea that we have to change some of our convictions or habits to secure this priority. I see that often in pre-teen children in my practice who are distressed because of a problem that occurred in their relationship with a close friend. Often, they want this friend for themselves and want this friend to behave in a way that aligns with their wishes.

Peer pressure is experienced more subtly in hunter-gatherer societies. In that model, humans are connected socially to goal-oriented activities related to life's needs. Social activity is well controlled by the larger social structure of the community. The existence of the powerful instinct to survive makes the idea of having a serious conflict with our social surroundings hard to take place, and peer pressure is hardly any pressure at all.

Our brain is wired to have us form friendly relations with our peers as well as our parents and relatives. We appreciate the difference in the mechanics between these relationships, and usually, they do not compete with each other.

In fast-moving, changing societies, similar to what is happening in our time, we easily can see differences in values from one generation to another. This has prepared the ground for the birth of the concept of peer pressure in the modern sense.

This, in turn, has changed the rule which governs the traditional model of bonding with our parents, other family members, and neighbors. In this current time, we pivot toward fast-changing circumstances with new rules and adopt these new rules continuously. This makes the possibility of a social clash between the new generation and older ones more likely to occur even in remote communities, which may seem far from the center of the industrial world.

The Adolescent Stage

I tend to feel that this is an artificial stage in our life created by the newly formed social and economic structures of the past two hundred to three hundred years, starting in the west then moving to the rest of the globe. It is a stage mandated by the new society mechanics, which will give us, when we become adults, bigger inner baggage of struggle related to memories. This stage mandates that we should be in school for many years after reaching puberty and we should be focusing on studying for a long period of time. For some of us, it is a great stage in our life. We may see it as fascinating and enjoyable. We experience the pleasure of learning and interacting with other students, making friends, and preparing for a fruitful academic, scientific, or business future. But for some of us who have a problem with sitting down and focusing for many hours every day, this stage becomes a source of agony.

Some of us are better functioning when we are working with tools and moving around and have absolutely no interest in some of the mainstream school material that we have to study year after year. To add to that problem is the backward way of teaching, designed to discourage any critical thinking, and to deprive the material of its fascination and beauty. An example is how science is taught in schools and colleges. Students are guaranteed to forget ninety percent of the information a few days after a test is taken. Add to that the disaster from the exposure to drugs and bullying.

I can argue that in a simpler social structure, the adolescent stage is simpler and shorter. Young people become more responsible and mature faster, ready to form successful families at an earlier age. I always hear the argument that the frontal lobe takes twenty-five years of life to mature, as MRI studies show, but it is not uncommon to see a twenty-year-old fully mature human who is balanced in his/her decision-making process. Could an immature social environment delay the maturity of our frontal lobe? Consider the necessity to party and drink during spring break for example, which is created by society: could that make the frontal lobe less mature and take a whole twenty-five years to mature?

Media Influence on Peer Pressure in Modern Times

The content of any show we watch on TV is a subject that is created by humans whom we are not interacting with. The show is presented to us by actors. With this magic technology, the social influence of movies is immense. While we are watching any show, our limbic system is scanning the environment without our awareness and taking notes. It is registering for example what is fun and what is not. Our social needs are being created in the reward system and the inner cells of the limbic system. The nucleus accumbens, the hypothalamus the amygdala, the prefrontal cortex and the cingulate gyrus are being programmed to influence our social needs and create our norms.

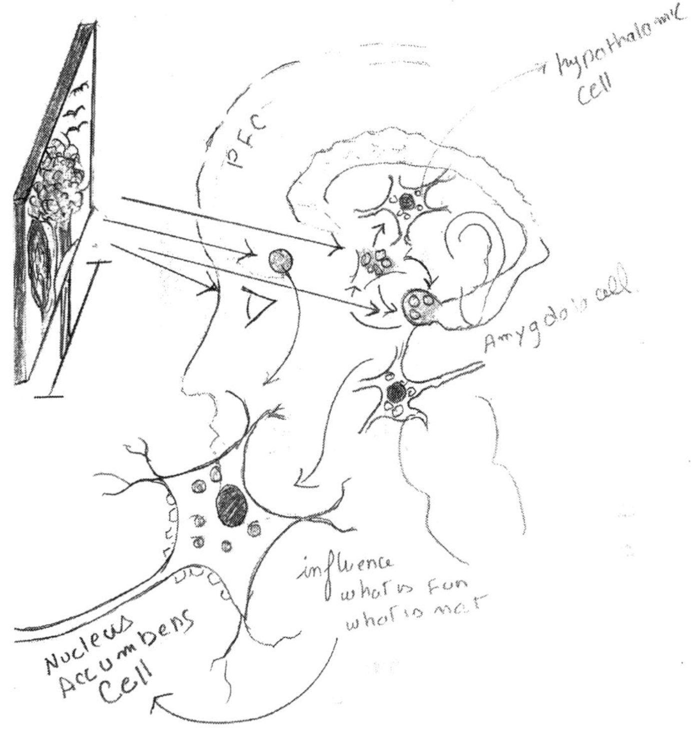

The media also elected to create movies for children, movies for adolescents, and movies for adults. This social programming prefers us to have a separation between people according to their ages, an idea that is accepted by the majority of us. But the potential outcome for that is a slow alienation of vulnerable children from their older relatives and parents. This in turn will strengthen our need to be accepted by our friends and peers in school.

Group Forming

Peer pressure may make us form small groups of people with strong bonds and commitments to each other. Sharing certain behaviors among the member of the group may become so powerful that it takes precedence over the need for our behavior to be in harmony with the overall society values. Many circumstances will contribute to the group forming we get involved in.

When paranoid thinking is associated with adopting victim identity, a group may rationalize antisocial behavior, as in the case of gangs. In this case, the group is adopting behavior, which is completely out of synchronization with the rest of society and often may involve antisocial activities. Sooner or later this group will face direct conflict with the larger society or with one another. This might escalate to violent activity inside the group, leading to unnecessary human suffering. In my practice, I saw one of my teenage patients come to me with a bullet still sitting in his chest after he was shot. The surgeons told the mother it was better not to remove this bullet at this point. I asked the patient what happened. His answer was, "I was with the wrong crowd."

Sometimes it is a lesson learned or loss of life is the result. In some cases, after the recovery, the patient may go back to join a similar group of individuals with similar antisocial values. This is due to the lack of other choices or alternatives. Alternatives should be structured by sound social institutions, confidant in finding rehab plans for individuals who were involved in these situations and able to put preventative measures in place. Religious and other social institutions should take the lead in teaching youth the highest ethical standards that would help them have functional lives. They must take full responsibility for dealing with and preventing these problems from taking place. But do they?

The prison system that we have currently offers no better solution to this problem. This system should also take responsibility for helping to fix this misery, by offering intense education for the prison inmates to achieve excellent rehabilitation. Prisoners should not be left as victims of a toxic environment that will give them no insight about how they can conduct their life after they are released.

I try to use this analogy on my patients, by saying you know that Earth is not all desert; we just have to keep walking and be persistent and the desert will end. Then we will see a different face of the planet Earth.

As we discussed earlier, in hunter-gatherer and traditional farming societies, there is not much difference in values between generations. The daily living activities are accommodating to maintain a balanced interaction between all the members of the social groups. While we are children, we all probably prefer to run and play with friends other than our parents. Our parents understand that preference and give us space to fulfill this need.

As you can imagine, if we happen to be living in small tribes, like in the case of a hunter-gather society, the tribe will be the main form of social and economic structure for us. Society is forming a group that must include people and relatives of various ages. The group is not too large, and it has clear objectives and values inherited from a powerful culture.

Physically harsh life demands food, safety and a place to live. Coordination, cooperation and harmony among the member of this society become essential elements for survival. Our daily needs as individuals are by themselves our survival needs. The hierarchical structures of society are maintained and observed as sacred structures with clear values. Often children have a role to play and work to do.

Yes, children still want to play with others living next door, and they want to behave in the manner they behave. But the variety and options to behave in different ways are limited, as are the toys and available activities. Peer pressure in the modern sense, for this group, is not much pressure.

Children are not going to leave the boundaries of their area if they think about leaving the tribe without protection. If they wander into the forest they will be eaten by a predator, or maybe kidnapped by a rival enemy tribe, if there is such a thing. Their natural environment sets clear boundaries. Their mind does not have to work very hard on making choices. The path is simple and clear.

At the end of the day, they have to sit down with close relatives to eat as they are really hungry at that point. Then, maybe after some unquestionable rituals, they go to sleep peacefully.

The New-Time Toys and the Old-Time Toys

Despite the fight to find our way around and the mini-drama that occurs during our early childhood while interacting with other children, we have the desire to have friends. You can see that desire in the eye of the child who is a little older than one year, forming gradually.

The normal interaction between children sharpens our social skills and improves our ability to smile, talk, play with others and be empathic. At this level of interaction, there is not much difference in comparing the hunter-gatherer model, with any other model.

When the child becomes older you start noticing a variety of activities related to the specific culture, like playing with toys for example. In primitive societies, toys are manufactured by an older relative or the children themselves, as these toys are very simple. Children have the opportunity to observe the way the toys are made and obtain experience in participating in this simple manufacturing. The pleasure is simple, without a thrill, but overall, it is satisfying.

In modern times, game activities are less connected to our immediate surroundings. Children play with toys created by other human minds, living far away from us. Take an example when we are playing video games: we are interacting with the minds that created these games but from a distance, without direct human interaction between the factory worker and the children. You can also see this in amusement parks. The excitement of the rides will suppress any question in our minds about the validity of these activities. The ride will take us, for a brief moment, out of our world, to a physical thrill, then brings us back down. The toys of modern times seem to add another alienating component to the life of children living in our modern times.

STOP 6

THE EGO

The definition of ego varies according to the situation and the circumstance that the word is used for, even though it is hard to give a clear definition. When you mention this word, no one is going to ask you, "What are you talking about?"

This word has been studied extensively for the past century by psychologists more than philosophers. Also, I see the word investigated by people who have an intense interest in the spiritual aspect of humanity.

This word is usually used to describe the self-enhancing side of the human being. This self tends to be distinguished from the spiritual self, which is referred to as a purely idealistic manifestation of the human psychological state. The latter is clear of negativity and does not need enhancement. Ego is a word used frequently with negative connotations. It could point to the weak structure of the self, and it is responding to the pressure of the materialistic and the negative social world. This world has a massive upper hand over us, mandating us to perform and enhance ourselves to fit well in an imaginary status in society. When the ego is fractured, it influences our deepest emotions to start work on serious repairs, so we can look for materialistic validation from the eyes of our peers and society, and ask them to give us an important status.

Often, what responds to and communicates with our egos are other people's egos. Egos sometimes are conversing, interacting, and making deals, and maybe making societies and even nations. Another side of the human being, is the spiritual. It is totally or partially absent, or dormant, forming the real universal dogmatic sleep that humanity is experiencing. Occasionally we wake up, to find that we have destroyed ourselves by denying the real side of who we are. But often we ignore this damage in a way that is similar to someone who has not slept for days. And when we have the opportunity to wake up we will choose to snooze and go back to sleep. When the alarm goes off the next time, we repeat the process, and on some occasions, we take a brief moment to ask, "How long have I been sleeping for and why am I so sleepy?" We realize we have been sleeping for a long time, then we will ask again, "Why am I so sleepy?"

The ego way of living is also a costly way of living. It can deprive us of possibly sleeping well at night and enjoying everyday activities. Our ability to appreciate the beauty in simplicity as we are looking at a flower becomes affected. Also, it deprives us of enjoying simple and rewarding human social interactions. This way of living interferes in sensing the presence of peace in our lives, and in our ability to accept the world without complicated thinking or being able to feel the world as a spiritual being. Our spiritual side can be present in every activity we do. When we talk, for example, our words have the potential of not just reflecting our self-enhancing mechanism but of reflecting the original source of who we are as a spirit or a soul.

Living as a spirit also entails declaring that conscientiousness is the main mode of interaction when dealing with people, as if God Almighty is sitting with us observing every single action we do. While we are interacting with other people, we are sensing the empathic presence from them, sensing the humane side of everyone around us, and expecting the best out of everyone. This will enhance our ability to make excuses for other people's mistakes and enjoy and appreciate all the work we do. It allows us to be grateful for the opportunity to have work, instead of protesting our compensation and looking for things to complain about.

The Ego and the Foundation of Our Thinking

The ego is occupying the regular state of our thinking but to different degrees. When this kind of addictive thinking takes hold of our mind, it undermines our potential and makes us less than what we could be, in regard to having clarity of mind and the sense of acceptance.

When the ego takes hold of all our thinking, it mutates our thinking into a negative social recording, repeating the same old story—the story of endless desires for more material and better social status. This way of thinking can also trigger us to complain about not achieving enough in life or about having bad luck. When these stories are running in the background of our thinking, they will not give us a chance to breathe peacefully.

To deal with it, we are approaching the world with a self-centered perspective. We try to work hard to achieve and elevate our status in the eyes of people around us, as well as our own eyes. We try to accumulate materials and enough money to give us a sense of gratification, not knowing that it is short-lasting.

The ego may play a different role for the people who did not succeed much in accumulating wealth and material. The ego may tell them that they are not as happy as the rich are. The reality is they do not know what is going on in the minds of the richer ones.

All of these activities prevent the hypothalamus and the endorphin system from having a balanced flow. Negative stories stress the hypothalamus and deprive it of sending the appropriate number of endorphins to the rest of the brain.

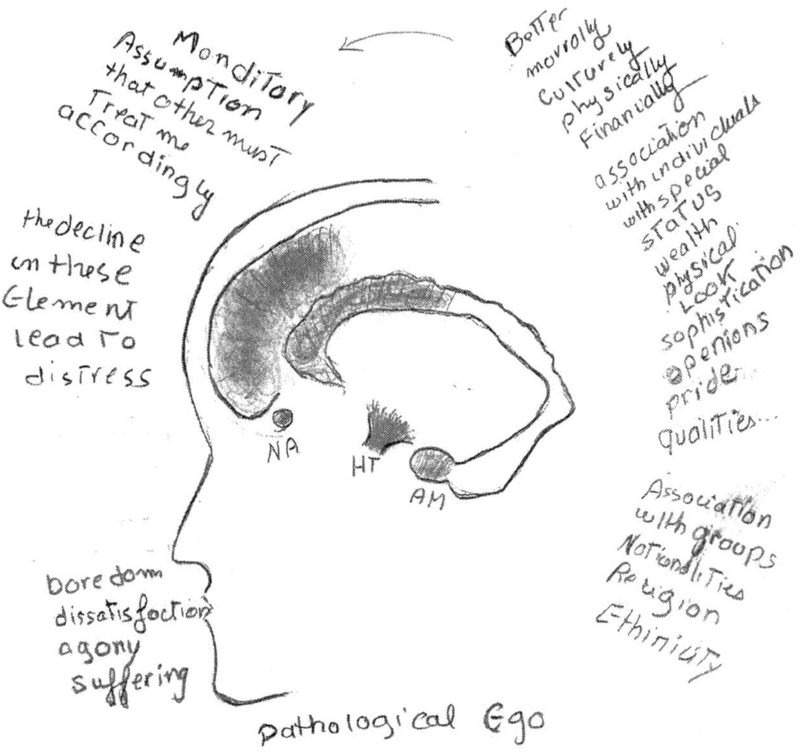

When our mind takes a break from all the social thinking, like when we are engaged in a functional activity like gardening, often we feel relaxed. We find great relief when working on a math equation if we happen to love this kind of work or studying other subjects of choice. A farmer who is reading about new methods of decreasing the use of fertilizer in his/her field and preserving the topsoil from undergoing further degradation is another example.

These functional activities release the mind from social thinking and from interacting with our ego or with other people's egos. But many of us fall victim to our egoistic mind, which tends to repeat these stories during our resting time, unfortunately endlessly.

The ego with its movies of thoughts was orchestrated in our minds over our past years. Initially, it is simple, a two-year-old child while interacting with others might cry about sharing his/her toys with other children. With time, to keep activating the reward system, the thoughts have to be more complex. Occasionally, when we are alleviating the unpleasant feeling coming from anxiety or depression, we give an easy path for the ego-centered thinking, not realizing that it will guide us deeper to more depression. Worse is when the ego-centered thinking has reprimanding or retaliatory elements toward others, fostering the negative feeling and making our lives more miserable.

Childhood Adverse Events

Many problems facing children contribute to shaping their egos. For example, children who are exposed to physical, emotional, sexual, and mental abuse in their homes will have resentment, and when they are exposed to the merciless techniques used to sell material, it will create in them a sense of need.

Sexual abuse is facilitated first by the disintegration of the family structure, which makes the children vulnerable and unsupervised or unprotected by their parents. Second, by the legal system being lenient toward the offenders, and leaving the internet a safe haven to expose children to sexual materials. Meanwhile, governments worldwide and the giant tech companies are not making any fuss about it. This practice is helping foster the next generation of sexual predators and victims.

Other Examples of Egoistic Thoughts

The need for more self-enhancement occupies a major section of our social brain. This will mandate us to adopt various techniques and these techniques are closely dependent on our various environmental elements. For example, the need to be powerful and able to dominate varies from time to time. Another pathological form of this thinking is the feeling of being threatened when an idea does not agree with our own.

The ego may create a need to have conflicts with others. It may lead us to believe other groups are conspiring against us. Here we can see the limitation of the word "we." It must have concrete boundaries, us versus them, and we cannot include them. "Them" on many occasions is translated by the ego-centered mind as "it." Daniel Goleman describes this idea in his book *Social Intelligence.* Treating others as "it" removes the human traits of others; we deny the fact that they have feelings and emotions like us.

We are better morally, culturally and physically, and these self-enhancing thoughts are trying to assure us of our ability to survive. The need for self-enhancement comes from these hidden doubts of our inability to deal with life events, and doubts about the role that society is assigning to us. We seek assurances from the whole world to calm this hidden view of ourselves as weak, incapable creatures.

These doubts are basically triggered by what we hear from people around us. Consider the words: competition and hardship. In our normal language, our unconscious mind takes the matter to heart without taking it easy or being conscious of the way our ego operates. We try to help these thoughts by being associated with friends or relatives with special statuses, like wealth, or by being proud of our physical qualities: beauty, knowledge, or being unique. We try to acquire sophistication, smart opinions, good financial status, or to belong to a special social or ethnic group, certain nationality or religion. Often the main religion we practice is a universal religion called hypocrisy. The latter practice was established by the mutation of the places of worship into theaters, with actors playing characters who perform to inflate our egos even further.

When our self-image is dependent on being wealthy, then any threat to that wealth may lead us to serious discomfort and a feeling of loss of identity. Adopting this way of thinking will make it easy for us to go through suffering and agitation when things do not go our way. Peace does not find its way to our hearts easily. We are busy with being upset when we do not get our way. After getting our way and becoming this unique person, boredom soon takes over the menu of our thoughts, and the initial excitement will evaporate.

Another ego-made ailment is the habit of judging other people's behavior. This serves as a self-enhancing process. It proves that our opinion is the right one in our eyes and the eyes of others.

From reading all of the above, you will conclude that the word "ego" is associated with negativity. Could this be questioned? Why would self-enhancing thoughts and actions have to be all about negativity? You can look at figure 6.2 and find that the reward system is a fertile ground for positive thoughts. You will find that all these ego-centered elements are grown in the limbic system and become part of who we are and how our brain operates.

Is it not part of our human nature to seek self-improvement? Is it not part of our nature to be preoccupied with social thinking? Is it not part of our nature to be associated with successful entities? This is true, but when these elements take on narcissistic extensions and become too exaggerated and take over our thoughts, they lead to our suffering and the suffering of people around us.

Why can't ego-driven activity be structured around positive ideas and actions? This would be a functional picture, and there would be no reason for me to write this book. Let us look into this idea further. Why does the ego have to be built on unethical and unintelligent structures? Why wouldn't the self-enhancement be structured around positive values? This may result in having citizens who are not tormented by their needs for self-enhancement, and they are fully functioning humans! A practical goal is to have an ego interested in our idealistic goals instead of the narcissistic ones. If our emotions and energy are being consumed in materialistic goals, it will only lead to our agony or boredom in the end. A non-materialistic home and social environment are going to help make this balanced creature. This will allow our behaviors to be in line with our positive desires. These desires will be programmed to be naturally accepted by the most idealistic version of humanity.

Anxiety and the influence of our ego do contribute a great deal to the movement of societies in regard to great achievements and inventions. These goals may be based on the desire to acquire wealth or fame, which will push humans for hard work. We can see these achievements, especially in the fields of agriculture, mechanical engineering, and medicine. They lead to a decline in the rate of poverty and disease prevalence. But when these achievements are accomplished by a person with a healthy and wise ego, we will have the ability to look meticulously and see the big picture of what we are doing, and we do not need to suffer the side effects of these great achievements. An example of a hard achievement is the extremely cheap price of sugar which makes it available in huge quantities for consumption. This contributes to the epidemic of diabetes on one hand and global warming on the other. At the same time, we are consuming the topsoil and dumping tons of fertilizers that reach the open ocean creating negative effects for us and the environment. If society had healthy and wise egos, perhaps we would not be in this situation today.

Any idea that has grown in our mind and is forming the brain circuitry and intracellular programming of the reward system becomes essential in our life. The disruption of this circuitry places the brain in a depressive-like state. Imagine a reward system engaging in a project of drawing many mental pictures for success. A failure of that project would leave the vulnerable subjects shutting down the activity in the reward system. The same may apply when we face a decline in health, which is inevitable, or when we have a financial crisis.

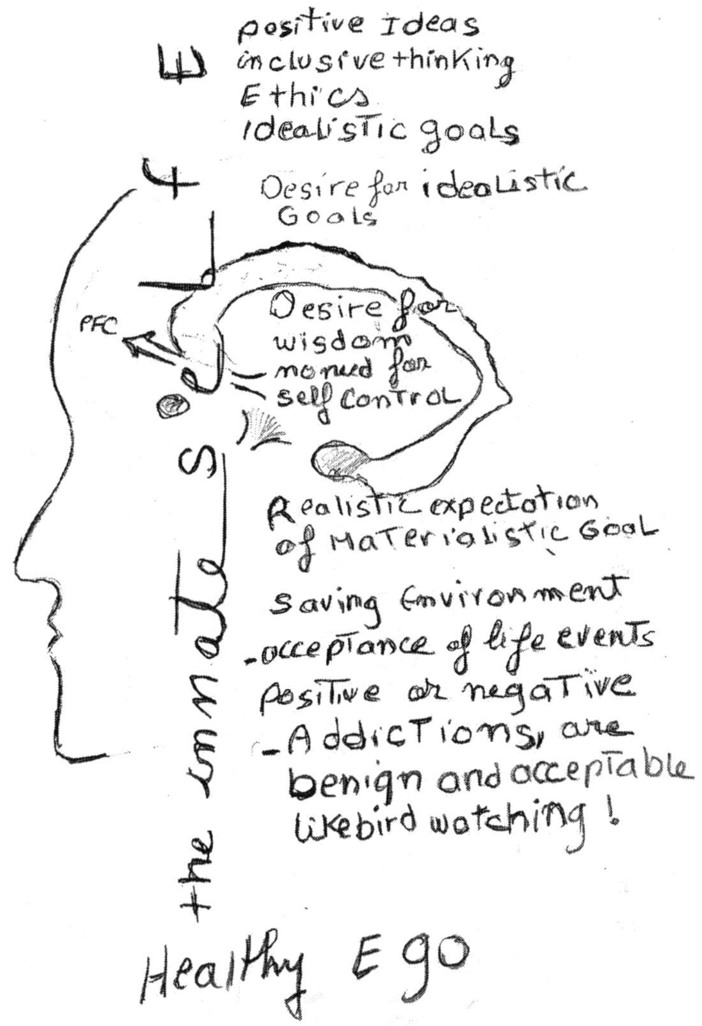

Disengaging from the ego is very hard to achieve. It is like knowing ourselves. We live life letting our brain take us on a long ride, and we push the cruise control button and hope that we will enjoy the ride. We try to avoid the feelings of internal discomfort as much as we can. We let our biases, desires, addictions and our self-inflated image take control of our imagination and behavior. Our reward system is stuck in the same circuit over and over, leading to suffering and aiding vulnerable humans in acquiring psychiatric illnesses. This suffering can both put pressure on us to change our approach to life and adopt wisdom or to understand ourselves and break away from the pressure of our desires.

Initially, disengaging from the ego will lead us to a state of discomfort, or even anxiety, even when confronting the ego makes the most sense to us. Disengaging from the circle of the thoughts we used to adhere to our whole lives might put us in internal turmoil for a while. We wonder if there will be a light at the end of the tunnel. But with persistence and patience, this can be done, and meditation can be used for this purpose also.

It is the responsibility of society with its social institutions, the media, TV, the movie industry, the educational system, and our parents, to promote a healthy ego—an ego that will adopt functional behaviors as part of the innate self. Why not? We can do better. We can do better in improving the technology of computers to make them miraculously sophisticated, but we do not like to put any effort into helping the semiconductors of our brains. We keep thinking that leaving Earth to Mars and adopting artificial intelligence will make us happier, but why don't we try to better our lives and minds on this planet Earth.

A healthy ego could also be promoted by the media and schools. They could urge us to desire to look outside our narrow selves and acquire wisdom. They could urge us to desire wisdom instead of fighting with our desires for wealth, power and control, by using ruthless means. We could have healthy egos derived from a healthy society and healthy media. Healthy egos contribute to the stability of our personalities and decrease the chance of acquiring psychiatric diseases. Healthy egos will make us have mercy on the planet Earth and ourselves and be satisfied with our lives on Earth, so we do not have to go to the planet Mars.

A healthy balanced ego that has realistic expectations of the materialistic world, can handle the negative situations much better. We could be living in peace to the last minute of our lives, provided there is a healthy society promoting healthy egos to its members. The idea of zero egos in society is unrealistic and impossible to achieve, even though it is a great idea. It would be a great idea if we all become priests and philosophers meditating all day, working for the service of others, and giving up our wealth to others. It would be nice to have zero crime rates and zero cheating rates. There would be no need for policemen on the streets and the courts would close down. No ego is impossible to achieve, but a healthy ego is possible. A healthy ego is up for grabs, but first, we must shift our desires from material worshiping to wisdom.

STOP 7

THE THINKING BOX

Thinking is the silent massive engine that defines who we are as human beings. Thinking is not a very hot topic in neuroscience these days, maybe because of my ignorance of the modern literature written on the subject, or maybe because neuroscience is very busy dealing with depression, anxiety, and other demanding medicinal applications. But thinking was a hot topic during ancient times. An example of that is Plato's theory of forms, commonly referred to as Platonism. It is a live theory that was adopted by many people from ancient times till our time.

The theory of forms is claiming that the real things in our world are the abstract side of things. We call them the forms. They are the real structure of the thinking brain and what we use to examine the physical world.

The forms are the ideal versions of materialistic items in our world, but they reside in our minds. We use them as standards to compare other physical structures that our senses can sense and our minds can comprehend. An example of that would be when we touch a tree with our bare hands, we feel that its bark is rough. When we let go of the tree and we turn our face away from it, the idea of roughness stays in our mind as an abstract entity. When the concept of roughness occupies our mind, we may think of a tree or any other physical item we can attribute roughness to, but we also can think of nothing other than the concept, roughness.

Plato sees many of us living in the cave of our senses, not realizing that our senses can only tell us only about the shadows of the real things, and not the things themselves, the forms. The mysteriousness of thinking is an element that was appreciated by Plato. This matter did not change at all in our time, but it tends to be ignored.

When writing started, approximately six thousand years ago, the early languages written allowed us to transfer the thoughts of the mind to symbolic letters and words. This allowed the development of many linguistic sciences like syntax and semantics. Using meaningful written language was a huge step in human history. It allowed the human brain to take off and bring the complexity of our modern life into existence. This is what transferred science from the older version gradually to newer ones and allowed the current structure of scientific achievement to be built.

Writing, in addition to the invention of the scientific instruments, allowed our ancestors' observations and work to be used in our time. The scientific atmosphere influences our achievement in current and ancient times. For example, Galileo's work: Just imagine that writing or the use of a lens did not exist in his time. Would Galileo ever come to the beautiful work that he did in describing the mechanics of the solar system? While we are using science to explore the world to our benefit and improve our lives, we try to use it to discover the tremendous potentials of our brain. The existence of these potentials for me is more than shocking.

Before the scientific revolution, humans were intrigued by their ability to think. People wondered how we could make sense of the world around us. They wondered how we were able to see things, and how we were able to draw conclusions.

By taking a glimpse at a table we can decide whether we can place a heavy object on it or not. For some of us, miracles cannot get more complicated than that.

It is very hard to investigate how animals are able to make sense of the world around them because they have no way of reporting back to us their thoughts. Some of us, including myself, have no problems adopting the concept that humans and animals operate similarly in navigating the world.

Why do we have the ability to do mathematics as part of the basic structure of our thinking? Why do we have the concept of a straight line, oval shapes or a square? Why are these words making any sense at all? Why was our brain prepared six thousand or ten thousand years ago to do complicated mathematical work as soon as writing started? Why does this massive analytical machine exist? Plato's theory of forms at least pointed the finger at this problem using an extremely sophisticated argument. Why is the brain of a hunter-gatherer living in the jungle so equipped with massive potentials to do advanced math, physics, and philosophy even though they do not need these capabilities to survive? Why did a giant leap happen? How come we came to the point of questioning our origin and stumbling on the issue of consciousness? Are elephants or whales worried about consciousness in the manner that we are? Do they ask what happens after death? Do they question how come we have gravity or how gravity works? Maybe they do but we are not understanding their feelings and thoughts. Are they more intelligent than we are in many areas of thinking?

How Do We Deal with Thinking?

We have no option but to think. Rene Descartes attempted to make peace with thinking by stating, "I think therefore I am," and he came to the point of reconciliation with thinking. If we try to define thinking, we find it impossible to do. We are imprisoned in this tight box called "thinking." For us to describe it we have to get out of this box, and we cannot because it is beyond our reach.

Drawn by Al-Ado inspired from a portrait by Frans Hals

The thinking box seems to have many defects, making sitting in it a very uncomfortable experience. This situation suggests for us to get out of the box of thinking.

As soon as we try to get out of this box, we crash down falling into the box again. Thinking about this concept is beyond our capability to think. Some examples that are beyond our capability to think would be the concept of time, gravity, infinity, and whether the universe has limits or a beginning.

Furthermore, when we try to look inside the box and try to examine it, the box makes the task even harder and frightening. We try to live life ignoring the subject of thinking altogether. Let me give an example to clarify this situation.

The spirit in the language

There are words in our language that we can find a definition for. Let us take the word "logic." We can say logic is a principle based on sound reason. You see here that for me to define the word logic I had to use other words, like the word "principle." Let us imagine that a young child hears the word principle for the first time and asks, "What does the word principle mean?"

Someone may say it is a foundational truth. The same child or maybe an adult, may ask, "What does foundational truth mean?" Now assuming that we are familiar with the language we are using, it might seem silly to keep going with this line of questions! At one point, we will stop. But why do we have to stop? The main question should be how come we can stop? We stop because we are born with this capability to understand the language through description and explanation without these ideas being based on experience. Understanding is the miracle that we have that would allow us to stop asking endlessly about the meaning of the words we are using in our language. I am really trying to tell others that the use of language by itself is a very frightening experience when we think about how we speak.

I see this issue to be the heart of the problem of thinking. We are using many tools in the box of thinking, like language and grammar. We are relying on them in our communication with each other, and we have no idea how this process works!

We have no idea how we understand any language, but we use it anyway. Children with severe autism may look at us talking; I only can imagine the thoughts going through their minds when they hear us. They may think we are bizarre. They may wonder why we keep talking and talking and we do not understand the implication of our language. Could children with severe autism have a special wisdom that we do not understand?

Going outside the box makes us uncomfortable. Similar to when we ask the big questions in life: How come we are here? Often, we create a simple story. We say there was a chemical reaction that happened thirteen billion years ago, called the Big Bang, which led to the solar system, then led to life on Earth, and with time it became us. By creating this story, we are trying to fix the thinking box to our liking, to calm ourselves down, and we are trying to make the box of thinking more comfortable.

For some of us, this story that we created may help calm our questioning mind. For others, this invention not only does not work but makes the thinking box more uncomfortable. Similar to when we prescribe medications for a problem like ADHD only to find the patient having a psychotic reaction.

Trying to fix the box and make it suitable seems more difficult at present when depression is at an all-time high. But do we really want to fix the box? Are we serious in trying to fix the box or do we prefer to live ignoring the box altogether?

Looking inside the box also makes us uncomfortable, because looking is challenging our comfortable reality, and challenging our day-to-day simple function.

When we converse with someone, we can sense that we are sharing with that person similar concepts and thinking structures and this will allow us to understand each other. It is an amazing experience when we meet someone and find that we are agreeing on many concepts, and our conversation becomes more interesting when we agree on the minute details. But often we run into situations when the communication breaks down. Then we try hard to explain our position, but it does not always work.

Thinking has numerous shared elements among us. That is why we can converse with each other, and we can go even beyond simple conversations to discuss philosophical ideas.

Language is by itself a metaphysical mental structure: a structure we cannot examine by using our senses. Besides the grammar rules of language, the linguistic component of thinking is a structure we are born with. It is enhanced with learning and experience. It is the real mother tongue that allows us to learn other languages. Our conventional mother tongue is just the programming of the speech center in our brain, in coordination with a motor center in the cortex and many other fine-tuning centers located in different places in our brain. This allows us to be fluent while talking to others. While thinking, we use our original mother tongue, and in addition to that, we use our learned mother tongue and other languages that we are familiar with.

When we are emotional, our linguistic thinking gets suspended, allowing our feelings to take over. For example, when we feel extremely joyful or fearful, often we express these emotions with our body language and facial expressions. Crying and laughing are words of the universal emotional language that all humans as well as animals that live close to us like our pets, understand. When we use them, we drop all the tools in the box of thinking and let them chaotically fall to the bottom, declaring that we have another dimension of communication between us and others.

We are designed with built-in structures to acquire languages. Some philosophers call it innate language. This innate language is a tool for us to express to others that we are making functional sense of the world around us. It is a tool to help us inquire about the world beyond our immediate experience. We also use the functional imagination segment of our thinking to look into the experience of others, without us being the experiencer.

Mathematics is another dimension of thinking, and it is a subsystem of language. It allows us to make computational sense of the physical world around us. Mathematics allows us to use our brain as a platform to do experiments on time and space without testing tangible objects.

Emmanuel Kant considered time and space as modes of thinking. Kant wrote the most sophisticated book describing these tools of thinking that we are born with, the famous book *The Critique of Pure Reason*. Kant responded beautifully to the empiricist movement that swept Europe in the eighteenth century. This movement, led by John Locke and David Hume, regarded the brain as just a blank slate where sensations become memories then memories become ideas.

Consider when we are facing the world with our senses, the sense of vision with the variety of electromagnetic radiation falling on our retina, the airwaves hitting our eardrum, the multiplicity of chemicals reaching our nose, and the tactile stimulations affecting our skin. How are we dealing with these inputs? We classify them, categorize them and prioritize them. Consider when you walk into a store to buy a part for your car, and the store also happens to sell groceries. You are going to the section that sells car parts, but what made the store so organized? Are the items of this store just stuffed in the space randomly, or there is a mind, which examines every single item and places it in the appropriate location in a nice way. Like the organized store, so is the human mind when it is dealing with the senses. Every single sensory input gets screened and placed in the appropriate spot. So, the mind cannot be just a passive organ, or just a victim of outside stimulation, as Emmanuel Kant explained in *The Critique of Pure Reason*. We are using these tools from the second we are born, and so does every other living creature.

Animals, at one point in their life, do have more advanced thinking features than humans, without being based on learning. Take for example when a newborn deer is born. If the mother leaves the fawn alone and it senses danger, it will sit down and be still without making the slightest noise until its mother is back.

The fawn has an advanced built-in system, valid, sophisticated and wise without being based on experience.

Emmanuel Kant considered our brain's ability to face the world using time, space, cause and effect, necessity, limitation, reciprocity, and others, which make the system that we are born with and gives us innate tools to make sense of the world. This allows us to come to a confident conclusion, that the sum of the internal angles of any triangle, equals 180 degrees. We confidently confirm that without trying to measure the angles of any triangle we see around us when we are working on a construction project, for example. We conclude that the shortest distance between two points is a straight line, but we should ask ourselves this question: "How come we have this confidence?"

Animals use math and physics in applicable ways. When a cat jumps from one point to another, it measures the distance accurately and applies the necessary muscular force, so when it lands, it does so with stability and grace. But as far as we can see, cats do not spend time just thinking about time and space, or maybe they do, but they use an operating system different than what we use.

Part of our thinking follows the computational functional system that exists in computers, but this is only a minute aspect of our thinking: Using math, starting from a simple equation like 1+1 =2, creates the concepts of adding to make things bigger and allows our senses to have the chance to examine the physical entities around us. Unfortunately, our ego may take advantage of this function and connect it to the reward system. How could that be? I would like to give an example: Sit down with your friends at a social gathering where the ego is in action and take a moment to analyze their conversation. You will find that it is hinting toward things becoming more or less like made more money or less money. If we visit places, we describe the experience as good or bad and often we make a judgment concerning other humans in the same manner.

Often, we enjoy going further beyond the simple math that we use during our daily activity to more complicated math. This allowed us to write the laws of physics, like the law of gravity.

The Thinking Domino or the Thinking Human

Thinking governs our mental activity and presides over any intellectual maneuvers we try to do. Look at the idea of free will. These days in the media, many people are discussing this matter. The scientific views are centered on the concept that the nature of our body and brain is all about materials. Minds are the product of this chemical convulsion. We try to use reason to come to this conclusion. Our thinking and function in life are based on the laws of physics. I am going to try to convince you that if you believe that this concept is correct, that the mind is just matter, this means there is no such thing as thinking. By accepting this choice, you are denying the entire thinking toolbox. While discussing this matter with someone else, you are telling them, "I do not believe that you have a toolbox called thinking, the latter is only matter moving according to random chemical reactions. But at the same time, you are asking others to use their toolbox to understand your opinion!! This is an obvious contradiction.

Emmanuel Kant in his book *The Critique of Pure Reason* discussed this matter beautifully. It is saddening at our time to see our concepts going backwards and science going back to being naïve!

Believing ourselves to be robots is an impossible thought. Maybe it is easier to consider others as robots, especially when others are behaving like zombies. I can agree with the statement "I am a robot" linguistically, but it is impossible as a concept or a thought. The sentence "I am a robot" only creates more defects in the thinking box and makes it more uncomfortable. When I look at myself in the mirror and say, "Who is that? It is only me." The sentence "I am a robot" means my thinking is not my thinking. The word "I" that I am using is dissolved, and I have no existence anymore. Now you can see that the problem of consciousness is back.

How could we interact with one another if there was no free will? While we are communicating with other humans, it is impossible to consider others as matter or robots. When we speak to others, we feel that our consciousness is communicating with theirs. We do not think that physical matter is communicating with physical matter. We can lecture about the concept that the mind is all about matter. While we are doing that we are using a metaphysical structure, called language, to explain a metaphysical structure, called the mind, and we have no idea what they are and how they work! Is that not a very weak argument?

We are dealing with the world around us based on the concept of free will even though this concept is very hard to define using language. It is extremely connected to the idea of the self, me and you. Without it, normal interaction between us and others, using our thoughts, becomes impossible.

We as human beings use innate language as the main tool of the thinking box to test hypotheses. But we have no clue how this innate language works since it is in the metaphysical domain. Also, we use reason or the brain as a tool for testing hypotheses, and again we have no clue how it works. Then we have consciousness sensing all of the above, and we have no clue what it is.

This goes hand in hand with the argument that when we judge anything if our judgment is based on the natural deterministic laws of physics and chemistry working in our brain, this means that thinking is just a chemical domino effect and that this judgment is just an illusion. And if you want to believe that your opinion is just a chemical reaction, then you should not be taking yourself very seriously. Why do you want us to believe you if you do not even believe yourself? Free will is a tool that every one of us supposes that others have when we interact with them. It is one of the simple tools that we pull out of the thinking box when we converse with others. It is a metaphysical structure that we cannot examine or judge.

In practical living, we follow the input of the senses: vision, touch, taste, smell and hearing. We have the means to verify any experiment and examine the physical world. We interact with each other on the basis that the thinking boxes are reasonably similar, and that free will is an essential tool that we use all the time.

The same concept will apply when we are dealing with math: no two people are going to disagree about the result of 1+1. Math and clear natural laws and the input of our senses are not disputable; otherwise, we can argue about anything and everything.

This matter is the heart of philosophy since before the time of Plato. Plato himself discussed this matter extensively, then he came up with the theory of forms. Descartes and the rest of the rational philosophers of his time also did. Now we come to the twenty-first century. We are telling our students in school that there is no such thing as free will. Also, not seeing that we are submitting them to having a mental stroke, and not realizing that living in the world as a human is different from living in the world as robots. How much do we want to have depression, suicide, and drug addiction rates rise before we wake up to realize what we are doing?

On the contrary, we should tell teenagers ethics is real and ethics must be categorical imperatives in our lives. We should tell teenagers we are responsible for our choices; we have choices, we have free will, and we should not have bad credit. Ethics, honesty and integrity are our responsibility. They are the ABCs of living. They are here to serve us and make us have a decent life, and they are the preventative tools against depression, drug abuse and suicide.

Drawn by AL-Ado, inspired from Portrait
by Johann Gottlieb Becker

As soon as we tell people that there is no such thing as free-will, we are outside the box of thinking. When we go outside the box of thinking, intelligible communication with others becomes impossible. The denial of free will may produce momentary amusement, suggestive of the sophisticated speaker, but it is going to produce confusion and chaos in the human mind. This way of thinking will make the self a fragile entity filled with struggle and facilitate the state of depression.

Thinking and Our Daily Life

Our daily life includes many mini-thinking dramas regularly, created and sustained by our ego, and it is hard for these dramas to produce anything positive unless our thoughts are directed and nurtured by the environment, and unless they are controlled by us; but who is us? Consciousness! What is consciousness? It is the real us when we are facing the outside world and when we are facing ourselves. We feel it in every moment of our life, but we tend to ignore it, and we have no idea how it works. It is something that we are most confident about its existence, more than anything else in our life. It is the operating system that we use to face the world, but we do not admit that we use it. Frequently we deny it, and I see that as very normal because it is outside our thinking box and it is impossible to define. Sometimes it looks obvious but very elusive to describe using our language. We feel it, but we cannot figure it out. It is intimately connected to our physical structure, and it is interacting intimately with the chemical and physical world around us, but we have no idea how.

When we look at our brain, we see the brain circuits firing and responding to every little bit of change in our psychology. The changes in the physical world around us influence our behavior and feeling, and the changes in the material structures of our brain, also influence our feelings and behavior. For example, the change that occurs when we take a drug causes rearrangement of the cellular components of the social centers in our brain. We are embedded in the physical world, by means of the materialistic structure of our brain and our senses.

These mechanisms that influence our feelings look similar to those in other creatures, especially mammals. So, we can have meaningful interactions with them and with each other as social creatures. Born of these two kinds of interactions is our ability to interact with the planet Earth and the universe. Do you agree that this is the most bizarre ability to acquire?

As we have the opportunity to interact with other creatures, consciousness allows us to feel the psychology of animals, their joy and sorrow. We enjoy having spiritual interactions with them. When we look at a lioness who lost her cubs, we can feel her pain without difficulty, and when we look at two cubs playing and jumping around together, we see that they are happy.

The demise of any physical structure in our brain affects our interaction with the physical world and limits the ability of our consciousness to interact with it, but in a difficult way to predict. An example of this is when someone is going through a massive surgical operation on his/her brain, like removing half of the brain or when having a massive stroke. In some cases, large elements of their personality do not change. Try to do that to a robot and see what happens. On the other hand, our behavior may change a lot after an accident that may not look so severe.

The quality of our feeling, sometimes called qualia, preoccupies our consciousness and influences our thinking, especially when it comes to depression, anxiety, physical pain, material loss, material gain and desires. Disengaging from these feelings is very hard. Working on this matter should be a task that we are trying to achieve till the end of our life. Spiritual training may shed some light on these ideas. Some of this training may include:

1. Knowing that many of these feelings, like fear, anxiety and depression, are in the end computing problems in areas of the brain's social center, interfacing with consciousness. We can break away from their influence on our thinking by reiterating this concept subtly.
2. Directing our attention toward empathy, consciousness and conscientiousness, and defining the positive role that the social part of the brain can potentially play in improving our life and the life of people around us. Consciousness when it comes to our choice of monitoring our behavior and conscientiousness that has to be adopted by society to be the social platform of operation, as we discussed in the chapter "Healthy Ego."
3. Being engaged in other mental activities and being able to concentrate on what is necessary and constructive in our life. So, we are not sitting down and watching movies all day and blaming others for our problems.

4. Being able to enjoy simple activities we do all the time, like cooking or walking, deserve our attention, appreciation, and enjoyment. We do not have to wait until a vacation or a planned trip to be emotionally fit and positive.
5. Meditation, and meditation all the time, meaning the concept of God is present with us during all our regular activities and interactions with others. This will bring a higher value to these activities and emphasize the highest ethical standards in our life.

Critical Thinking

We tend to define critical thinking in many ways. If you examine how people use the term, you will find that we use it to examine other people's statements and ideas. It is not about the observable empirical events that our senses can see, feel, or touch. Critical thinking is about involving the old tool that we are proud of called REASON. It is located in the box of thinking that we have no idea how it works. Often, our ego tries to get involved in servicing this tool and maintaining it. This tool is another dimension of our thoughts that we have no option but to use, despite its many problems that philosophers like David Hume and Emanuel Kant have written about.

To make this tool function better, it will require us to be watching and examining our emotions, biases, and evaluating the current status of the thoughts that we have at one moment. When we hear a statement, it is important to try to discover more about that statement, like what is the real emotion behind it, the intention, the reason behind the choice of words, the neutrality of the speaker, how intelligent the speaker is, how deep the speaker is sinking in her/his own biases, her/his fears and desires, how serious and passionate or how conscientious she/he is.

We misuse the tool of reason when it becomes ego-centered, full of preconceived judgment and paranoid feelings. Lack of an empathic dimension makes the situation even worse.

Critical thinking is a goal that we are all trying to achieve. Some steps of critical thinking are going to be sending signals to the amygdala and the hypothalamus, and some of these signals are going to make us uncomfortable. This discomfort becomes obvious when we discover the merit in other people's opinions and it is evidence against our own. Opinions that differ from our own interfere with our biases. Nevertheless, we should seek fairness and extreme honesty when we evaluate other people's opinions and disregard our biases.

Critical thinking should be one of the arts of mastering the self and the ego. From that point on, we can look at the world and other human beings with constructive eyes. We will dive less into our primitive emotions and our harsh negativity. Then we will give space to our consciousness so it can have mastery over our ego.

This process will make us endure discomfort, especially initially, but with time, the ideas that are causing discomfort become less stressful. Pure reason often tries to find a middle way between our biases and what we find close to being the truth and may find a resolution to the conflict. Meanwhile, our conscience is trying to approach the matter on very neutral ground. After all, the ideas we are dealing with are created by a fellow human being.

By trying to be fair to other people's ideas, critical thinking becomes sharper. Critical thinking is connected directly with controlling the amygdala, by the depressive obsessive cycles coming from old memories and past experiences. It allows our psychology to be at rest, and our skills to decipher the data in a better way. The waves of discomfort in the limbic system become calm and reach a state of equilibrium after much back-and-forth instability.

Critical thinking is almost suspended when we are stuck in a state of paranoia. Our thinking becomes hijacked by fears and suffering, and we look at the world from a very narrow tunnel. But when we get sick and tired of doing things the old way, we decide that we have had enough of the suffering. When we are using critical thinking in a neutral may to our biases, this process becomes a habit which may have fruitful applications in our life. I see it as a great way to a more balanced, happier, and sharper brain.

STOP 8

DRUG ADDICTION AND OPIOID ADDICTION

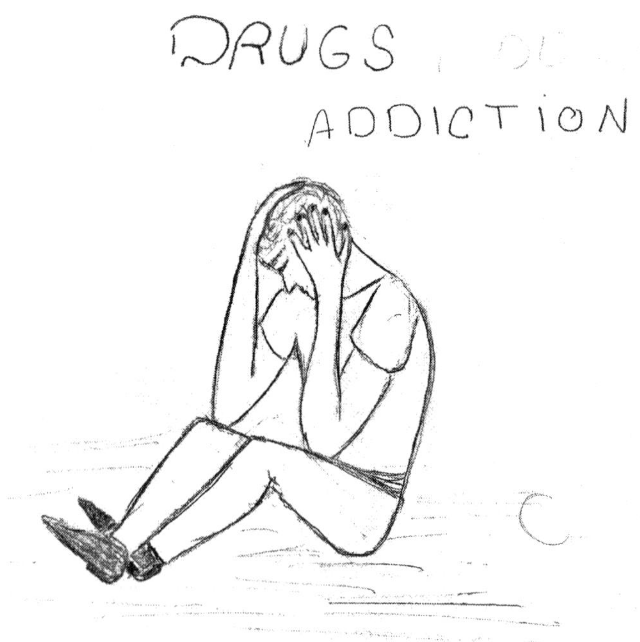

The best time for us to fall victim to drug addiction is when we are depressed and under pressure. The difficult environmental factors that lead humans to drug use are similar to conditions that the rat Hoover was subjected to in the experiment that we discussed in the natural reward system. Hoover was bred in the lab, placed in a cage, and an electrical wire was placed in the reward system in his brain. We were not surprised to find Hoover pushing on the lever, an activity that did not make any sense. We, as humans, also find ourselves engaged in many activates that do not make sense. The act of taking drugs is not much different than the act of a rat pushing a lever that will lead to the electric stimulation of the reward system.

The rat would not choose this destiny for itself under normal circumstances. A stressful environment pushes us to seek a way out of the unfriendly environment we are living in. This unfriendly environment is primarily composed of unfriendly people around us. They are either abusing us physically or mentally or neglecting to treat us as human beings with emotional and psychological needs.

The negative and harsh social environment leads to a very powerful influence on drug-seeking behavior, especially when drugs are available everywhere. Imagine that these drugs are not available, and we have never heard of them. Will we ever seek their use? Our tortured soul would look for different outlets, maybe functional ones. This harsh social environment was constructed based on vicious cycles, going undetected by scientists, philosophers, and religious institutions.

With the strange availability of these drugs, despite their illegal status, dealers are offering drugs at cheap prices initially, until the student in the school is hooked, leading to a potentially disastrous situation. You can figure out by now that street drugs are going to hijack the reward system in the brain and alter its responses.

The reward system's response to drugs varies from one person to another. For vulnerable people, drugs can take hold of that system leading to extreme exhaustion of its intracellular subsystems. The euphoria that occurs initially when the drug is used does not last for long.

In people who have a tendency toward addiction, using drugs will leave the reward system too weak to function when dealing with regular tasks or when dealing with other functional activities. Happiness and euphoria become dependent on drug use and taking drugs becomes glamorized initially by people. Some of my patients will go on arguing with me about the safety and the benefit of taking a drug and how it makes their life more relaxed. Maybe their life became relaxed because of the suspension of thinking about their social pressure. Their brain becomes sleepy and less aware of the dysfunctional environment and their difficult social past.

Soon many patients find themselves dependent on taking drugs to live normally, and the initial euphoria declines. We keep taking the drug after that to stay out of the anxiety that we can experience from even the thought of stopping the drug.

In some cases, when the addiction is less powerful, the person may live with chronic functional daily use, with variable degrees of suffering in their social and personal life. Due to drug use, the normal dopamine levels operating the reward system and natural opioids secreted by the hypothalamus drift to subnormal levels compared to an average human.

Drug users waste their time finding their dealer or other means of obtaining the drug. From time to time, they find themselves bringing chemicals into their system to try to decrease their suffering or to feel normal. Their commitment to other aspects of their life does not matter at that point because drug use is now the main priority. After a while, even if the patient is functioning okay, he/she will be living life dealing with a senseless act, wasting time, money, physical and mental efforts. For sure this is not a satisfying situation for the long run no matter how legal or illegal this act is. It crosses the mind of the addicted patient that there are other human beings, equipped with the same brain in essence, and their life is not dependent on taking any drug.

Increasing the dose of the drug for some of us is necessary, but higher doses will lead to more profound brain circuit alteration and intracellular changes in the nucleus accumbens and hypothalamus. The potential of a deadly overdose becomes reality when the drug can suppress the vital brain centers that are controlling the respiration and other autonomic functions.

The deadly overdose effect in the past few years became a more familiar scenario to me. Mothers are bringing their children to the clinic without a father, telling me that the father has died from an overdose. Children are coming with their grandparents, telling me that both parents have died one after the other from an overdose of heroin.

Babies born to mothers who used opioids during pregnancy are kept in the intensive care unit after birth for an extended time. They have withdrawal symptoms from the mother taking narcotics or street drugs, and they will not be released until the dangerous withdrawal symptoms are treated. It is a condition called neonatal abstinence syndrome. The babies with this problem may have sleeping, feeding or breathing problems, and in some cases, more complications for a certain time. This problem has certainly been on a sharp rise and adds to it the wide use of the teratogenic drug called alcohol, which is available to pregnant women. It has variable consequences on their fetuses, especially when consumed during the first trimester of the pregnancy.

During my regular office work, entering an exam room, the parents are present with the child. Smelling cigarette smoke or weed on parents is a very familiar problem for me these days. These parents bring me the child for a coughing problem, and when I enter the exam room, I start coughing from the smell of smoke in the room, which is called third-hand smoking.

The Physiologic Effects of Taking Drugs

After the initial introduction of a drug, the brain cells in the nucleus accumbens become intoxicated with a high level of dopamine. These cells will reduce the number of receptors of this chemical on their membranes to decrease their response to the drug and reduce their risk of cell toxicity.

When drug use becomes regular, a common scenario will happen: the brain expects the use to become regular, so it will change to recalibrate and balance the production of the neurotransmitters governing the arousal system and the endorphin release. The drug now is only causing the brain to function normally, back to the state prior to taking the drug, while leaving the feeling of addiction to stay.

This crisis is quickly sensed by the rest of the limbic system, like the prefrontal cortex, the amygdala and the hypothalamus. The neocortex becomes shocked and isolated, especially with taking meth, cocaine, and narcotics. The circuits in the brain that are used to integrate the nucleus accumbens with the rest of the social brain are neglected. Adding to that the toxic effect on the cells directly, especially in the case of alcohol, will lead to decreased brain function, and priming the brain to show more signs of depression.

In the case of extended narcotics use, the production of internal opioids is disrupted, and the opioid receptors are flooded with these exogenous drugs. These chemicals play important roles in regulating our overall social behavior and feelings. After these centers are altered with high doses of narcotics, the production of internal opioids that mediates many functions in the brain decreases, and we become more dependent on the exogenous drug. When we suddenly stop taking the drug, anxiety, seizure, agitation, and gastrointestinal symptoms become obvious. Since narcotics mediate some of the physiology of the vital centers, sharp withdrawal could lead to death.

The Effect of Chronic Drug Use

Let us suppose that a person is taking drugs in moderation and able to control himself. Maybe he has been using these drugs for a long time. Someone may assume that this is a safe situation, but let me show you what is going to happen in this case: A healthy reward system, as we discussed, is essential for us to move toward achieving any goal, even walking to the kitchen to get a glass of water. This complicated machine has a life span that will make it last till the end of our life. By using drugs, it is now consumed for a senseless reason, and it is being used up over a long time. It leaves us toward the late years of our lives socially, physically, debilitated and burnt out. Taking drugs chronically for the long run will lead to mental stagnation, and our social judgment becomes blunted and unwise. Ultimately, chronic drug use will lead to a physical depression presented with weakness, feeling low energy, and decreased motivation toward doing daily tasks.

Alcohol Use

Alcohol is not only accepted socially, but you could be subjected to bullying if you do not drink at a social gathering. Exposure to alcohol comes from friends and loving relatives. In addition, medical media is listing studies showing the benefit of a small amount of red wine consumption daily. The benefit of wine is coming from a chemical found in red grapes; they just forget to mention to you that you can have all the benefits of red wine by eating a few red grapes and avoid not only the addiction risk but also the potential medical complications that are countless. Many medical studies are popping up, one after the other, pointing out these facts.

If you have a gene for alcohol addiction, it means that you are prone to becoming addicted to alcohol after you start drinking. Physiologically, you would experience endorphin release in addition to the sedative and anxiolytic effects of alcohol on your brain.

Alcohol addicts are at a disadvantage when they start drinking, and these people do have hope with medical intervention because of the use of medication that blocks the opioid receptor in the brain. Some of these medications, like Naltrexone, could be implanted underneath the skin with lasting effects for months, which is also used to treat opioid dependence.

Heroin Use

Internal opioids are called endorphins. They are hormones secreted by the main hormonal regulating system of the brain, which is the hypothalamus, and by other opioid-producing areas. The receptors of these chemicals are widely distributed in the brain and spine. When activated, they can ease the pain in case we are experiencing serious medical illness or bodily injury.

Endorphin production is a potential language our physical brain uses to translate to us the good feelings coming from an event, like looking at a flower, working on a piece of art, or the feeling that a mother will have when holding her child after being separated from her or him.

When a mother is prevented from seeing her baby, she will experience a serious decline in endorphin levels. The reunification will lead to a surge in the endorphin level. This surge is connected to the intensity of this feeling, which will calm down after the situation is back to the routine of permanent reunification. You can see that this system is disrupted when the mother is addicted to heroin as we see that clearly in hospitals. After the mother gives birth to her newborn, she may leave the hospital in the middle of the night, leaving her newborn baby to the hospital staff to take care of him/her, and she will never return to see the baby.

Meth, Cocaine and Benzodiazepine

Meth and cocaine work on the reward system and their targets, as we discussed, in the nucleus accumbens. These drugs make dopamine more available in the synapses which will boost the prediction of the real euphoric effect. Benzodiazepine works on the amygdala, and this is how they have their anxiolytic effects.

Eighty percent of the world's pain pills are consumed in the United States, and around seventy-five percent of recent heroin users began their addiction with prescription drugs. About 194,000 people have died since 1999 from overdoses involving opioid pain killers.

A solution to these problems resides in acknowledging the negative societal conditioning of its members. Changing the entire dysfunctional social system, which is composed of the media, religious institutions, schools and universities, in a way that would address human social and spiritual needs, becomes necessary.

The medical research system is working hard on introducing new medication and strategies in dealing with drug addiction, and fair success has been achieved in the past few years. Medical clinics, hospitals, the insurance system and social organizations must encourage addicts to seek help and make the services related to this illness affordable and economically possible.

STOP 9

SEXUALITY AND THE SOCIAL BRAIN

Whether sex is extremely overrated or underrated is in the eye of the beholder. Who has the final say on this matter? It is the media. The media in our life, like TV stations, the internet, books, and magazines can influence our feelings and opinions. Also, add to that what friends are talking about, how the educational system is dealing with this matter, what our relatives and friends are admiring and appreciating, and how religious institutions are judging the matter.

In traditional media, the word "sex" is now standing freely not connected to any other function. Many people may not really agree with me, so I do understand. However, there are a few points here I would like to make. If my views on the subject are very traditional or contemporary and agree with the media, then what is the point of me writing this book in the first place? It is going to add nothing to the common views that are prevailing at this time.

Sex is a word that is often used as a free-standing term without a meaningful definition. Frequently we can encounter many other terms connected to it, like addiction, freedom, or revolution.

Sex was once viewed in human history as being connected to a specific function: the creation of a human being. Sometimes we see this word connected to love and intimacy, but often we do not see that connection.

Sorry to say also that sex was part of the military weapons, in the form of rape, that was used to attack the enemy in wars. I wonder if this action has been suspended yet.

Sex with its main function to satisfy physical desires is greatly emphasized in our time compared to the function of having children. The latter is also a very powerful emotion, but it is not as emphasized in our traditional media.

In my opinion, if someone has three children and this person has only had intercourse three times in his/her life, this is not going to make life more or less interesting for them. Humanity for sure is not going to lose any of its real achievements, or humanity's achievements may have been more creative, less destructive, and wiser.

I know this sounds crazy, strange, and different. But may the next few lines explain what this idea is about without necessarily sounding like a lesson for priesthood or celibacy.

Look at a child while having immense pleasure from doing very simple activities like jumping off the bed, playing with a ball or riding a bicycle. Would you have the same immense pleasure from jumping off the bed or riding a bicycle? What is preventing us from experiencing pleasure from the simple things to do in life?

It is the habit of being an adult. Being an adult means that we live in the grip of what the media call it: sexuality. The reward system of adults goes through a drastic transformation during adulthood. Many ads on TV are trying to remind us that we are not children anymore and emphasizing the idea of the necessity of being attractive physically. Take, for example, TV ads about creams that can preserve our youthful look. Our social surroundings remind us frequently of the importance of being young adults. This implies that when we grow older, life is going to lose some of its values or pleasure. I see this idea to be very naïve!

During my work, I look at a child running around with lots of excitement and happiness. I see that to be a source of wisdom, which cannot easily be grasped and comprehended by adults. Why? Because they are adults now, and adulthood is defined by the media as being needy. It says we have to have another human to satisfy our needs. Therefore, we are described as dissatisfied creatures. Without having him/her, something is missing, and we become miserable, and often she/he becomes a necessary object to own. I am not denying that we are hard-wired to have a mate to share life with. But what I am suggesting is to employ this need to better the lives of humans rather than to contribute to our misery, such as when a couple spends a year of their life going back and forth to a divorce court! The prevalence of divorce is undoubtedly a clear example of a dysfunctional reward system that is not bringing any reward to their owner!

Often when we find that special one who is going to make us happy, we experience a sharp increase in our positive feeling, and expectedly this initial excitement fades with time. Dealing with other human beings as objects consumed by our reward system will put our relationship with our spouse at the mercy of the mechanics of its biology. When the decline in the interest of the reward system reaches a certain level, our culture may allow us to try to return that object to the manufacturing company as a defective product, one that did not meet the manufacturing description. We try to find someone else to fulfill our ever-demanding needs for emotional and physical fulfillment.

Jumping is an activity that provides children with lots of pleasure. Often, we have the opportunity during our adult life to be around other children. When we join them in their activities, we feel some relief from the duties of what the social environment assigned to us as adults. Sometimes, we wish that we could become children again. As sexuality becomes pathological addiction, it contributes to our misery on a daily basis. It takes control over our reward system, then moves to hijack the neocortex and the entire social brain to deprive us of having sound social interaction with other humans.

The media occasionally describes sexuality as the ultimate pleasure, especially for men. The idea is placed in teenagers' minds from an early age. The internet, by showing nude scenes available to youth to watch without restriction, enforces this notion and contributes to the human misery that we are experiencing. On the other hand, drug addiction and sex addiction are synonymous these days. Men, compared to women, have an easier tendency for sexual addiction to soar to the status of drug addiction without actually trying this drug. This addiction is induced by societal hints, like a friend in school hinting to a friend that touching women or doing other sexual acts induces powerful pleasure. Just like that the drug is now in the system. If you have been listening to the news before the COVID-19 pandemic, you would find that a small portion of the news is talking about sexual crimes, like harassment and assault even from our experienced, wise, and socially intelligent politicians.

As sexual addiction builds up, dopamine floods the reward system, giving the brain a mental stroke, similar to what a street drug or alcohol does. As in any other drug glamourized by the media, the desire to test it pushes us to go on with another step, which is finding a partner. If this partner is a sexual partner only, meaning the relationship is very superficial, it means that we are using a human being, especially women, like a drug, and we could be reducing each other to drugs.

Again, the media and what we hear and see from our friends and relatives for sure are playing a major role in setting a sexuality structure in our brain in this era, as in any other eras in the past.

How Children Learn About Female and Male Relationships

In hunter-gatherer societies, children have enough of a chance to observe the reality of the relationship between the sexes by living with their parents and observing their behavior, as well as the behavior of other close members of society, until the time they die.

This experience has been cut very short these days. Many children live with a single parent and do not have the opportunity to observe the relationship between their parents. The media also gives us a short concise version of this experience in a movie that describes male and female interaction that is condensed in an hour or two. These movies give us strong conclusions about what social life is all about, while our thinking is suspended. Many movies picture humans behaving like robots, stripped of the reality of interacting with the social environment, as realistic emotional creatures. Often, the plot of the movie does not add much to the viewer's knowledge, since the ideas of the majority of these movies rarely bring a life sample from the most common human interaction scenarios in our cultures. It is rare to see that the goal of the movie is to educate the public and improve human conditions.

Real Life

A normal society has to have a system that would report the cases of rape or sexual abuse on women and children daily and an effective system that would deal with these social diseases. The morning news gives you the traffic jam reports and how you can save more money if you buy this item today. You do not feel that society cares about what happened to its youth the night before. What President Jimmy Carter wrote about the subject of human trafficking is an eye-opener on this topic. It is nice to see a senior politician who cares and is not only looking at the members of the society as mere economic entities.

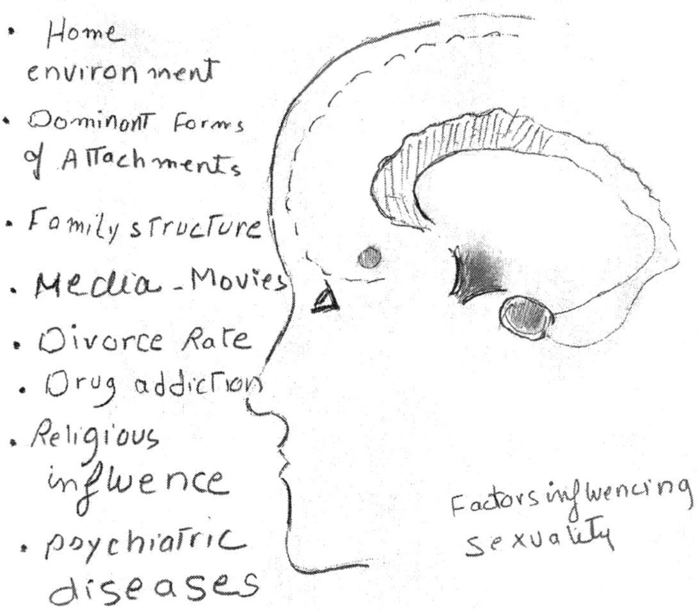

Watch the many shows on cable TV and you see the rate of crime connected to sexuality. Look around you and you will find a long line of women living in poverty and taking care of their children, and they are very poorly equipped to handle life. Society calls them single mothers. In reality, society has created this phenomenon, and we are all guilty of creating it.

Sexuality as a realistic element of our life is poorly applied and understood. Often, in the media, it gets mixed with the emotion of love on the surface only, without any practical or realistic application to the formation of our emotion or society. It is often presented as a necessary tool to meet personal temporary needs.

Sexual Transmutation

The first time I heard about this subject was when I was going over some of what Napoleon Hill wrote in the last century. Napoleon insisted sexual transmutation was a prerequisite condition for success in achieving goals. Napoleon described how very successful people achieve their most success after the age of forty or fifty when the grip of sexuality becomes less powerful in debilitating their minds.

Napoleon thought that young people, mainly men with extreme vitality and powerful sexual energy, are at an advantage when they can put this energy into productive forms and use this energy in worthwhile projects. He used the term sexual transmutation to describe this ability. Napoleon did not put an actual mechanism of putting the sexual desire under complete control, and I want to shed some light on possible mechanisms to enable the reader to do that.

Freud also showed that the great artistic and scientific achievements and other creative work of humans came from the process of sublimation, by channeling sexual energy into good use. He described the process of seeking honorable alternative sources of pleasure for forbidden desires through the process of sublimation. I see that Freud and Hill were talking about the same thing here. In the case of an eight- or nine-year-old child making a great achievement in school, here I do see that sublimation is a silly concept to try to explain the energy that this child has, since he/she, I hope, has no clue what sexuality is. I do see Freud maybe insisting that what I said may not be true! I would say to him, "Okay, no problem."

But before entering the subject directly, let us get introduced gradually to this idea by shedding some light on the brain function in regard to sexual function, then try to add a practical tool to implement sexual transmutation.

After puberty, most of us do not get engaged in wild sexual acts and take what seems to be a wise, reasonable approach to the emotion of sex. As we are examining our society's values, most of us conclude that the emotion of sex has to be placed within the context of a loving relationship. As the culture shapes the reward system in our minds, most of us grow feeling that having children and a family is something rewarding. All of us grow up feeling that being loved is a strong emotion, and the pleasure of sex is limited and short-lasting. Sexuality cannot by itself replace the rest of the activities in our life. So, this activity becomes self-regulated by the mind and placed within an acceptable social system called love relation. Love relation includes unquestionable commitment between the partners, and the idea of separation is not at all on the table. This goes further to form a social union or marriage, and this union is blessed by God in all cultures in the East and West alike.

Marriage and Divorce

With time the marriage union became a thickened contract. This contract became complicated, even though the marriage certificate process seems to be very simple and does not involve much paperwork. If divorce happens to take place and end the relationship, legal consequences are often a serious matter to both sides. The wise legal system sets the rules for that. These consequences do not talk about the emotional catastrophe that is about to happen or talk about the disintegration of love institutions in society. These regulations care less about these things. They care only about the pennies and the bits of materials that are going to end up in the trash in the end. The real serious consequences are the ones affecting society in terms of the disintegration of the family structure.

The legal system, with the high prevalence of divorce rate, teaches men and women that marrying someone with a lower financial status, is an idea that needs to be taken with caution. This programming sometimes may not be formulated at the get-go of the human emotional life but will show up in their subconscious mind as society draws the picture in slow motion in our brain. Worse than that is when this picture becomes digitally formulated at high speed and hits teenagers in their early years of maturity. On one occasion, a teenage patient of mine told me that he was not going to get married because he did not want somebody taking his money! These negative elements are shaping the reward system with regard to sexuality and love.

Women are more protected from this toxic effect to some extent, because of their more advanced empathic characteristics, and their different nature in regard to sexuality. Also, women during their early age of maturity come to realize that they are very attractive to men, especially during their youthful age. For women, the emotion of love and sexuality are tightly connected to having children. Having children to them is by itself a very powerful and hardwired desire in the brain. That desire is also very powerful in men, but maybe not as hard-wired! How come? How outrageous of me to say that? That is based on the charts of my patients. For every ten households comprising a mother and children, there is one comprising a father and children. And when the father has the children, the mother is usually a drug addict who has lost custody of the children, or she has died from a drug overdose or some other way.

Animal Kingdom Mechanics of Attraction

I felt I need to speak a little about this subject to prepare the reader by discussing an easy example from the animal kingdom. After that, we will go over this function in humans. I would like to give an example from the animal kingdom on how the mechanics of sexuality work in the brain. In mice as in many mammals, pheromones, chemicals secreted by specialized glands close to their rear end, play a major role in how a mouse can identify the sex of surrounding mice. Mice use this clue to identify the sex of each other. The existence of the vomeronasal organ in the nasal sensory system is what gives them this ability. When pheromones reach this system, they bypass the normal sensory process that is used to process the sense of smell and interact directly with the vomeronasal organ.

The vomeronasal organ directly signals the amygdala. The information gets processed there, then sent to the hypothalamus for further processing and to form an appropriate behavioral response. This area in the hypothalamus controls the social behavior related to sexual activity. As you can see, this route avoids the higher cortex where the sense of smell is processed. When a male mouse loses his ability to discriminate between the pheromones secreted by a male and the pheromones secreted by a female, he loses his ability to discriminate between sexes. This sense that mice have is, in reality, a sense that humans do not have; you can call it a sixth sense if you like! This introduction is somewhat important for the reader to get an idea about the immense complexity of sexual behavior in general.

If you look at two mice, male and female sitting side by side, it is not easy to know which one is the male and which one is the female. This could be the case for mice also when they look at each other for the very first time if they have never seen each other before. Mice must use the vomeronasal system to detect the pheromones secreted by males and females. In other mammals, it might be easy to figure out the sex of an animal by looking at them, like in lions. The vomeronasal system, in this case, will not do the exact job that it does in mice, but still has a significant role in their mating behavior.

In the case of birds, like peacocks, it is easy to see the difference between the male and the female: the male has his amazing fantail. But in the case of canaries and many other species, birds pay attention to other clues like the singing of the birds, the body posture, the behavior and other very subtle physical differences.

Humans do not rely on the vomeronasal system to know the sex of other humans. The shape of the male and the female is strikingly different, and the human brain is extremely well designed to detect these differences. When other animals look at us, they may or may not be so impressed by these differences, depending on the species and how frequently we are in contact with them.

We have no reason to smell each other to know the sex of our next-door neighbor because we are using our sense of vision and hearing. We also interpret the body language and the behavior of other humans.

Our sense of vision is the fastest sense to give us this information. Visual processing information in human males, when looking at a female, will lead to mating behavior as well as other social connecting behaviors which include, love, platonic love, the desire to have company with the opposite sex, and I will leave the rest for your imagination. All these sensory inputs that we discussed will go through the amygdala to reach the reward system and the hypothalamus. The latter two areas can collect information about this person of interest to us, from other sensory areas in the brain other than the amygdala.

Pornography in the Human Example

Now with the invention of TV and the internet, the media shows females and males partially or totally naked. Porn shows naked females/males ready for mating, and this is a scene that denies any other function that these humans have. This is an extremely unrealistic scene. Porn tries to convince us that humans are basically zombies.

This situation can change the behavior of the viewers and trigger mating behavior, especially in men. This stimulation for mating behavior is based on unrealistic, fake scenes. With repetition, the male hypothalamus, the amygdala, and the nucleus accumbens systems will be programmed accordingly. These delicate centers in the brain that we have been discussing in every chapter of this tiny book, are extremely sensitive detectors, more than what we give them credit for. So, what does this imply for humans? It implies that we do have innate mating behavior, but it is subject to adding many additions and modifications, at least in vulnerable people. But how? Let us consider the facial expressions of people who are performing in a pornography scene. Every tiny facial expression gets registered in these centers—the hypothalamus, amygdala, nucleus accumbens systems—subconsciously.

No matter how these actors disguise their inner psychological dialogue, which will include anxiety, depression, drug addiction, past sexual abuse, and poverty, these sensitive agents can detect them. This will lead to negative programming of the arousal and sexual excitement circuits in people who are watching these scenes. This will facilitate creating pathological behavioral traits, in regard to mating behavior. Some of this pathological programming includes the programming of the sexual arousal centers to be stimulated by scenes of actors who are depressed, abused, have no social support, living in poverty, addicted to drugs, etc.

Picture manipulation becomes sophisticated in the super-technical age we are currently living in. The pictures of the females are manipulated so they look very young at their prime ages of attraction. This creates a very phony, deceiving unrealistic scenario in the mind of the males who are watching. These young females are smiling, looking friendly and inviting. But at the same time, they seem to be intoxicated with sexual feelings and promiscuity, lacking other emotions, and they are behaving like sex addicts. Even though in reality they could be drug addicts or humans not living a happy life. These women likely are victim to psychiatric illnesses and abusive social environments. This miserable life, we are all responsible for; it is our creation and society needs to wake up to this fact.

This is the world of pornography! Recently, in mainstream pediatric journals, we started to see a screaming article talking about the negative effect of pornography on the brain of youths and how easy it is to go online and be able to fall victim to watching these scenes. This will contribute to creating the next generation of sexual predators and victims.

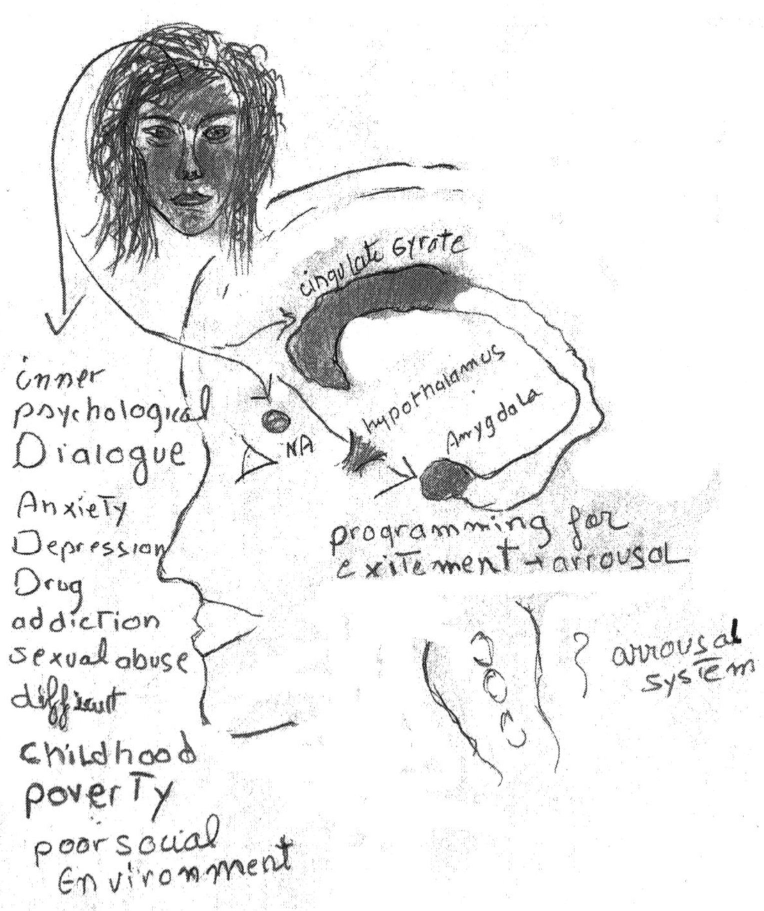

Psychosexual maturation in teenagers now is influenced by, and it is under the mercy of the visual media. This maturation is moving parallel to the reprogramming that is taking place in the reward system. Watching movies is a very common leisure activity teenagers and adults do regularly. Let us discuss a scenario in a PG-13 movie showing a bunch of teenagers engaged in social gatherings and often alcohol is shown. Curtsey of the producer, they show you a couple leaving the crowd to a private room trying to have an intimate time, of course without any sex scenes in this kind of movie. I would like to describe this scene as mini-porn which could be worse than porn because now it is exploiting the emotions and the feelings of the teenagers. It is affecting the inspiration of the human and the values of society in these scenes. Worse than that, when a movie shows teenagers behaving without emotions or with shallow emotions, it creates a stereotype of human behavior through conformity. These movies can get inside our home, spreading the same message to teenagers worldwide.

Sexuality: Neuro-Hormonal System

Now let us go briefly over the neuronal-hormonal system that manages sexuality. Adding to the very complex role that the hypothalamus plays in sustaining life, it also takes a leading role as a master regulator of sexual function. The hypothalamus secretes the gonadotropin-releasing hormone to target the pituitary gland. This in turn secrets the follicle-stimulating hormone (FSH) and the luteinizing hormone (LH) to stimulate the ovaries in females to produce mature eggs and to stimulate the testicles in males to produce sperm with the help of testosterone. Before puberty, the part of the hypothalamus that takes this role is dormant. At the time of puberty, it starts working gradually to a point of full maturity in a few years, then gradually declines till the end of our life.

What triggers this biological clock is not known. As in many biological clocks, like the beating of the heart, mechanistically we can describe it with ample knowledge, but why does it beat? We do not know, and there is a very good chance that we will never know.

The Emotion of Love

Love is the mother of all human psychological connections, and love is defined as a psychological dependence that is activating the reward system when the human engages in thinking of the beloved person. In this state, dopamine reaches the nucleus accumbens at a very high rate which leads to a strong euphoric state, and likely this is associated with activation in the endorphin system.

When the rest of the brain neocortex is engaged in thinking about the beloved person, it is trying to find a solution for all the obstacles to meet this person. The neocortex is involved in imagination about how the situation is going to be when seeing the beloved one, and this in turn is going to further influence the nucleus accumbens.

It is hard for us to imagine that while a person is engaged in thinking about their beloved one, they can solve a math problem at the same time. Lots of resources from the entire brain and the entire limbic system are responding to these thoughts. This will create a state of prediction and expectation to see the beloved one which will influence the nucleus accumbens to be in a state of hypersensitization to any stimulation that is connected to this person.

If these predictions do not materialize for a while, this might create a state of desperation similar to what happens in drug withdrawal, which is a sad feeling. If these two people get together and the relationship goes to a stable mode, this will leave the reward system with a slightly increased level of dopamine above the baseline. Depending on the stability of the limbic system and the reward systems, the relationship is sustained. Cultural, religious, and social factors play a role in maintaining this stability.

The structure of love in our minds is influenced by our social surroundings, including media and other people's opinions. In our time, love tends to be mixed with physical addiction and sexuality to a great extent. We all have the concept of what the word love means, but it does not have to involve physical addiction. Poems from all cultures tend to describe love as pure, giving emotion, and not based on fulfilling physical needs. If you watch

TV and movies, you will see the domination of the concept of physical attraction in human relationships. After a few meetings with the beloved one, the couples are in bed. Most movies tend to emphasize sexuality and physical contact as a core part of every love relationship.

The human being is pictured as looking for someone to make him/her happy and satisfy their hunger for physical contact as well as psychological demand for company and interaction with the opposite sex. This hunger, as I described earlier, is partially created and shaped by the media. We tend to introduce sexual addiction and use the human being as a material, or as a drug, covered or hidden under the emotion of love.

In a relationship that is initiated by physical addiction from one or both sides, to satisfy the demand of an addicted partner the emotion of love in this example does not even exist. People in this scenario allow themselves to be consumed like drugs are by an addict.

As in consuming any drug, the effect of this process will not be sustained with time. This will lead to the breakdown of this fragile relationship. Subjected to societal programming, males tend to emphasize physical contact as a core part of their relationship with females as compared to playing a more emotional-spiritual role, but this is not always the rule.

Neuro-Mapping of Love

The emotion of love in its pure form acts as a powerful brain stimulator that can shut down the sexual impulses without much struggle and a hug will suffice or a smile will do. For that reason, it is logical to think that the centers of the emotion of love in the hypothalamus are not far from the brain cells responsible for sexual feelings and sexual maturation and puberty.

The cellular architecture and the specific design of the hypothalamus centers in each human allow us to merge the feelings of both love and sexual attraction for our beloved partner to result in a lifelong functioning relationship. I hope you agree that there is a big difference between having sexual feelings supervised by the emotion of love, and sexual arousal that is supervised by the visual media. The brain function during these experiences is totally different. The emotion of love, when very active, changes the brain's metabolism immensely and allows us a humane experience. We find these humane experiences surprisingly in abundance in the animal kingdom's male-female relations. Often, when we observe animal behavior, we find what we can interpret as romantic and tender affection between partners. When a human behaves sexually in a violent and abusive way, society has the responsibility to look into environmental elements that would contribute to this disastrous programming in the limbic system of this violent person and try to fix them.

The influence of the emotion of love on the limbic system goes beyond supervising the emotion of sex. It positively stimulates the human. For example, imagine a depressed human whose feelings are submerged with negativity and depression, then all of a sudden they become very energetic with activity in the reward system. As we discussed in the reward center, we feel this change in the form of optimism and enthusiasm. The positive effect of the state of love could go on for years of our life unless sabotaged by the ego. From a neurophysiological perspective, it is a dilemma to try to explain how the brain's metabolism all of sudden can be changed with the emotion of ideal love.

Our Love for Our Pets

Love in the animal kingdom does exist for sure, and it plays a central role in the survival of animals and the continuity of the species. The tenderness that the mother bird gives to her babies, could rival any tenderness given by any human mother to her babies. The dedication that bird parents and many other species give to their babies, may exceed what humans can do in some scenarios. Humans take a break from their duties of caring for their newborns when they have to sleep and eat, which is very normal. Human females can go through postpartum depression especially when the structures of her home and her society are not ideal. From my experience with songbirds, a couple will give ninety-nine percent of their time to care for their babies with extreme dedication to allow these babies to mature and be on their own. When their role is done, the emotion of love settles down, allowing the babies to go their separate ways until the next reproduction cycle restarts.

Human investment in bringing children into the world has an implicit contract. It implies that we are assured that we will have a source to fulfil our need to give and express the emotion of love toward our children and receive it back from them. Letting go of our children will crash the limbic system and deprive us of this emotion. We tend to show this emotion toward our grandchildren when this emotion is difficult to show toward our mature forty-year-old daughter or son.

The new rigid social and economic structures, the demise of love in our super high-tech world and the rough demands of life often separate us from our children or will make us live in a small nuclear family. To satisfy our need to have more contact with loving creatures, we find having a friend from the animal kingdom to be of great value to our spiritual love needs. This offers us an outlet for our love emotion to be expressed. We treat our pets as spirits, and we feel them as spirits. The negative side of that is the unrealistic obedience that our animals give us because our role in this relationship is controlling and owning. We expect our pets to be where we want them to be, sleep when we want them to sleep, eat what we want them to eat, and do what we want them to do. We put them in cages and on a leash. This form of interaction is unrealistic between humans because we cannot own humans. When we love them we have to give them space.

Sexually Transmitted Diseases

The other issue related to this matter is sexually transmitted diseases. I would like to share with you the headline of a recent edition of a famous pediatric journal, named The Infectious Disease Journal in Children that says: the sexually transmitted disease (STD) epidemic in the US carries a staggering human and economic cost.

I am actually reading the edition of this journal while I am writing these lines, and I am going to share with you some of what is written in the article, word by word: "The rates of sexually transmitted diseases are at an all-time high in the United States, there is a need for more screening as well as better treatment and prevention methods. STD rates are rising and many of the countries' systems for preventing STDs have eroded."

What I see is that there is no lack of knowledge about the benefit of abstinence in preventing STDs, neither is their lack of general knowledge in the public about STDs. The real reason why this epidemic is taking place is ignored. There is a lack of spiritual dimension and wise social support in our life to help us make wise decisions. The habitat for humanity is not limited to just home for the body and knowledge for the mind. It should include a spiritual dimension, a sound culture and a stable family institution.

When a sexual act has been installed in the mind and reinforced to be okay with a partner whom the human does not have a spiritual and emotional connection with, or sacred societal ties or bonds with, a surge in STD rates is not surprising. The instinct that we have to protect ourselves from diseases and dangerous situations becomes disabled. We are left with a chaotic reward system that is unable to give us satisfaction and happiness on one hand and is leading us to psychological misery which makes us vulnerable for medical diseases on the other hand.

Sexual desire and ego-driven emotions sometimes feel like love, but they are not. Addictive physical desires by themselves, are not a strong factor in creating any long-lasting bond. And that is what I am seeing from dealing with teenagers. This way of living has a low rate of success and carries serious societal consequences, contributing to the misery of both sexes and the demise of society.

Compared to us, animals' mating rituals have a variety of models to fit their biology. They have a clear idea of what they are doing, and you can see the complicated design of the nest that birds are building before mating, with a clear concept of the purpose of building this nest. The nest is usually built-in one to two days and is glued somehow to the branch of a tree by using a biological glue they secrete from their mouth. They are taking into consideration that force of the wind that may shake the branch of the tree, so the nest may stay safe.

One day, I was looking at the side of the building where I work to find an abandoned nest, and it looked like the nest was built over the weekend by a red robin. The nest was abandoned, most likely because the bird realized that there is too much human activity in the area, and it was too exposed. When I tried to remove the nest, I found it to be stuck to the side of the building. My take on this is that the physical attraction between birds is not just about feather touching hunger and mating desire, it carries with it other desires like sustaining the species and having babies.

In the case of salmon, after a long journey back to the place where they came from, the mating rituals between a female and a male do not include any touching at all. These fish are driven by a powerful emotion to go back to the place where they were hatched from as eggs. This journey leads to their exhaustion and then death, but not before securing the eggs of the females to become fertilized by the sperm of the males. If there was lousy media in the life of salmon it would try to convince them that touching each other would be more rewarding than going back to the place where they were born.

Human life is way more complicated, and obviously, we are not repeating the same rituals that our ancestors did a thousand years ago. These days, when we get married, especially in the developed world, we do not even repeat the rituals of the previous generation. Our rituals are changing constantly. The sophisticated electronic devices we are creating, which are created by the higher neocortex, are coming down on us influencing our social brain. These devices have this opportunity because of the social emptiness that we happen to be living in during our current time.

In the past, it was commonly said that need was the mother of creation. These days, it seems to be the other way around: creation has become the mother of need. The neocortex is creating more possibilities for us to experience pleasure, and more possibilities will create new needs.

Back to Sexual Transmutation

Now let us discuss the main subject. Napoleon Hill, as we discussed earlier, gave the example that when a bricklayer transforms his/her sexual energy into something useful, he/she will lay more bricks. Napoleon insisted that many successful famous people became successful after the age of forty or fifty when the toll of sexual influence on the human becomes limited. Napoleon explained that a relationship that does not have a spiritual dimension does not bring to the human being any long-lasting positive reward in his/her life. Napoleon advised physicians to counsel their patients on this matter, to help them apply sexual transmutation, and that is what I am going to be doing in the next few pages.

Techniques to Help in the Transmutation

No matter how your views about sexuality and morality are structured, you are going to have some form of boundaries, and these boundaries are connected to society and culture whether you feel this connection or not. Even when you do not believe that social structures have anything to do with your sexuality, you are going to have some boundaries based on your own personal feelings and opinions.

Common sense and experience in life tell you that it is better to be in a relationship with a loving and caring partner, sharing interests, values and beliefs. This partner is trusting and trusted and you enjoy his/her company.

Sexual transmutation is about keeping busy at work whenever any sexual impulse takes place. So how would anybody achieve that? We are going to achieve it through our own cognitive therapy and creative imagination. An example of creative imagination in this instance involves rehearsing a scenario like this one:

Looking at a potentially arousing image, for example a naked woman, will use many pathways in the brain. It starts from the retina in the eye then passes through the thalamus. The thalamus sends signals in two directions: the first is toward the amygdala, the second, to the posterior visual cortex. This visual cortex also interacts with the rest of the neocortex and the rest of the cortical centers concerned with conscious experiences in the neurologic sense. What I mean by that is those that we can report about. The amygdala will decide whether the picture of the person is of interest or not. Also, face recognition cells in the brain will be activated. Then the nucleus accumbens is informed about the situation, and a reaction is formed. The memory center in the temporal cortex and the hippocampus will be consulted. From our past discussion, you might have figured out that a circuitry triad composed of the amygdala, the nucleus accumbens and the hypothalamus becomes active together. These centers will have the most say in how we are going to react ultimately to the experience of looking at the picture of a naked woman.

The result of this pathway will be influenced by all past social experiences, cultural biases, TV programs, movies and what friends are talking about. Also, religious influence will have a say in the way we respond to these messages.

What is considered attractive, may vary according to society. In some cultures less exposed to the media, the woman has to be somewhat on the heavy side to be considered attractive. It is impossible to know how much influence the media and other environmental factors have on our judgment of what is considered attractive or not. Some observation is coming up with general guidelines about the proportions of facial landmarks to be the standard of cuteness. The media is now worldwide, influencing all cultures in the same manner in regard to what is considered cute or not. It is hard to judge whether what is considered beautiful is hardwired in all of our brains or adopted from the media and society.

Finally, the signal reaches the hypothalamus and the endorphins are secreted. The hypothalamus is the last organ that receives the signal, it has the most say in the matter, and its role most likely is more important than the nucleus accumbens on how our response will be. Numerous centers in the hypothalamus are going to interact with the centers dealing with sexuality.

Many spiritual and religious teachings describe looking at a picture of naked women to be connected to enhancing the desire in the mind which will lead ultimately to suffering. Nudity also implies sexual slavery, abuse of women, human trafficking, and the degradation of women. There is a good chance that a woman is exposing herself to the world of nudity because she needs money to live, is a drug addict, or has a psychiatric disorder.

The influence of the hypothalamus on our feelings and psychology is subjected to the design of the neurocircuits of its multiple nodes and the way they are programmed intracellularly. How this biological programming is felt by us and the rest of our social brain is beyond miraculous. Turning our face away from a nude picture, when done consciously, is led by a harmonious limbic system. This will resolve the influence of this picture on our minds. Subsequently, the nucleus accumbens and the hypothalamus return to a neutral state. The nucleus accumbens is not in any state of deprivation or addiction state, and the hypothalamus goes back to keeping the body working and focusing on doing its other numerous tasks, as we discussed its many other roles in the introduction.

Now, how could we prevent this mental stroke from taking place in the first place? Someone who does not have a spouse yet, like a student in college, or someone who is looking for a partner with certain mental characteristics and has not found one yet, could benefit from sexual transmutation. It is a disaster for her or him, and for society, to sleep with people to get to know whether these people have the desired mental characteristics or not. By taking this chance, the risk of programming the sexual arousal to run by promiscuity may become well established as a strong drive in us.

For sure in the hunter-gatherers' model, everything is worked out by the close social network. The relatives and the chief will assign a husband to a wife. I do not know if they are going to ask the bride and the groom if they feel an attraction to each other in the modern sense. The naïve form of attraction is primed by the society, and of course by the physiology of the human. The husband and wife both are told that their ideal partner is waiting for them and the neurological construction in the forms of new circuits are being worked in the limbic system. Needless to say, that this construction project was prepared for years before the time of puberty. The tradition also structures the role of each partner, which will decrease the chances of disagreements between them in the future. Life here is too simple: a big chunk of human activity is structured around having some food on the table at end of the day, being safe, and enjoying the company of your spouse and extended family members and friends. The partners do not have a chance to disagree on which company they are going to hire to do their photography or to do their floral design. Their social obligations are spelled out clearly to them and endorsed by society. There is no need to argue about where the honeymoon is going to take place because it is taking place in their tiny new home, and other options are not even on their radar.

Techniques in Sexual Transmutation

Let us take this scenario: a person is faced with a stimulating situation, as in seeing a picture of an almost naked woman. The response to this situation may take different directions. The person who is implementing sexual transmutation needs to imagine themselves behaving in a way completely indifferent to what they saw, then has to imagine that they are getting a boost of energy as they are working in their usual work. The word "imagine" that I used sounds simple, but in this example, we should give it a bit of sophistication. For the imagination to be effective, it has to be amended by believing, and what I mean by that is believing in the ability to succeed in putting the emotion of sex under complete control.

This process of imagination could also be amended by a cognitive one. For example, understanding that living in the world of physical desire will carry unnecessary suffering. The image of a naked woman should be interpreted as a picture of a human being and not a material body reduced to become a drug to be consumed by an addict. If someone catches themself looking at any nude image, immediately they should imagine our friend Hoover the rat sitting in a cage with an electrical circuit connected to his nucleus accumbens and hypothalamus, ready to zap his brain and die. The viewer has to understand the concept that watching porn is equivalent to plugging their reward system into an electrical circuit and destroying their biological source of living, as shown in figure 9.5.

The human has to understand that describing women in the workplace or on TV as cute, referring to their body structure, means placing someone in a cage and placing electric wires in the brain, connecting the wires to a lever then pressing on it. A naked image stimulates meaningless chemistry in the brain with final results called suffering and maybe depression. This form of addiction is hijacking, then absolutely destroying the natural reward system that is designed for us to experience life and enjoy it as is.

This is a spiritual practice, and I will try to explain it in a modern neuro-circuitry sense. I am sure our ancestors figured this out without knowledge about the reward system or the hypothalamus. In the beginning, this may be a hard task, but with daily repetition for a few months, what do you think is going to happen in the brain? If you think this is not going to work, I suggest trying it first. The trial itself is an experience that is going to be harmless.

What is also going to help is listening to a spiritual talk and reading spiritual books. Many spiritual books discuss the negative effect of the ego and physical desires when they take over the mind. Eastern philosophies and religions do a fair job elaborating on this subject by insisting on preventing using the mind and thinking in the direction of desires. Also, Western religions tackle this matter effectively. Religions try to show the fleeting nature of desires and materialistic possessions, including inflated sexuality.

Other techniques of this transmutation may include meditation by imagining that the response to the visual stimulation is blunt. Before you do these meditations, you have to be in a very happy mood, otherwise they will be ineffective. You have to prime yourself to be in self-control and in a confident state. Then, imagine a nudity related scene and you are turning your face away from it, because pornography and the exploitation of the individuals is disgusting, and it is a very short cut to suffering, misery, and depression in the long run. You have to believe that this imagination is reality. The word belief is the magic of this technique.

If this technique does not seem to work, and rationality is not able to face the addiction the response has to be more negative and visceral. Imagine that you can modify the deep pleasure parts of the brain, the amygdala, hypothalamus and nucleus accumbens, as if they are mechanical parts. Imagine your amygdala giving indifferent responses to this stimulus, or shutting down and having no responsibility for any sexually-related stimuli, whether it is coming from outside, or from the neocortex. Better yet, imagine the amygdala having a repulsive and negative response to these stimuli. You have to imagine that your hypothalamus also is not responding or giving a painful response to any stimulus coming from the amygdala, which is translated to a negative dopamine/opioid balance, leading to a painful feeling. Imagine that your pituitary gland output stays the same and does not fluctuate, so the effect of sex hormones on the brain will be steady without fluctuation, so you can control any arousal effect influenced by these hormones on your mind. Imagine that the hypothalamic activity and metabolism are lessened in the area being stimulated to any sexual related activity. This result will be similar to what the brain of an eight-year-old does when viewing any naked image. It considers it repulsive and disgusting!

If that does not work, you have to up the ante like having nausea for sexually related ideas and scenes. In that case, you have to imagine that both the hypothalamus and the amygdala are sending messages to the vagus nerve which is connected to the gastrointestinal tract, and this in turn is moving the stomach toward vomiting! Imagine that you are going back in age and reversing the puberty changes enough to have your mind under your control. Please use your intelligence to find what would be suitable for you in case these examples do not work. If the movie industry will ever take note of what I wrote and make a movie out of that, they will get my blessing and I can assure you that I am not going to ask for any royalty or credit.

During this process, you need to be in a happy, confident mood; this is essential in the process. You need to maintain positive dopamine and opioid balance to succeed quickly. Not only are you going to feel happier for releasing yourself from addictive thinking that paralyzes your brain, but it is going to help you avoid behavior that you might regret. You have to do that at least two times every day and slowly you will see yourself mastering this skill. Relapsing to old behavior is going to happen without patience and persistence.

In the future when you find a suitable partner for marriage, all of this will be reversed: reversed in a manner to connect you with this partner, not in the manner the society wants to inquire about you by asking, "Are you sexually active?"

When we ask the question, "Are you sexually active?" We could be considering the human being's intimate relationship as a mechanical one that does not have a spiritual side. This is similar to when we ask, "Did you go to sleep last night?" a process that is deprived of emotion and connection to any human being, or when asked, "Did you eat steak yesterday?" This question is not suitable for the ideal and functional human society.

Bear in mind that a one-hundred-percent-suitable partner does not exist on planet Earth. Differences have to be accepted by each partner. Armed with these skills, when you go into your marriage your chances of success, without ending in divorce, are much higher because you give your brain a chance to think and evaluate. If you master this matter, I will congratulate you. Keep in mind that some of us do not need to go through this process. Their brain is put together idealistically, despite all the sexually related stimuli that are running the media.

Happiness must be envisioned through the eyes of a six-year-old child who is happy, not because she won the lottery, not because she is a sexual being, and not because the stock market jumped up a thousand points and doubled her money. A six-year-old child is much wiser than all the adults around her. She is not bothered by all of that chaos. Her life is simple. She is enjoying the simple activities, which do not have to be a big deal like sexuality or winning a lottery ticket.

What is going to happen when we are successful in sexual transmutation? The metabolism of the cells of the hypothalamus which have the most interface with our feelings and qualia, and the hormonal control in regard to puberty and sexual maturation, will slow down. Metabolically the biological activity in the neurohormonal systems that take twenty-four hours to occur; now it may take weeks.

The effect of the sex hormones on behavior, as demonstrated by studies done by Robert Sapolsky, does not have the last word on how we behave. The response to testosterone by the key social centers that control sexuality, the amygdala, the nucleus accumbens and the hypothalamus, is mediated by many other social and environmental factors and influenced by neuronal plasticity. The whole area before puberty was naïve and dormant; we can get near this stage psychologically with training.

Why not have the option of reversing the function of these areas in the brain that deal with sexuality? Why can't these centers have an intelligent role added to their own roles? Why do we have to leave ourselves subjected to our primitive instinct, functioning below the animals?

Animals are governed by sophisticated systems to keep their life in superb function and keep their species alive. Why are the most sophisticated creatures on the planet, us, living with no system?

Peer Pressure, Sexuality and Social Conformity

I go through the social history of my patients in the office, and I see that a huge number of my patients are living with their mothers. Where is the father? He just does not want to be bothered, and the battle is going on for child support in the court system. The father does not want to pay child support. The fact that makes me very surprised is when I hear about the selfish gene, as my dear friends in biology classes are talking about. The genes that are held by a creature are supposed to be passed on to the next generation and will be able to survive. I am sorry to say that I am not seeing that from my observation of human behavior. All that I see is hedonism and egoism. Which is stronger, the genes or the social programming? You decide. The father-child bond has the potential to become weak when social programming is against it, sadly.

Why is this scene taking place? It is due to conformity, which is the mental conditioning that took place over a long period of interacting with our environment and played a major role in structuring the reward system.

When the human sees and hears that the bond between the child and the father should be very strong, and the integrity of this bond is extremely rewarding, the reward system will be structured accordingly. Society can strengthen this bond by showing that it is an important source of pleasure in life, and we should sacrifice to keep it safe and strong, lasting till the end of life. The child's reward system and the limbic system should be structured according to these ideas. These concepts literally are changing the brain physically by connecting the abstract ideas, like children's parent bond in the neocortex to the prefrontal cortex, then to the hypothalamus and the reward systems. This becomes part of the personality of the human and constructs their biases subconsciously. When children become adults, they will wake up to life, carrying these ideas to heart.

Now compare that to a young man sitting with his friends on a street, listening to them bragging about the number of children they fathered with different women while still "enjoying the single life." The phrase "enjoying the single life" will be engraved in the human brain of the people who are listening to this statement to some extent. After that, it may reach the heart and limbic system, then the hypothalamus including the reproductive system. This will lead to restructuring the intracellular systems and the dendritic connection between the cells located in the hypothalamic area, the amygdala, and the reward system. You can imagine how desires are being formed slowly, and this young man will mature and not experience a different scenario. Or he might experience a different scenario, but he has in his mind conflicting scenarios making his life difficult.

When we interact with the environment, we are not a blank slate, as Emmanuel Kant tries to explain to us in his books, but the result of this interaction is not going to be always in our favor when the environmental forces in our life are not the best and the wisest. When the human is already brought up by a single mother and the father cannot be bothered, the child-father bond has higher odds not to be ideal. The father is either watching football, in prison, looking for a new encounter or in the hospital. The father may be in his second or third marriage after he acquired knowledge and wisdom to be patient in his new relationship. He for sure paid a heavy price for the knowledge that he acquired from his past experiences.

Serious and honest social organizations are needed to fix this crack in the societal foundation, and it is fixable. Schools, religious institutions, and universities have a major role to play, other than taking people's money.

The media might also wake up at some point and look over the disaster that it has created and realized that it is in the interest of nobody. Do we really have a purpose in producing a movie or program? Or it is only to serve our ego and deep pockets. Why do we allow our ego to make us behave like hungry beings, while we are not going to bed at night hungry? In fact, we are overeating, refluxing during sleep, and having heartburn, which could be from spicy food.

Where Are You on the Love Scale?

Are you a giver or a taker? Or to rephrase the question, since we all play both roles in every marriage or relationship, what percentage do you have of each of these elements? When you are playing the giver role, the role is going to be like this: you are a generous person in your relationship, having your spouse happy emotionally by using words and gestures. You are flooding your partner with generous emotions, beautiful words, compliments and persistent smiles reflecting your warm emotions. Do you support your partner when facing difficulties in life? Do you try to look for your spouse's wishes and try to make them come true? This point is tricky because hopefully, your spouse's wishes are not only materialistic. Are you able to cross the boundaries and rules of society to assure that your relationship survives? Are you a giver in terms of giving material objects, like showering your spouse with money and gifts within your ability, without charging your credit card more than it can handle? Do you have a spiritual dimension in this relationship? Do you give your spouse space when circumstances require?

Are you a taker, asking your partner to do things for you continuously? Is your relationship demanding a vacation, shopping, buying a new car, and a new house? Is your relationship with your spouse about addictive anxious attachment? Is your conversation with your spouse about your superficial daily drama only? Is your conversation full of worry about the future and your financial concerns? Are you always complaining that you are not getting the attention that you deserve from your spouse? Do you get upset if your material demands are not met? Do you have your spouse take the responsibility of making you happy and fulfilling all your needs? How much are you a giver? How much are you a taker?

You can ask yourself these simple screening questions to help you evaluate your emotions and understand your personality. Without a continuous effort to understand and improve husband-wife interaction, the relationship may lose a necessary element to keep it vibrant.

STOP 10

EATING DISORDER

Sharing a meal with other people at the end of the day has helped us satisfy the strong desire for eating and socializing, especially gatherings with other family members, friends, and extended relatives.

Food preparation is an essential part of human activity, and it is enjoyed by all cultures. However, in our modern times, many people eat in restaurants regularly or buy already cooked food. The activity of food preparation became less essential, and with our busy lifestyles, we are very quick at filling the time with other activities. This activity is close to becoming obsolete in many homes.

In the past, bringing food to the house was the center of human activity. The entire day's task was spent to secure this need. For example, in cultures based on traditional farming, and in hunter-gather societies, humans spent their days finding or growing crops, then storing them. Preparing food for eating was the real luxury activity of the day, and food security was the center of the family's economic planning.

The situation has become very different in our time. Shopping is the main way of bringing food home. Securing food in this way could still be time-consuming and potentially strenuous, especially in places where easy transportation is not available. In the developed world, shopping has become very easy, since people shop in supermarkets, simply placing the items in their carts and then driving home. This activity is becoming increasingly more convenient since many grocery stores offer online ordering and pickups from the front of the store. Better yet, we are now able to order and get the food delivered to our homes.

As you can see with time, the activity of putting food on the table is becoming less and less important compared to other activities. Assuming you have the financial means, there is not much worry about the possibility of going to bed hungry. This is no doubt, one of the greatest benefits of the industrial revolution.

Eating satisfies the powerful desire controlled by the complicated reward system. This system, when working in optimal conditions, will allow us to have what is described as an ideal body weight. The ideal body weight will help us live our lives with less of a chance of developing medical problems. The limbic system faces many challenges in our time, due to many changes affecting our lives. These are taking place at a fast speed and beyond our ability to adapt at the same rate.

Hypothalamic Control of Eating and Hunger

The hypothalamus exerts the function of eating through its two arms: the hormonal arm and the neurological arm.

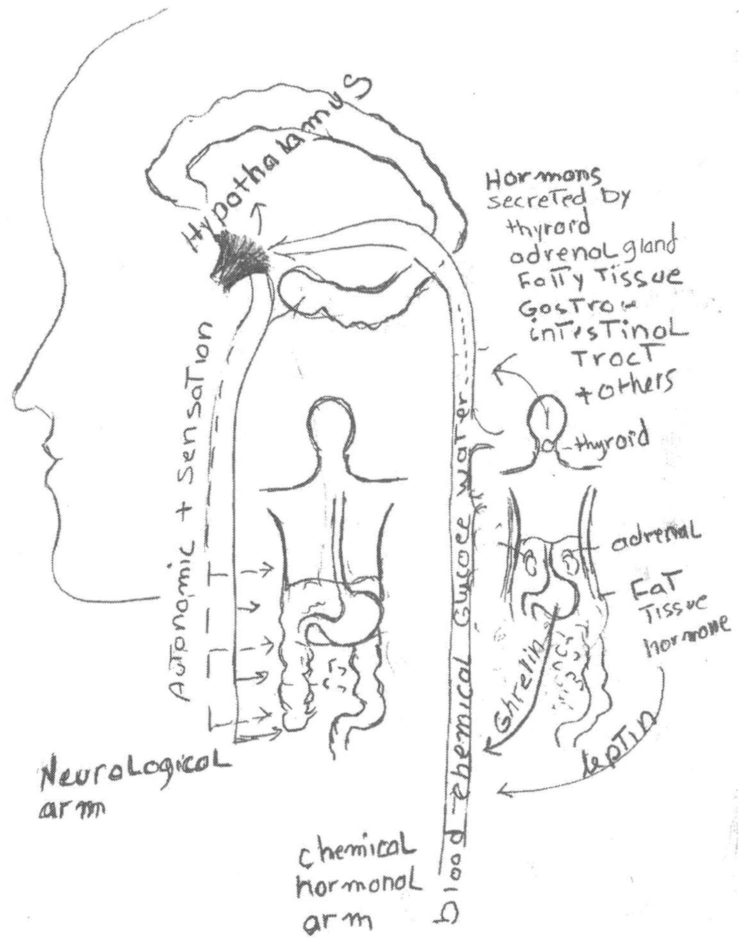

These two arms are designed for sending orders to the rest of the body and receiving information from it. The hypothalamus has the necessary sensors to do this function. It senses the status of the blood chemical components and hormones secreted by the rest of the endocrine glands, and the status of other organs through its neurological connection with the rest of the body. In this connection, the vagus nerve controls the parasympathetic functions in the stomach and bowels. This nerve allows the hypothalamus to connect to these organs and senses their status of readiness for eating.

The Hormonal Arm of the Hypothalamus

The hypothalamus receives signals from the rest of the body through its ability to sense the blood concentration of glucose, salt and water. Also, it receives feedback about the levels of hormones secreted by the endocrine glands, stomach, intestines, and fatty tissues.

In response to these messages, the hypothalamus miraculously induces the state of hunger which is felt by you and me or by the means of our consciousness. Then it mobilizes the organism toward this immensely complicated function of eating and drinking. The hypothalamus secretes hormones like orexin, which target the locus coeruleus. The locus coeruleus is the main part of the arousal system in the brain stem, which secretes norepinephrine and other chemicals. This system creates an arousal state, colored with the feeling of hunger and readiness to eat!

The epinephrine secreted from the locus coeruleus reaches the rest of the brain and the amygdala. The amygdala starts screening the environment for food, especially for what looks good and tasty. The amygdala is calling upon the hippocampus to revive memories, which reinforces the decision to eat a certain food.

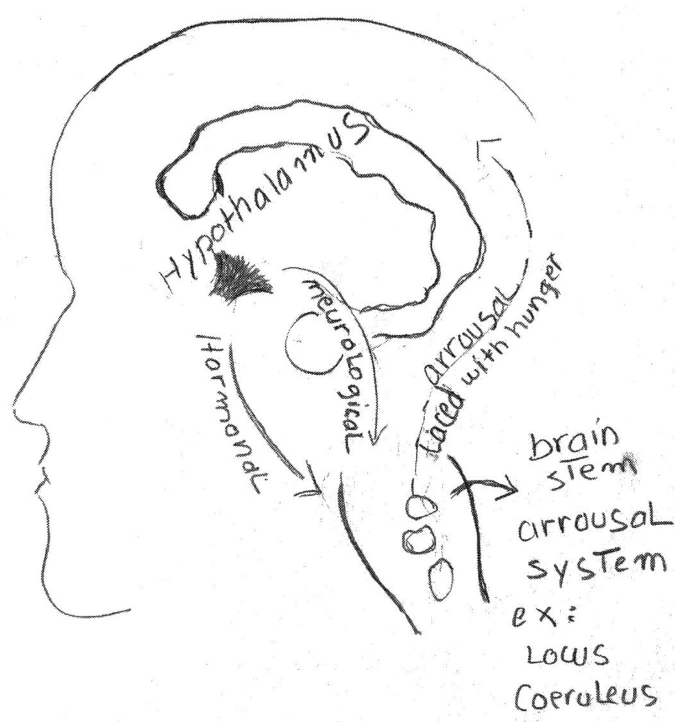

How is the Reward System Activated?

The amygdala easily connects with the nucleus accumbens, which is also one of the main target areas of the arousal system with its ventral tegmental area node, as we discussed during the chapter on the reward system.

This will create a strong desire for food and an urge to eat, making the body move and look for food. The complexity and harmony of this system are beyond what words can describe.

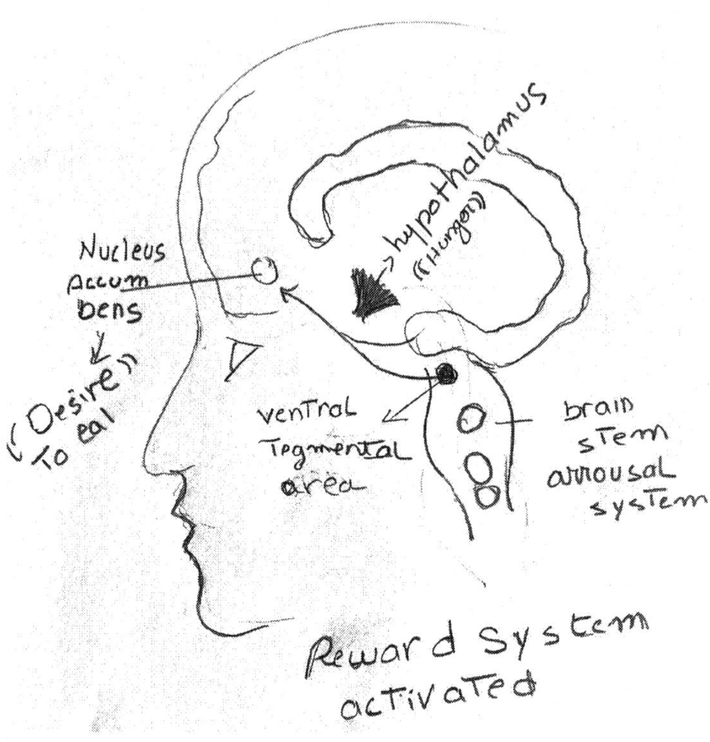

The Neurological Arm of the Hypothalamus

The vagus nerve is the main nerve that connects the gastrointestinal tract with the parasympathetic centers in the limbic system. The branches of this nerve allow the hypothalamus to sense the neuronal signaling from the stomach, the small and large bowels, the pancreas, and the liver. The function of the parasympathetic system on the gastrointestinal tract and organs is to prepare them for eating. It is sending information about the status of the food that was consumed, and what digestive state we are in. Is there a stool in the large intestine? Have we had a bowel movement today? It will provide the hypothalamus with this information. When the message is in favor of eating, it will start the series of events, leading to the activation of the nucleus accumbens, which will help create a status of temporary addiction to eating.

The nucleus accumbens, the amygdala and the hypothalamus are programmed over the years of our life by eating a variety of food, and this process forms our food preferences. This programming takes place in the intracellular structure of these nodes, as well as in the architecture of their neurological circuits. The ultimate role in the restructuring of both the intracellular architecture and neuro-circuitry maps is to allow us to eat the available food in our environment. In the end, this may lead to the release of endorphins which are part of the reward mediator to eating food.

This programming has been taking place since our childhood. The kinds of cheese we were exposed to, the spices our parents used are going to shape our reward system. Even the ratio of the variety of bacteria and yeast living in the environment have a say in this matter. These organisms have an important function in making ethnic foods like cheese, yogurt, pickles, and bread.

We grow up adopting our own taste for certain foods, which becomes a part of our own naïve personal preference. Since food is an important element of our culture, certain meals could be associated with certain occasions or festivities. This will leave a lasting imprint on our memory. Needless to say, the happier we are while eating a meal, the more likely it is that that meal will become a favorite one.

But how do we really enjoy food? Dopamine floods the nucleus accumbens while we are looking at food and moving towards eating, followed by the hypothalamus's secretion of endorphins before and while eating, as we discussed in the reward system chapter. After a few bites, this state of temporary addiction to eating gradually subsides and the dopamine level decreases as well as the endorphins secreted by the hypothalamus.

Without the idea of consciousness being involved here, our discussion of the function of eating is going to be deficient. This philosophical concept, the spirit, forces itself into neuroscience whether we like it or not. Ignoring it will make the discussion weak and anemic. The way I see it, any neurologic discussion without referring to consciousness is a discussion that is begging for life support.

During eating, food is in contact with the oral cavity, and the latter will be sending satisfying messages through a sophisticated system composed of the taste buds of the tongue, other receptors in the inner-cheek areas and the palate. When we swallow the food, hedonic messages come from the throat, esophagus, and stomach. This amazing system, like any other biological system, reaches its complexity infinitely.

As we discussed, after the first initial phase of eating, the pleasure connected to this cycle of chewing, swallowing and, feeling of hunger starts to decline, and the stomach during this time is not full yet. When the strong hunger state has subsided, it is easy for us to stop eating.

In the state of addiction to food, the sensitization is persistent, which will make it hard for us to stop eating despite the decline in the pleasure of this activity. The addiction forces us to charge this system by trying to find a different food or resorting to eating sweets after we are done with the main course. Later we go back to regular food, preferably different from the main course. In the state of addiction to food, hunger is not much involved in eating; hedonic addiction is the main drive for eating.

When the nucleus accumbens and the hypothalamus are insisting that they are not satisfied yet, we will continue to eat, until the stomach is no longer able to fit food anymore, and the experience may become painful. In this scenario, the amygdala and the hypothalamus will send a reprogramming inhibitory signal to the nucleus accumbens to shut it down. In drug addiction, we do not taste the drug, but we feel the urge to use it. This is similar to the state of addiction to food.

The Control Module

Let us consider another scenario. Imagine the person is on a diet or is diabetic and cannot eat many sweets. In this case, we are trying to place this eating system under supervision, by involving other structures from the limbic system like the prefrontal cortex, the executive center of the brain, and the neocortex in the process.

One of the ways this could happen is by having a thick connection between the prefrontal cortex and the amygdala, and from there to influence the nucleus accumbens and the hypothalamus. This may help in allowing us to put the eating activity under control. This gives the amygdala the strong ability to control the nucleus accumbens without much effort and agony, which may reduce the difficulty of controlling eating. The ability to control our eating will give us a sense of confidence rather than a sense of weakness and inability to manage the situation. The lost sense of control over our emotional behavior is frequently a cause of agony for humanity.

People with ideal weight, likely have a balance between their hunger and reward system, which governs the initiation and cessation of eating. This coordination allows our eating experience to become more enjoyable. Eating is mainly initiated and stopped according to the feeling of hunger, and the stomach is not left overfilled at the end of the meal. The hypothalamus increases the feeling of satiety by decreasing the secretion of the hormone orexin. Endorphin production also slows down. Dopamine reaching the nucleus accumbens, slows down, the expected pleasure from eating decreases, and the brain is ready to be stimulated by other activities.

The Peripheral Hormonal System

This hormonal system works to help us achieve the ideal body weight by secreting hormones from the GI tract, like ghrelin, and from the fatty tissue, like leptin. The level of these hormones in the blood reflects the status of the gastrointestinal tract to handle food and digest it. Ghrelin is secreted by the stomach when empty. The hypothalamus interprets higher levels of ghrelin as readiness to eat, and this stimulates the feeling of hunger. Leptin, on the other hand, does the opposite. It is secreted by the fatty tissue, and it stimulates the feeling of satiety. It circulates in large levels in the blood relating to the amount of fat storage that we carry, and it lets the hypothalamus know that we do not need to eat because we have enough fat storage.

When the hypothalamus receives a large input from the sensory organs regarding food or other parts in the brain, like the neocortex, it will become subject to the influence of these systems. For example, the neocortex can supply us with vivid pictures through the miracle of imagination about what the food looks like and the variety of food items. Our senses, mainly the senses of smell and vision, bring us complicated details about the food and how tasty it is, and these factors will stimulate our appetite.

Living in our modern time with sophisticated cooking techniques and a variety of fast food options stimulate our senses toward making changes in the hypothalamus in favor of eating more. We can look deeper at the influence of the environment on our eating habits by looking at other cultures and what they eat. Let us discuss a special case. The diet of an African tribe named the Maasai is composed mainly of milk and blood that they extract from a superficial vein from their live cattle. I wonder whether they get bored with this diet or if they are just as happy as we are with what we eat.

The body image of some of us may play a role in influencing our appetite and the feeling of hunger, especially in young individuals. The body image of these teenagers could be very important. In the case of anorexia nervosa, the young patient has the wrong idea about their weight. They may look at themself in the mirror and see an obese person, when in reality, they are very thin. In this case, the human's emotional response to the self-image is much more powerful than the physiologic effects of the hormonal and neurological arms that are influencing the hypothalamus. The social centers that control eating become the target of reprogramming.

Often after eating, our arousal system output declines. This is common especially around the afternoon time when the function of the brain is generally less sharp than in the morning. This is the time when people want to have a post-lunch nap or have a cup of coffee. The opioid circuit related to food shuts down and other circuits related to other activities are activated. The autonomic nervous system controlling the GI tract changes from ready to eat to working on digestion.

This process works on maintaining our weight in an ideal condition and keeps us away from acquiring illnesses related to overeating like diabetes. So why do we overeat? Because not all of us have perfect systems as we discussed earlier, or we lack a functional social and spiritual life that would allow us to control our eating habits.

Factors Making us Overeat:

1. The abundance of food and the variety of processed food in the developed world and many developing countries.

   We are not worried about having food on the table for the next day. If we go back two hundred or three hundred years and look at human average weight, we would likely find that the epidemic of obesity and diabetes was not as prevalent at that time as it is now. Muffins, cakes, sweets, and ice cream are becoming part of our regular daily diet and humans have always tried to improve the taste of food. Spice is as old as human culture, but the process of food enhancement has become very sophisticated in our time. This might lead vulnerable humans to overstimulate the reward system for eating.

2. The process of getting food is oversimplified.

   You can now get food delivered to your door with the click of a button, or you can go shopping to see a huge variety of already cooked food packed and ready for consumption without much work. We are not doing anything in the morning when we are spreading peanut butter on a piece of toast. We have a boring passive role in the process of preparing food.

3. Habitual eating.

   I see parents carrying bags of dry food with them everywhere they go, and they offer them to their children as a way to calm them down. Bagged, spiced, salted and dried food is loaded with calories. It is appetizing and easy to overeat. The child's postprandial time, which is the time when we stop eating and work on digesting the food, becomes very short.

4. Failure to elicit a proper postprandial period.

   The postprandial period is the time spent without eating, which is a resting phase of usually a few hours. Failure to do this will not only set the wrong program in the hypothalamus but will also disrupt the whole circuit composed of hormonal interaction between the hypothalamus and the gastrointestinal tract. The invention of sippy cups makes it too easy for parents to be able to give soft drinks to their children anytime and anywhere. This will make it more difficult to give these children a healthy postprandial phase.

5. Endless adds on TV reminding us that food is available and needs to be consumed.

6. Depression and anxiety.

   Food gives us a temporary break from our thoughts of pain and suffering for a period of time. While we are eating, food is supplying us with higher levels of endorphins and dopamine.

7. Loneliness or lack of social life.

   For some of us, this is a catalyst to supplement the hypothalamus with the activity of eating. The lack of friendship and weak interaction with others forms the idea in the neocortex and in the entire limbic system that we are living in an unfriendly universe. An unfriendly universe makes it easy for us to find supplemental external activities such as comfort eating. Perhaps we are not having a pleasant time while we are mixing with others in school, or perhaps we are getting bullied at school.

   Socializing and mixing with other humans is a natural source of pleasure in our life, and all of sudden it becomes the main source of our misery and anguish. It is no surprise many children want to be homeschooled, a phenomenon that I see only escalating in my office. Do we have friends to enjoy the time with? Are we left alone socially? Even though there are people around us, why are they busy in their own world? Sometimes while I am examining the child in the office, I see the mother shopping online for clothes using her cell phone. Children need to feel their mother is present mentally and physically in their company.

   Human connection in its ideal form is a mood elevator and stabilizer in our life. Some philosophers are telling us that happiness is an inside job and should not be dependent on outside sources. I think it is possible to convince a very small portion of humans that happiness is an inside job: we call these people, philosophers. Most of us, including me, want to enjoy life using the social element of our surroundings, and not by listening to these philosophers.

8. Lack of other interests.

   I remember when I was ten years old, thinking that sitting down for a meal and not playing was a waste of time.

9. Lack of physical activity in our overall daily schedule.

   To convince you of this idea, let's try this experiment. While you are in the middle of eating, stop and go to a treadmill and start running gently or do a task that demands physical activity. Watch what happens to your desire to finish your meal during this scenario. Exercise gives us an amazing ability to stimulate the arousal system, the endocrine and the hypothalamus in a favorable way. It requires us to have optimum equilibrium and balance. While moving, the autonomic nervous system is helping us move the blood to the muscle. The motor cortex of the brain is recruiting the blood to supply its activity. There is a huge difference in the brain function between us sitting down and running.

Eating the Right Food

No one is unfamiliar these days with the phrase "healthy food." The good media is bombarding us with endless programs from public stations displaying guidance and rules about what to eat and what not to eat. Many books are written about the benefits of eating fresh fruits and vegetables and decreasing the amount of processed food especially carbohydrates. Most of my patients are familiar with healthy eating but do not practice it. Once in a while, I see a teenager or a parent who is not very familiar with healthy eating, so I spend time educating them on this matter. Some of my patients keep gaining weight. One of the reasons is that they get money from their parents, and on the way back from school they pass a store that carries entertaining food. They spend their money on snacks and junk food. Do they not have will power?

Willpower by itself is a strange system. It is a spiritual practice that is performed best when guided and encouraged by society and practiced widely in a spiritually warm atmosphere. The economic system has to have elements of compassion and humane practices, even when it is based on a capitalistic functional one. It should take into account the best interests of society when manufacturing food and advertising for it.

Eating processed food once in a while in limited quantities during holiday time is not going to make a significant impact on our overall health, but the dilemma is when this becomes a daily routine.

Willpower and the Mind

Willpower without a mind means that our behavior is the product of mechanical coordination between the neocortex and the limbic system! Who said that the eighty billion to one hundred billion cells in the brain have to coordinate with each other? Is the blueprint for that included in the sperm and egg? How could we imagine that coordination is the product of trial and error? It is a miracle that these cells are working together in the first place to give us a talking and walking human. Running this system without consciousness proves to be very difficult. Can you imagine how the electric signals that are coordinating billions of brain cells residing in the neocortex and the limbic system can take place? What kind of system is dictating this rhythm? When the mind is involved in the process of coordinating these cells, the process of something called willpower might make some sense, and we may have something called a functioning brain!

Suggestions for Appetite Control

The goal is to have an eating system that would allow us to have pleasure by eating healthy and to only eat when we are hungry. Let us see if a creative imagination can help us in achieving this task.

We have to imagine that this way of eating should stimulate the visceral sensation of acceptance to eating healthy. Pleasure and satisfaction should be felt without the need to fill up our stomach. While we are driving, exercising, or doing other activities, we can imagine that eating healthy foods, low in carbs and animal fat, is a very satisfying experience. The feeling that comes from this imagination has to rise to the level of belief and we have to believe what we imagine. The more realistic this feeling becomes, the greater the success. Also, you can imagine specific foods like eating a delicious salad with walnuts and strawberries in moderate quantities to be very satisfying. The closer the imaginary picture is to reality, the better the results.

This process may also be supplemented by negative creative imagination, which is about having negative feelings toward leaving the dinner table with a full stomach, especially after eating unhealthy foods.

The addictive pressure from the reward system and hedonism over our feelings have tremendous dictating power over our behavior. Also, the reward system could become very activated with a negative concept like hate but only when we avoid what we do not like. We can use this negative element to our advantage to avoid overeating and becoming sluggish after over-indulging.

We can learn from picky eaters to curb and control our eating. Some of us tend to hate many food items and are referred to as picky eaters. The reward system in picky eaters becomes activated when they avoid the food that do not like. Understanding this concept, for some of us, may be helpful to succeed in case we are struggling in dieting. This may be achieved when we convince ourselves that we hate certain unhealthy food!

When we use creative imagination in this case, it has to be about imagining confidence in achieving success. The more vivid and realistic the feelings emerging from this imagination, the greater the success that can be achieved. This confident feeling, we call belief. Belief is the essential element of any recipe for success.

This creative imagining can be done while we are doing easy activities like walking, which do not require serious concentration. We need to repeat the process multiple times during the day until it becomes a habit or routine, occupying some of the background of our thinking. With time this will create confidence and this will give a sense of satisfaction and contentment. With persistence, not only will the reward centers be reprogrammed, but our digestive system will be adjusted to eating less.

It is a very good idea to look a little bit at our menu of daily food and try to match what would be considered a delicious food with what would be healthy. It is helpful to stress the idea that eating has to be an enjoyable experience. Also, it is important to remember that the first minute of eating carries with it the most pleasure followed by a decline in the taste of the food after that. This idea helps us cognitively to engage the neocortex in influencing the limbic system to eat less food.

A larger rotating menu may be a good idea for some of us who get bored with the same food day after day, as long as we stick to the main plan, which includes healthy delicious foods, in moderation, and avoiding filling up our stomach.

A process that would add a boost to successful dieting is doing daily weight checks, recording the weight, and keeping track of our caloric intake.

We should have sympathetic thoughts toward our internal organs, like the heart, the pancreas, the brain, and the backbone. We should be living in peace with these organs that are working very hard to supply us with health. In return, it is smart to return the favor by adopting healthy eating habits.

Other Ideas for Appetite Control

Imagine that we feel that our eating habit is completely under control. The reason we eat is to survive. Every cell in our body is asking for food and we eat for this purpose. While we eat, we enjoy the food, but when we overeat the food starts to become toxic. We have no desire at all to eat more than we need. So, the reason we are not going to eat the cake sitting in front of us is that we have no desire to do so. In fact, we hate it because we are a picky eater and don't like dessert. It is easy for us to avoid eating dessert, something so many people wish they could do.

Eating under control is more fun, more rewarding, and the food will taste better. In the end, the feeling of being in control of your overall health is beneficial. This idea has to be there all through the process of eating. Our lifestyle often requires us to sit down for many hours but needs a system for healthy eating and exercise. With practice and consistency, these methods become much easier to apply.

It is so important before eating to *prepare* the mind that the food is delicious and tasty. Prepare the mind to have the conscious feeling that eating is a great experience and the timing of it is very appropriate. We decided already what food and how much we are going to eat. After we are done eating, train your mind to have a great pleasurable memory about the event. The idea of eating is done for now, and the desire to eat has no place in the present. Be very thankful for the ability and health to be able to eat and not have medical problems preventing us from eating. We are basically creating a satisfying experience by eating, creating a mood-boosting station for the mind. We do not crave dessert since the food we ate was satisfying enough.

If these ideas are not working, we can try completely bizarre ones, especially when the food is very good, and we are eating in response to compulsion. I would like to introduce an idea of the heart and the lung. Imagine that the food is going inside the lung and the heart to give them energy so they can function. You can also think of the heart as the only recipient of the food with every single bite. When the food goes down the esophagus, it is going to settle in the heart and when the heart is full of energy, we are satisfied. This may take the edge of the strong desire coming from filling the stomach. While we are eating, think of the heart getting very full and starting to suffer, then take a deep breath and imagine relieving the pressure of the heart with every slow deep breath.

This maneuver allows us to have a spiritual presence while we are eating and to be conscious of every step of the process. The last thing we want is for eating to be an unconscious process dictated by hormones, anxiety, depression, addiction, resentment and dissatisfaction that is derived from the negative events in our daily life. The negative events in our daily life could create mini depressive moments in our minds and have negative effects on our ability to control ourselves. These negative events may push us to continue to eat after we are no longer hungry. Understanding this concept is important in dealing with children when they are overeating.

Parents have to understand this concept and have to provide the right environment for the child. Putting harsh rules and regulations in place may make the child more dissatisfied. Generosity and empathy will work better.

Spiritual Dimension and Meditation While Eating

Enjoying the time of eating could be present in our life in different ways than the traditional way that many of us experience. A spiritual dimension could be rewarding, and it could be joined with prayer.

Beyond the traditional means of prayer and meditation, which are important and recommended, we add an element that would look into our intricate body design. Start with appreciating our sense of vision. Let us imagine how complicated and intricate the inner layer of the eye is and how it works like an amazing solar panel, miraculously allowing us to see the world and the food we are eating. Let us think of how complicated the system of the taste buds in our tongue are as they work tirelessly to transform the chemical stimulation coming from food to the feeling of internal comfort as we eat.

When we look at the food, we can feel the beauty and sophistication in the making of what we are eating. The food was originally made in the form of plants, growing from the seeds through magical events. When we start eating, we can imagine how lucky we are to have the endless coordinated effort to chew the food and swallow it.

We can feel how these simple affordable functions of imagination can fuel our minds with happiness, satisfaction, and positive experiences. Let us be assured that a positive mood is easy to achieve without owning expensive material. Eating has the potential of being a station for improving our psychological state. This will prevent the eating experience from becoming automated or a hedonic activity.

If you have a religious dimension, you can include your prayer in the process, thanking the creator for the gift of eating and all the positive feelings related to it.

If you still have difficulty controlling your appetite, try to have a dialogue with your body at the beginning of the meal. The dialogue can be related to what your body needs. Try to feel the discrepancy between those needs and what the desire centers in the limbic system are requesting us to do. Let us try to go with the wiser choice. It is interesting to tune into our bodies and feel what it needs. Tuning in allows us to feel the state of hunger and decide to eat accordingly.

STOP 11

SLEEP DISORDERS

It does not take a neuroscientist to see that when we are experiencing sleeplessness, we feel exhausted and we function on a depleted battery. Sleep controls our overall outlook for the day. Making mistakes during work is more likely to occur when there is a lack of sleep. The seamless flow of steps that we take while we do any task becomes disrupted. When the degree of sleeplessness is severe, we may function like an intoxicated person. Sleeplessness also causes a lack of vibrant enthusiasm, with a special taste to it. Sleep restores our brain energy after a day of hard work. A good night's sleep will make us cheerful, energetic, and optimistic.

If you happen to be watching TV at two o'clock in the morning, you will see adds advertising a medication trying to solve a sleep problem. It is not a secret these days that this problem is very prevalent and that the pharmaceutical industry is working on making medication to help us solve it.

The Anatomy of Sleep System

The hypothalamus is the initiator of sleep. Again, the hypothalamus is the tiniest section in the brain that has the most diversity of functions. Anything less than a miracle in describing this area would be unfair. It is working hard every single second of our life and not taking any breaks, day or night.

The suprachiasmatic nucleus in the hypothalamus is considered the initiator of the circadian rhythm, the famous rhythm that influences us to sleep during the night and to be awake during the day.

Obviously, the light during the daytime plays the main role in regulating and stimulating the hypothalamic circadian rhythm. As you see in figure 11.2, the optic nerve brings the light signals from the eye to the optic chiasm, which sends signals to the suprachiasmatic nucleus.

The connection between these two regions brings the information to the hypothalamus about the status of the world around us, letting us know whether it is daytime or nighttime.

After that, the suprachiasmatic nucleus connects to the ventrolateral preoptic nucleus (VLPON), which is the node of the hypothalamus that triggers and control us to sleep! The VLPON is most active during sleep! It works hard on inhibiting directly the arousal system or by inhibiting another node inside the hypothalamus itself, which works on stimulating this system. Its ability to shut down that system gives it this magic influence over our sleep. As we discussed in the previous chapters, the activity of the arousal centers is what makes us awake and alert. The role of the VLPON adds tremendous complexity to the function of the hypothalamus. The location of the VLPON, which is in the heart of the social brain, makes it subjected to the influence of our emotional status.

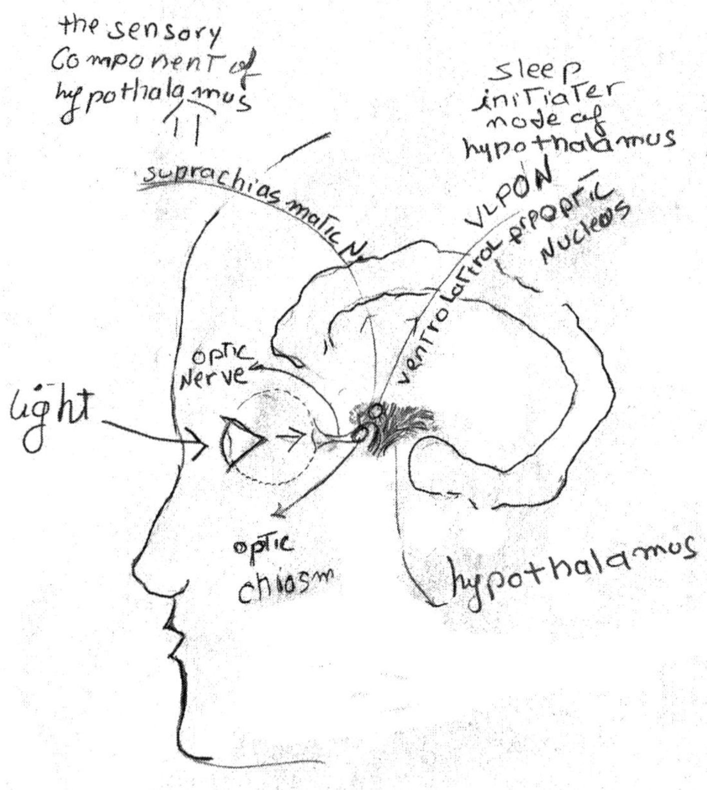

The arousal system is located in the brain stem and the midbrain area. Its centers have been known to us for many years: the locus coeruleus secretes norepinephrine, the raphe nucleus secretes serotonin, the basal forebrain nuclei secretes acetylcholine, and the ventral tegmental area secretes dopamine. The mammillary nuclei reside in the hypothalamus itself and not in the brain stem; they secrete histamine, an important chemical of the arousal system. The mammillary nuclei are considered part of the arousal system even though they are not residing by their sisters in the brain stem!

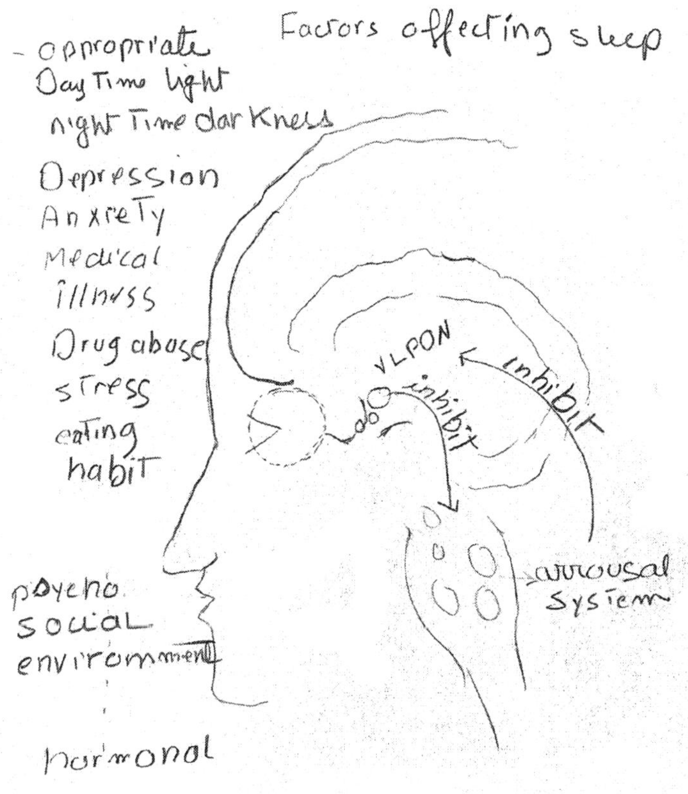

During sleep, the VLPON has to work hard on keeping these centers inhibited, until we wake up. At that time, the VLPON will have a break.

What also influences the function of the VLPON is the energy status of the rest of the brain cells. Signals sent from neighboring circuits try to inform the VLPON about how tired and exhausted the rest of the brain is, and how much energy is available for the brain cells to keep engaging in mental or physical work. When the level is down, it does not matter what time of day it is: day or night we might fall asleep.

Habits also tend to reprogram the communication between the suprachiasmatic nucleus and the VLPON concerning sleeping at night and being awake in the daytime. If we are trying consistently to stay awake during the night, this communication between the suprachiasmatic nucleus and the VLPON will be disrupted. The stimulation during the night when the TV is turned on can further disrupt this communication. When the lack of synchrony becomes prolonged, the circadian rhythm may become changed to a point where it will become difficult for it to synchronize daytime with wakefulness and nighttime with sleep.

The psychological state affecting the rest of the brain and abusing drugs could disrupt the signals coming from the rest of the brain signaling the VLPON about the energy status in the rest of the brain. We can imagine that synchrony between many neurocircuits is very necessary for this function to be possible.

I have dealt with many cases of insomnia in children; some of these children have psychological disorders, which may help explain the problem. Some patients with sleep disorders have a normal environment and no obvious psychological or medical problems. These patients want to stay up late at night and wake up late in the midday.

When the arousal system stops firing to the rest of the brain, we go to sleep. You can see that the VLPON and the arousal system are trying to inhibit each other, so each can do the best that it is designed to do. The VLPON is trying to put us in sleep mode by calming down the arousal system, and the arousal system is trying to calm the VLPON, so it does not interfere with its function of putting us in an awake state.

What I wrote is an extreme simplification of the function of sleep. And I did omit other nodes in the hypothalamus that have important roles in sleep to make this function simple. The rest of the wiring in the brain, you know by now, has a say in the matter. Fear and anxiety that are interrupting our life can put the amygdala in a defensive mode, which is going to stimulate the arousal system on one hand and directly affect the hypothalamus on the other hand. Now you can see how some people who are plagued with anxiety have disrupted sleep.

Watching TV in the evening not only is going to affect the circadian rhythm by emitting artificial light, but also by sending stimulating massages to us that we should eat this food, buy these clothes, and drive this car. Shows on TV that display social drama, violence, action scenes and loud music are sending messages to the brain to keep us awake.

All other events happening during the daytime that stimulate the limbic system to have a strong influence on the amygdala and the hypothalamus are going to change the rhythm of the hypothalamic nuclei. To add to the complexity, there is a hormonal effect called melatonin released from a single gland in the base of the brain, the pineal gland. When secreted it enhances sleep. The pharmaceutical companies were able to manufacture it and put it in pills, to be sold over the counter.

Many hormones secreted from the distal glands are controlled by the pituitary gland and an example of that is cortisol. This hormone is secreted from the adrenal gland, which is located above the kidneys. The cortisol level is higher in the morning, which tends to put us in an alert state. When I give a patient a high dosage of cortisol as a medicine, for a reason like an asthma attack, I like to give it in the morning and avoid the evening dosing when the situation permits, so the medication will cause the least sleep disruption. Another example is the thyroid hormone, which plays a major role in controlling energy consumption and metabolism in the rest of the body, which makes us more active during the daytime.

We probably all know someone who watches TV at night or who works during the night and has no problem initiating and maintaining sleep at various times. One way to explain this situation is that having a very healthy VLPON can override the arousal system anytime the brain is tired. In addition, there may be an indirect connection with the reward system that raises the status of sleep to an addictive activity, but with some control from the prefrontal cortex and amygdala.

Excessive sleeping is a rare complaint in children and adults, but we are not going to discuss that. You can imagine the explanation of this phenomenon when you have a too powerful VLPON, which is sensitive to any drop in the intensity of light or the energy supply in the brain cells. Another possible explanation for this condition is that the VLPON is working as an autonomous node, not regulated by the light, and the arousal system is not able to inhibit its function. In this case, the VLPON can shut off the arousal system for long periods of time, until it becomes exhausted.

Good sleeping is essential for our wellbeing and for having an energetic brain. The age of the human makes a difference for how many hours we should sleep. The younger we are the more hours we need, which is a minimum of twelve hours for a child, and six hours to eight hours for an adult. The high metabolism and fast growth in young children require more energy storage in the mitochondria, the power generator in the brain cells, as compared to older humans.

Solving a sleeping disorder is easier when other matters affecting our sleep are solved, such as solving psychiatric problems like anxiety and depression.

Suggestions for Improving Sleep

If we have difficulty falling asleep or we wake up in the middle of the night, we are not going to help the situation by becoming upset about it. Allowing any negativity to reach our mind will lead to less self-confidence in dealing with the problem and we will become more anxious. We can say thank you for the ability to lay down in bed and not be in any pain. Let us have complete acceptance of this moment and try not to leave the bed. Let us bring our thinking down to a minimum, focus on deep slow breathing, try soothing meditation, or prayer. We can also focus on enjoying the moment of comfortably resting in bed. If we feel we have to leave our bed, let us benefit from this time. Try not to eat unless you are extremely hungry or drink anything except for water in a small quantity if we happen to be thirsty. We are going to use this time doing something useful. Let us finish easy work that does not require ample attention or read something soothing and meditate. Waking up mad, then turning the TV on will not help us solve the problem.

Watching TV in the middle of the night will make us forget our problems of not having enough sleep for a brief time, and when we are done watching TV, we will have the feeling that we wasted precious time on an addictive activity.

If one day, we feel that we are not in the mood to do any work during the night and we want to watch TV, it would be no problem as long as it does not become a habit. When we make headway to resolve this matter, the problem of watching TV in the middle of the night solves itself.

The feeling of how enjoyable it is to be in bed could be enhanced by a creative imagination by a variety of scenarios. Let us imagine that we are on vacation and the main purpose of this trip is to be in bed to sleep. Falling asleep is the fantasy of our dreams, and the only thing preventing us from fulfilling it is our schedules and our demanding work.

We can use our creative imaginations to create different scenarios describing the process of falling asleep as a very enjoyable experience. We have to imagine that falling asleep is very easy for us to achieve, and in fact, it is overwhelming. We need to imagine that our problems rest in the opposite, meaning the inability to get up and leave our bed because of sleeping in.

This creative imagination is trying to activate the reward system and to invite the secretion of endorphins from the hypothalamus when the thought of being in bed is crossing our mind. This means that our sleep is a very enjoyable activity.

These thoughts have to be our thoughts while we are going to bed, even if falling asleep is easy and our main problem is waking up in the middle of the night. This habit will bring consistency in thinking while we are in bed. Feelings are suspended during sleep but the moment right before falling asleep is enjoyable. Let us bring this feeling vividly to our imagination and this may facilitate going back to sleep.

If we find ourselves waking up at a certain time every night, some physicians suggest having an alarm clock go off a few minutes before this usual time. When we are awakened by the alarm clock, the cause of waking up is external, and the spontaneous awakening will be suspended. Therefore, bed and sleep are our friends at this moment, and our relationship with sleep and our bedroom is not dysfunctional. Let us try to keep the same pattern of waking up by the alarm clock around the same time for about a week. After that, we can delay the alarm clock to ring fifteen minutes later than the usual time that we are used to. This could help repair the relationship with sleep to a more favorable one. With this method, the problem is changed from the inability to sleep through the night to I have too much work to do, so I have to get up early to do the work. Otherwise, we would have normal sleep, and we would not have a sleep problem.

Needless to say, how calm we are and how our entire psychology is relaxed will help this plan go to reality. During that time, our adherence to other changes to our diet, exercise, and meditation is just as important in improving our sleep situation. It is important for our success to believe in what we are doing and having a gentle self-confidence to know that we will succeed.

Finding a solution to the sleep problem is very easy, especially for an adult who is committed to finding a solution; let us put the nodes of the hypothalamus to work in rhythmic mode.

Your sleep plan has to be in harmony with your daily activity. Some of us have the time to have a nap in the afternoon. If you are unable to take a nap, then you have to count on your nighttime to get the sufficient seven or eight hours of sleep. Remember that the hypothalamic nodes are sitting in a tiny area very close to each other; any disruption in the rhythm of one them will affect the rest. For example, eating late at night may encourage a gastroesophageal reflux and a feeling of thirst for some of us. In addition, unscheduled eating may affect the VLPON directly by changing the level of hormones and glucose in the blood. Another example is exercise, since exercise shocks the hypothalamic region in a positive way, and for sure, we want to use this function in a rhythmic way. Exercising at the same time every day, at least initially, is helpful. The best time for that is also subject to our schedule and ability. Exercise could be done in our home, because going to a special place may not be affordable for everyone. Exercising at home allows the process to be consistent.

Daily meditation, or prayers for those of us who follow a religion, have to be consistent and rhythmic. Prayers in general consist of a few ideas and rituals, but the main ones are feeling gratitude and thanks to the Creator and feeling a warm psychological connection with God. Moreover, concerning the difficulties that we face in life, we should take advantage of these scenarios to enhance our connection with God. It is during these difficult times that we are at the most need for this connection. For the believers or unbelievers, prayer or meditation should be adopted in the form of ethical, merciful interactions with others. We can extend this mercy to our interactions with all humans, animals and the planet. Consider these categories as an end by themselves and not as a means for personal goals.

Creating a new element in the background of our thinking helps us deal with sleeping difficulties. Writing down a short story about how you want your sleep to be. For example, you could say, "My sleep is very sound. It is very hard for me to wake up in the middle of the night. I am very sleepy at night. I have no problem falling asleep. The minute I go to bed, I fall asleep. Bedtime is one of the most enjoyable moments of my day. The alarm wakes me up in the morning from a deep sleep."

Anytime the sleep issue comes to mind during the daytime this short story has to be in the background of our thinking. I do not mean we need to recite the story, but the essence of this story has to be this feeling about falling sleep. However, for some of us reciting these kinds of stories and repeating them might have a positive effect on our subconscious minds.

The social environment and inner limbic system environment, discussed in the previous chapters, influence our sleep. Any output from the limbic system that is going to go out of control at nighttime is going to disrupt sleep and challenge the VLPON. The direct connection between the amygdala and the hypothalamus is one way to explain this influence. Consider all the negative habits and feelings as disruptors of sleep, from the simple negative emotion like fear, envy, and jealousy, to the feeling of not having enough good luck in life, to the ultimate negative state of depression and anxiety.

Many people may respond to medication, and I see children coming to me after being seen in sleep medicine departments in some tertiary care centers. Medications are often used in children since it is hard to cognitively deal with the situation and the practice of medicine, in general, is shy from talking to parents as being a key component in their children's atmosphere, and they have to be the ones who initiate the change.

Over-the-counter medications for sleep are antihistamines. Antihistamines will block the effect of histamine secreted by the mammillary bodies from the hypothalamus itself, which is part of the arousal system. A side effect of this use is that we may wake up drowsy, and the effect of the medication may decrease with time. When taking an antihistamine, the depth and quality of sleep may not be as good compared to natural sleep. However, for some people, it may have a role when used cautiously. Let us suppose that we used an antihistamine at night, and we are waking up drowsy in the morning. We want to take advantage of that feeling to replace the habit of thinking about our inability to sleep with a new habit about how we are sleepy all the time. After that, I suggest stopping the antihistamine after a week. If difficulty in sleeping resurfaces, we can focus on the memory of being drowsy that was experienced when we were taking them and put us back to sleep by establishing a new pattern. Newer FDA approved medications that antagonize Orexin are very promising.

The idea that being in bed while sleepy is very fun as we discussed earlier, as long as we can regulate the daily activity, we could maintain this pattern.

Melatonin, as we discussed earlier, has the benefit of initiating sleep and possibly maintaining it for some patients. The benefit for some people may outweigh the potential endocrine problems that it can cause when the insomnia is severe, and this medicine happens to work well without any side effects.

What happens with sleep during illnesses? During the flu season, many of us experience the sense of being very sleepy and can sleep almost all day and night. In this case, the hypothalamus employs all the resources of the body to get rid of the virus in an unbelievably amazing way. It wants to shut down body activity to send energy to the immune system that is going to be in a very excited mode. The hypothalamus also raises the temperature of the body to make it inhospitable to the invading virus. We can experience the power of the hypothalamus while exerting its influence on our wakefulness and sleep during the time of illness.

After all the hard work that you did to solve the sleep problem, one day you find yourself overeating in the evening or when you receive sad news, and find yourself slipping back to a state of dysfunctional sleep. No problem, start the repair process all over again, without frustration or sadness.

STOP 12

MEDITATION

Are you meditating without even being aware that you are? You could be meditating when you wake up in the morning and find yourself happy for no apparent reason. Perhaps you look out the window on the way to work and see the beauty of the road, the trees, and the creatures around you and feel very excited about the day.

Meditation can exist on a higher level. Perhaps a friend betrays you and somehow everything is still fine. Or perhaps the stock market collapses, and you lose a large amount of money, but you still respond with a smile. Perhaps your kids do not follow your advice and things go wrong, yet your heart is clear from any negative feelings about the issue. If you wake up in the morning feeling grateful about your place in the universe, and if you feel blessed to find yourself in some state of health, even on the last day of your life, you are meditating.

Meditation can be as simple as admiring the sound of rainfall or appreciating living even a simple life. Little things, such as waking up in the morning and seeing water run down the sink, will suffice for happiness. These are examples of meditation that do not include religious rituals. As beautiful as they feel, meditation is even more enjoyable when it is connected to religious rituals and feelings of connection to God.

Meditation is becoming a significant topic these days due to the discovery of the positive effects it has on our health in general. The benefits reach the intracellular level of each organ in the body. Even medical insurance companies have started to acknowledge this.

Materialism, as some scientists are telling us, is what life seems to be all about. It is somehow forcefully being linked to the scientific revolution, although it is a philosophical idea. Materialism has changed the state of religion to take a more reduced role in our lives. Meditation in the modern sense is becoming more and more devoid of religious connection and performed as a separate activity. It is often pictured as a person sitting down with their eyes closed and a gentle smile on their face in a state of suspended or positive thoughts, with increased dopamine and endorphin levels in the brain.

A state of suspended thinking is difficult to achieve, as our minds are usually racing with other thoughts. Our thoughts are the mold that all of our mental activities fit into. As mentioned earlier, our social thoughts tend to become weaker when we are engaged in functional activities. For example, if a mechanic is working on fixing a car, and her/his mind is absorbed with personal thoughts, then she/he is missing out on enjoying the job she/he's doing.

We all eventually must come to terms with the fact that we are merely visitors in this world for a very short time. If the end of this journey means nothing, this will make it very hard for the rest of our lives to have any meaning. Of course, these are just my personal beliefs and others may have their own views.

The part of the human hypothalamus that craves ritualistic behavior has been neglected by modern medicine. Although our culture often disregards this part of the hypothalamus, it is still neurologically and physiologically part of our brain. This creates a vacuum in the hypothalamus, which is the main area that responds to the thoughts connected to religiosity. Some of us try to fill this void with other things, such as recreational drugs and other activities, but this does not always work. Other neocortical centers in the brain also crave answers regarding where we come from, the afterlife, and how our brain is making sense of the world around us. This other vacuum we have created has to be filled with other activities to distract us to keep us from going crazy with inquiring about matters that are out of our control.

Modern society, through its new scientific orthodoxy, tends to associate religion with superstition and illusion. It considers spirituality as being contradictory to science and logic. Meanwhile, there is evidence on the benefit of meditation and the positive role that religion has on the lives of individuals and the fabric of society. It has also been shown that depression rates are low in societies where religion has more existence in people's lives, a fact that is frustrating to a good portion of our modern-day scientists. How can we be preaching godlessness while we are seeing the decaying effect of this notion on the psyche of society? I hope that these same scientists are mixing with citizens on the streets and seeing the effect godlessness has on society. I'm sure they would find out that worrying about status and being politically correct does not achieve much in the end. Unsurprisingly, a high percentage of physicians tend to believe in God, because of their social interaction with a large number of people on a daily basis.

Meditation these days tends to be practiced individually rather than being celebrated by a community of people. Shared activities are now dominated by newer ones reflective of our modern times with prevailing means of entertainment, dominated by screens of cell phones and televisions. The power of conformity and collective peer pressure easily explains the status of humanity at this time. We are absorbed by a large, powerful materialistic vacuum. Sometimes it can give us temporary satisfaction by acquiring more materials, art and sophisticated tools. But it cannot give us a stable social foundation or deal with the high rate of psychiatric diseases.

Kindness and wisdom are not advertised today on many social platforms. They do not seem to be as important as making money. Indulgence in materials is not going to give us the lasting thrill that it is promising. Soon after we acquire what we once wanted, we become used to our new lifestyle. These limits on the excitement of having lots of money are not felt by most average people living normal lives. Many of us do not experience the high life of multimillionaires. Instead, many average people live their lives in a dream state of becoming rich. The majority of us may not have the opportunity to mix and mingle with kings and queens and feel the depression and misery that many of them live through even though they are rich!

When we seek peace through the spiritual or the religious world, we often find this world corrupted. Religious institutions are no longer able to play significant roles in people's lives. These institutions are basically falling gradually into the materialistic vacuum affected by the behavior of the majority, and the spiritual dimension is in decline. You can see beautiful large religious places filled with worshipers, powered with beautiful talks but with a poor influence on society as a whole despite their apparent strength.

The media, depending on the mood and the agenda of the people in charge, can show that faith and reason can be met, either clearly and directly or in subliminal messages. The notion of faith meeting reason is similar to the notion of having faith in general. As discussed in an earlier chapter, how you *feel* about this idea is what is going to form your answer to this question. In other words, the answer is going to be packaged and ready for delivery with all kinds of explanations according to our biases and desires about the matter.

Therefore, the answer to whether or not faith and reason can be met depends completely on your desires—not necessarily physical primitive desires, but the mental and psychological ones. Is there such a thing as mental desire? Can mental desires be connected to physical desires and serve the deep pocket? I believe so.

The activity of the amygdala in response to any idea influences the activity of the reward system and the hypothalamus. An outcome is the release of comforting neurotransmitters, mainly dopamine and endorphins. All these systems dictate how we deal with any dilemma we encounter. Having a heightened level of consciousness may allow us to block the influences of our desires on our decision-making skills. This allows our brain to decide an outcome that is in the best interest of the whole rather than of the self.

Meditation involving religious rituals, without a doubt, is very powerful and enriching to the human psychology and is the most beneficial form of meditation. This form of meditation may be used to improve the ethical standard of society, which aims to make us exemplary citizens, who do not cheat, steal, or engage in physical or verbal violence against others. It helps us become citizens who are hardworking and who do not waste time on adultery and other useless pleasures.

Some may argue that religion is inherently violent, yet, if studied, you will find ample evidence to support religious tolerance to all, even nonbelievers. Treating others, the way you want to be treated is the foundation of all religions. It is up to us to look for this truth in every tradition and that the study of religion teaches us to be peaceful and fair with each other. Religion is meant to encourage everyone to spend their time and energy in worship, doing good deeds, and being of service to others, rather than being consumed in materialism.

Doing the above leads to a much more beneficial society. Firstly, if we become less materialistic this will lead to a decrease in human conflicts and war, because the disguised motives for any war are really to fight for power and resources. Secondly, it will relieve us of the obsession of figuring out the nature of God and the meaning of life. Questions we often ask ourselves such as "Why did God create the universe?" or "Why did God allow evil to exist?" or "Why would God talk about heaven and hell?" are often mind-consuming. Knowing that there are no satisfying answers to these questions that will relieve us from the burden of trying to figure them out.

The ultimate goal is to be righteous humans. Some believe religions ask us to behave like saints and figuring out the nature of God is the excuse for us to avoid doing what we are supposed to be doing, which is behaving as Godly humans. We cannot figure out the nature of the atoms that make up our bodies or the matter of Earth, and it's possible we never will. It would be very hard to answer these questions; figuring out who God is would be even harder. Atheists who blame the problem of humanity on religion are falling into the same trap. We should all treat each other the way we expect to be treated and we get attracted to people who treat us with the highest ethical standards, regardless of whether they are atheists or theists. There is no reason for disagreement or bullying, from either side. The ethical principles of human interactions are universal. Therefore, we should keep all of this in mind and do better to communicate with each other like rational, educated adults rather than bullying each other for having different beliefs.

STOP 13

CREATING THE BRILLIANT BRAIN

How do you make a brilliant brain? We will be discussing the importance of two concepts in improving the brain's ability to function and excel: the first is the overall status of the limbic system and the second is self-image.

The Status of the Limbic System

Imagine a morning you wake up with no interest in how you look and what people say about you. And imagine you are free of any negative emotions or any physical desires and your ego has no grip on your mind. Would your mental faculty operate differently? I guess it is an easy experiment you can do: assign an ideal day of the week and try to function in that day as being free of desires or addiction and free from any negative social interaction.

When interacting with people, look at them as souls, not bodies or physical entities. Their physical structure does not have an imprint in your mind, and if they happen to make mistakes on your behalf, these mistakes are not committed by their soul, they are committed by their ego, which is the materialistic mechanical conditioning of their limbic system by the environment. Try to prevent your ego from interacting with their ego. Consider that people's mishaps all originate from a faulty reward system, dysfunctional amygdala, or traumatized prefrontal cortex.

Imagine freedom from material desires, like owning an expensive car or house, and freedom from drug addiction or alcohol consumption that will destroy your brain. And imagine freedom from excessive food consumption and from the pressure of sexuality that will make you behave like our friend rat Hoover when he is electrifying his brain.

Imagine you are living a day free from being obsessed with thinking about negative political events or other negative emotions, like sadness, anxiety or fears. And do not forget to make that day free from dwelling on the negative events from the past.

All these activities consume the brain, overwhelm the senses and change the metabolic design of the brain. This will create negative neuroplasticity and lessen your ability to use your brain in a very fun way.

We want an amygdala that is approving most of the events around us not taking things to heart and active only when we are about to encounter a bear in a forest. Encountering a bear may not be a common event in our modern life, but equivalent to that would be avoiding a car accident on the road and driving responsibly. We want a brain that is not stuck in thinking about the artifacts of life. We want a brain free from fussing about what he said or she said, so we have brain energy to put to good use.

The second concept has to do with what kind of image you have of yourself in regard to your ability to have a great memory, sharp analytical skills or to improve your math and physics skills. Do you believe that you have great ability and intelligence that will give you an ample memory and a problem-solving ability?

How do you connect the wiring of the neocortex, which carries its ability to do physics and math, with the reward and the opioid systems? If you can wire these systems together the result will be an awesome ability to function without being exhausted or stressed by the time spent on this kind of work. Studying math and physics will no longer be work because work becomes leisure.

Imagine that math activity or learning how to multiply large numbers has strong relevant representation in the reward system and can stimulate the pleasure centers in the nucleus accumbens and hypothalamus. What will happen to your math ability? It will get much better.

Does that mean your IQ is now going to improve? Call it what you like. Does that mean your ability to do well in math will be escalating from that point on? Does that mean that your neocortex will be operating with an advanced operating system?

Do we all have the ability to perform well at extremely high levels of function? We all have massive computing power waiting to be tapped. When our self-image is positive, and we believe that that we have this massive computing power, our performance will change.

This massive computing power will be available to benefit us and humanity. When the ego is settling down and taking the back seat and the association with material is reduced to what is necessary to maintain a reasonable life, the brain will start communicating with us differently.

We always hear about people with massive memories who might have autistic traits. Many of these people are actually socially simple. Socially, they act like a child. Children may not have a great interest in presenting themselves to the world as significant social entities worrying about their status. These genius people with massive memories must be fulfilling their basic functions in social life. If these people have children and families, they must take care of their families. They must not deliver to the world dysfunctional children and lead their families to disintegration. We should have both social intelligence and functional intelligence.

A positive self-image about our ability to learn fast will get better results when our self-image is structured in the mind during the first few years of our life, even if we seek this image at any stage in our life.

If you believe that when you are on the way to work your eyes are working like a camera recording all the street numbers, this self-confidence, coupled with a positive relationship with numbers will increase endorphin production when dealing with hard to memorize numbers. Your trip to work will never be the same. There is no more socially corrupted mind or negative interfering thoughts affecting this relaxed state. This will also have a positive reflection on your social life in general.

This relaxed state becomes spontaneous and natural with practice. You will not need to work hard on controlling your thinking. It becomes self-induced psychological therapy. The large part of the brain, the neocortex that defines us relative to other creatures, often works at less than its maximum potential.

This is most needed for people with depression when they understand this concept of shifting the thinking from circuits related to negative thoughts to functional positive thoughts, through the available mechanism to all of us, which is called neuroplasticity.

A positive relationship with numbers, for example, means that this activity must generate positive feelings in the limbic system, and create receptors in the nucleus accumbens and the amygdala through intracellular programming, followed by endorphin secreted from the hypothalamus. It is initially a hard task, but you can see that it is an emotional one, rather than a mentally strenuous task. And when you achieve it, you will have the key to a great gift.

Let me give you an example: Each number is connected to your memory already, so the idea is any combination of numbers is not strange to us. Take the number 462. Each of the three digits of this number is familiar to us and imbedded in our deep memory, but how can we combine them?

Suppose you are trying to learn this combination by heart. You can see that this simple number does not generate any emotional response. Now, if I tell you that your wealth will be multiplied by 462 times today, what will happen to your emotional center? It will likely be stimulated, but why? It will be stimulated because you are living in a world that programmed us to be psychologically stimulated by the concept of materialistic gain. Could you learn to have emotional responses to the digits 4, 6 and 2 without other materialistic benefits? When you do that you will acquire the capability to deal with numbers without having to employ strenuous efforts. The combination of 4, 6 and 2 will form a new emotional entity in your mind, and you will have this series of numbers occupy a definite special location in your memory bank.

The Media and Youth Intelligence

It is up to the media to bring a generation that has confidence in itself to achieve. Broadcasting ideas hinting that the only reason for living is to fulfill our temporary physical needs that are changing from day to day will result in two scenarios:

The first is in creating a generation that can only think about the fulfillment of desires and needs and is therefore addicted to drugs or engaged in non-purposeful activities like watching movies all day. This generation wants to be on vacation all the time and may become broke from credit card debt. They might face challenges in regard to caring for a family appropriately, even when they have the appropriate emotion and desire to have a family.

The second is a generation who engages lots of energy in studying and hard work to achieve wealth to buy the car and the house that the media is showing. This generation can do very well financially. The problem will be when this generation has limited vision and all that it cares about is connected to material possessions. Life achievement will be measured by materialistic achievements only. The picture that this generation can see becomes narrower and they are easily tempted to make a financial decision without much regard to our earth's health. An example of this would be buying a so-called gas guzzler being more important than decreasing carbon dioxide emissions and global warming. When this generation is faced with any failure it will be hard to fall on a spiritual cushion to absorb the shock and recover, and when the end of the road comes, meaning death, there is not much to reflect on in terms of the meaning of life.

When is the media going to realize that it has a great influence on people's lives and employ its tool to serve society better? Is it going to lose anything by becoming a constructive force? No.

STOP 14

CONSCIOUSNESS

Consciousness took a prominent position in philosophers' search for the nature of reality, from before Plato's time till our time. But during our time, the word consciousness has many other meanings.

In medicine, physicians use the term consciousness to describe the patient's level of alertness. Fainting is always described as a loss of consciousness, a problem that is very common in pediatrics, and it is a very frequent cause of emergency department visits.

Spiritual teachers use this term to describe the spiritual dimension of humans and often consciousness used to describe our state of being alert and observant of our behavior, impulses, worries, desires and state of our mood. When advanced, we become able to disengage from the elements that we just discussed and go into a state of suspended thinking, described by spiritual teachers as a spiritual state. This state can influence our psychology positively and elevate our mood. I do see that as a great achievement. But it is hard to have every human being on Earth do that. I cannot tell you the percentage of people who cannot achieve this spiritual state. Most of us want to live life without becoming spiritual teachers or philosophers.

Neuroscientists often use this term to describe a state of being aware. Also, it is used to describe the ability to feel, hear or see and to later describe those sensations to other humans. As you see, using this definition in neuroscience makes it hard for us to ascribe consciousness to animals or to have their consciousness studied, since they cannot report to us the experience they went through. Neuroscientists also use the term qualia, to describe what certain sensations feel like, and their ultimate emotional response.

At one time in our life, perhaps during our late childhood, we may have encountered the word "spirit." When we are introduced to this word during this stage, we usually accept it without further consideration. By the adolescence stage, we will have another encounter with this word but mixed with many shuffled concepts we can hear about at home, in school or religious institutions.

Is There Consciousness or Not?

It is easy to put up a philosophical argument that is elaborate and lengthy to show that a spirit does not exist and conclude that consciousness is just a product of the brain's chemical activity. What it takes to adopt this concept is to create a positive emotion in your limbic system in favor for it; the rest is easy. You might even study all the brain circuits down to the electrons produced at the end of every chemical assembly line inside each brain cell. You can figure out how the electron spins to convince yourself that the world is all about materials. If you happen to stumble on quantum entanglement in physics, just block that phenomenon out of your mind and ignore it, because according to that phenomenon, consciousness has direct interaction with how the electrons behave. Mysteriously, this electron behaves like matter when we pay attention to it, and like a wave when we do not.

You can use the laws of the thermodynamics against consciousness or try to prove from your observation of human behavior that qualia do not exist. The hidden motive behind that work comes from our desire to discover who we are! Are we only sophisticated computers, meaning are we only dust? Are our brains only bags of nitrogen and hydrocarbons, accidentally arranged in a sophisticated combination through endless lines of chemical reactions that began after the formation of Earth?

Is who we are a chemical reaction that created bacteria, and the bacteria became sophisticated, then they got together and became larger organisms? Did these organisms then figure out that they had to reduce themselves to sperms and an eggs to have babies in case they died? So, with time, the bacteria became us then we became conscious and conscious enough to try to look out for our origin. Is consciousness a necessary element for life or a mere accident?

I would like to invite you to read contemporary books regarding the theory of mind, which may shed some light on the human way of thinking in this century in regard to the matter of consciousness. Unfortunately, at the end of this search, I found no conclusion. Often, I see a statement saying advanced neuroscience in the future will tell us more about the problem of consciousness and will tell us who we are. It seems to me that this statement is reflecting what the heart desires. The passion of believing that we are all just material, seams to hijack the neocortical circuits and paralyze them, then forces them to comply with the idea that we are no more than dust.

Do you like to call them atoms? So, we are just a collection of atoms, and their function is determined by the laws of physics and chemistry, creating chemical reactions. From that chemical reaction, we were born.

Knowing that the materialistic world has a major role in our life, we have to understand the chemistry of the stomach to make medicine for it. But the dilemma we face every single second of our life is how to make sense of the world around us! How does our language make some sense to us? How are we thinking? How are we feeling our emotions and sensations? These issues force us to consider other dimensions to who we are in addition to the chemical reaction.

To Make the Story Short

When you wake up in the morning and look at yourself in the mirror, what do you think? Who is that? Whether you are an atheist, theist, fake theist, or righteous one, when you look at yourself in the mirror in the morning, you are not going to treat yourself as a piece of material. You are going to treat yourself as a soul. This spirit can make choices, understand the good and the bad, and have feelings plus concerns. It provides for us the essence of being rational agents.

All the terms we use in psychology are defined only when we are considered ethical beings, as we can differentiate between good and bad ethics. We are sophisticated enough to understand the limitation of our thinking and thinking of ourselves as material is not a possible thought. I can always say that I am just material, but I cannot actually think it, because it implies that I am nothing! If I am nothing, I am denying that I even have thoughts. I should then admit that my thoughts are not mine! Linguistically, I can say what I want, but realistically I am fooling myself.

Philosophers who are subscribing to the idea that life is all about chemical reactions are trying to destroy this institution of philosophy without being aware of what they are doing.

Scientists are still struggling to discriminate between physical and metaphysical, between empirical data and data based on reason. The philosopher who wrote extensively regarding this issue about how practical knowledge is structured is David Hume. He lived from 1711–1776, and understanding David Hume is very important. I see David Hume as the least understood philosopher. I claim that a child becomes an adult only when they understand David Hume on the point of how humans acquire knowledge. We are going to discuss examples of what it means to be an empiricist in your thinking.

I would like to define science this way: science is knowing how things work based on direct observation and not imagination. An example of science would be the following short story: Let us suppose we are running a business and have multiple computers in a modern office. The business has paperwork and to complete it, we need a printer.

To get a printer, we go to a technology company. For example, we go to Hewlett-Packard (HP) and say, "HP please make us a printer." HP hires a huge number of programmers, engineers, and chemists to bring us a sophisticated machine.

The people who made this machine know every tiny detail of how it works. What does that mean? It means the eye of the human had direct observation of the last minute of the details of how this machine is put together. We have an assembly line to build this machine. This is a clear form of science.

When I buy this printer, I ask the seller if they would guarantee that this machine will work when I take it home? Does it have a warranty? How much do I owe you? The seller tells me that it will definitely work, that it has a one-year warranty, and that it is a brilliant deal for only one hundred dollars. I get ready to write a check and give it to the seller folded. Before the seller can give me my printer, they have to verify that the check is reliable and the amount is correct, but if I tell them to trust me and not open the check, they will be suspicious of me. The seller is using his/her sense of vision to verify what I am doing. This seller is a scientist because the seller is using his/her vision to verify what he/she believes to be true.

The process of making printers is a science that has a real application in our life that we are willing to pay money for. Science has been around since humans have been around. This scientific method is as ancient as we are. It does not belong to one civilization, neither the East nor the West.

Take another example: Suppose you want your grandmother to make a burger. She knows the exact ingredients and the way you like your burgers to be made. Under the direct observation of her sense of vision, she fixes up the burger to your expectation.

Let us take another example of a janitor at work. We have a school with bathrooms that are beyond messy. We hire a janitor to fix this problem.

The janitor uses his/her sense of vision and knows the chemicals to use because of their experience with the job. This person is a scientist. Why? Because the janitor is using his/her sense of vision. The janitor knows how the tools work, how the mop works, etc. After the janitor is done, we inspect the bathroom. Lo and behold we find a tiny piece of dirt on the toilet rim, and we tell the janitor that their job is not finished. How did we come to this conclusion? We used our sense of vision. And the janitor uses his/her sense of vision to find the piece of dirt and wipe it off. I can see David Hume, who is a classic empiricist philosopher, smiling in his grave with these examples.

The grandmother, the janitor, and the workers of the technology company are not using metaphysics; they are functioning in the physical domain as it appears to their senses.

While we admire the nature around us, we can form another science. It is based on descriptive observation. For example, the science of botany is a descriptive science we are willing to pay money for because it has an obvious application in our lives. In this kind of science, we do not know the minute details of the flower in the same way we know the minute details of the printer when we buy a printer.

Metaphysics is making claims about the world beyond our direct senses, and I am doing that right now by using this example: I am going to say that a chemical reaction started four billion years ago on the surface of the earth. The chemical equation looked like this:

> water + carbon dioxide + methane + hydrogen sulphide + phosphorous + other chemicals → human

Then humans happened to stumble upon a tool, call it the brain, but we had no idea whatsoever how this tool worked. It looked like a useful tool to make burgers, cars, printers, clean a bathroom, you name it. All of a sudden, we found ourselves asking strange questions, such as "Where do we come from? Is there life after death? Where is God? Is there a God? What is infinity? How can we define the word logic? How come we have language? How come we have qualia?"

For sure we can study the brain in detail and find that when we hear the word "I," we measure all the chemical reactions and structural changes in the brain cell and come up with a mathematical formula to describe it down to the electron. This nice work is very useful in its medical applications. But, in regard to the question, what is consciousness, this idea seems to fit better in the metaphysical domain.

Consciousness has a twin sister: the origin of life. They share the same complexity and difficulties to study. They both require the metaphysical domain. Studying the origin of life by using our senses is impossible. We cannot go back in time to use our sense of vision to see how life began on Earth. If this concept sounds naïve to you, I will ask you to give it more thought and reconsider all its aspects.

But how can we solve this problem? We tried to solve this problem by using a new invention called "reason."

"Reason" is a new human invention used when the picture we are seeing is not complete or invisible and we have nagging questions to answer or a phenomenon to explain how and why it is happening. For example, when we describe a chemical reaction that started four billion years ago that created the human brain, we hold these kinds of reasons sometimes very close to our hearts. Often, we are seeking a sense of comfort for our emotions, and it helps our psychology to settle down. But this remedy has many side effects.

If we live in isolation from the rest of the world, there will be no problem, but that is not the case. Other people have their own reasons that do not agree with ours. They see our reason as a dysfunctional invention, and they are doubting our conclusions. They are judging our reason, of course by using their reason. They see theirs as being much sounder, more objective, and less emotional.

Their toolbox of thinking has a different set of tools than the ones we have, and if we try to defend our reason we have no option other than opening the toolbox again to look for a new tool. This is not going to solve the dilemma. In this situation, we often find ourselves using another reason to defend our original one. Reasons have to rely on other reasons to prove themselves. As you see, we could be in a much more difficult position than the janitor who is trying to clean up the bathroom as we discussed. The janitor's tools are very simple, and he/she can use their sense of vision to verify their work in the same way a scientist would.

The other dilemma we have is that both sides at one point may decide to take a look at the tools of their thinking boxes and examine how these tools work. A major difficulty arises; we have no idea how they work. Let us dive a little more into this argument by giving easy examples.

One day I was trying to use the vacuum cleaner, but it did not work. I checked the electrical outlet and that was the problem. The outlet did not work, so I decided that I was going to change it myself. I bought a new outlet, disconnected the circuit breaker and opened the outlet cover. I could see the electrical wires clearly, but I was afraid of touching the wires for fear of being shocked. How could I be sure there was no electricity running through the wires? I went to the hardware store and bought a power sensing device to test the wires. When I placed its sensors in the electrical outlet, a light on the device would turn on if the electricity was reaching the outlet and the outlet was functional. Now after turning off the circuit breaker and testing the outlet, I could be sure there was no electricity running through the wires, so I could touch the outlet with my bare hands.

This example shows that I could use a tool and have an idea of how it works. In addition to my senses, I only needed a very simple reason that all of us can agree on. By looking at the light sensor, I could tell if the electricity was off, so it was safe to touch the line with my bare hands. Now I could install the new electrical outlet. This is an example of a simple reason we all have in our toolbox, and we do not disagree on it. In fact, humans and animals use this simple reason. No one would argue about this kind of reason.

Now let us look at the human brain as a tool. Clearly, we have no idea how these electric circuits in this device are translated to thoughts, but this device can give us reasons beyond simple ones. These reasons are not going to be verifiable, and often they try to twist the arm of our senses to make us consider it valid. In a practical situation, we do frequently take this kind of reason as fact, especially when we are under pressure to follow our emotions. But be advised not to use this kind of reason to test any electrical line when we are afraid of being shocked and we only use a tool that would allow us to use direct observation.

From this example I would like to take you back to the original question that we discussed: Is the human brain a product of a thirteen-billion-year chemical reaction that started with the big bang, if you like, then consciousness came with this reaction? Who is in favor of this conclusion and who is against it? Be aware that both sides are using reasons and necessity. Each side has a scale measuring different reasons and comparing which ones weigh more. Which set of tools is better, mine or yours? What is going to tip the scale, in the end, is desire and passion which will settle the endorphin and dopamine systems and put them in a positive ground. Desire and passion settle the metaphysical question.

What is controlling the endorphin and dopamine system? Many elements like genetics and environments are easier to study, but we have two other elements, the embryological blueprint and consciousness, that I see as impossible to search.

So, what is my conclusion? My conclusion is that both sides are sinking in the same metaphysical ocean. No one will argue about the fact—the simple reason—as discussed with the circuit breaker. For example, there would be no arguments about the following statement: In the state of Montana, three feet under the crust of the earth, we found a huge bone of a creature. It resembles a huge reptile, and its height is thirty feet. We tried to find its age by measuring radioactive carbon-14, but we were unable to do so. We ran many lab tests and used a variety of machines as well. The person who ran the test is Mr. So-and-So, and by the way, he has a credit score of 850, for example. Also, he never told any lie in his entire life!

No one will argue about that at all, but a human has this natural tendency to dive into the metaphysical ocean. We call our metaphysical work, science, but in reality, we live for our passion. We have psychological passion and desires that often get out of our control. Our spiritual passion, when mixed with resentment and closed-mindedness, will also lead us to depression and make us consider other people's reasons as a negative force in society. Meanwhile, I am not denying the benefit of imagination and coming up with theories or stories to try to explain the existence of biological and non-biological systems on planet Earth. On the contrary, I think it is part of human nature and it could lead to valid conclusions. But it still needs not to be mixed with science until it becomes observable science according to the scientific methodology that is as ancient as human beings are. Otherwise, scientists will be fooling themselves first and fooling the public and this will lead to serious consequences on the social psyche.

Human Robot

Let us suppose that we have the most complicated technology to build a robotic human using the best artificial intelligence, and this human machine is constructed of multiple systems. The movement system, for example, is connected to sensors to sense where the feet meet the ground. The visual system analyzes all the objects in front of the robot. The robot also needs a way to perceive the sense of taste and smell. Now if we believe that the reaction to every sensory experience this robot has, is interpreted through social interpretation and analysis, then we need a separate system to do this job. This new system will be called "the individual." This novel system has to do the following: On a functional level, it has to tap into every tiny sensory function these separate computer systems are registering. It also has to coordinate between these systems and combine them into one unified social entity. After that, it has to respond to the billions of sensory experiences brought in every single second during the life of this robot. Logically, the social sensory system is connected to an ultimate qualia or feeling, which will interact with the social centers. Qualia, or feeling, would be an essential part of that system. In human beings, qualia and hedonism are the centers of the socially functioning individual. In a robot, this has to be another subsystem.

The function of any sensor of this immense machine will be useless socially unless it reports to a command center—a central computer that is programmed to make sure the rest of the systems are serving its social agenda. This central computer will coordinate with all other social experiences of the past, which has to be stored in its memory. Then it has to respond according to a goal, but which one? The ultimate vision or goal reflects what is in the programmer's mind. This is what defines the purpose of the robot. In humans, this function belongs to the human spirit or the mind working on the human brain. In the end, all the systems in the brain must report to one entity. This entity will deliver feeling, sensation, acceptance, comfort, happiness, sadness, elation, and many other feelings.

I am making a metaphysical claim, not a scientific claim, that when the function of animals and humans is analyzed, it is easy for our mind to accept the idea of a spirit. It is a central system that can communicate with the rest of the brain cells and make sense of all the inputs coming from every single one of them. This makes way more sense to me than the idea that our brain is a bag of chemicals or modules that accidentally happens to be working together. Why do these cells have to coordinate with each other? Why are we not having seizures every single second of our lives? Why do these 100 billion brain cells work together according to our feelings and desires? Why do we have to make sense of the world around us? If you happen to examine the words "making sense" and put them under a microscope, you will find that this single entity is communicating with every single cell in the brain. How can an electric circuit in the mush of the brain make sense of other circuits?

In the case of our robot friend, a central social computer has to be able to be more sophisticated and has much more computing power than the rest of the computers working for it combined. It has to do the following: compute what other computers are doing, make sense of their function, supervise their function, then unify their function to serve its agenda.

When I look at the human brain, I see many centers and I can identify the function of each spot. The prefrontal cortex happens to have some supervisory roles but still has a specific role. We could still function very well while the prefrontal cortex is dormant or when its role is not needed at one moment. An example of that is when we behave according to the social code of society, as we discussed in the introduction, and the prefrontal cortex does not have much input.

Every one of us implicitly agrees about a unified entity called "self." In the practical world, this entity demands to be treated well, even in schizophrenic patients. What does this mean? It means that we want to be treated as a person, not like a robot. This entity demands to be treated with dignity and respect by other souls. When we get bullied, we do not say, "This is just a change in the airwaves hitting our ears." We do not say, "It is just a rearrangement in the physical matter inside our ears." This entity or soul does not like to be treated as worthless material. This entity demands to be treated as a spirit, and this is true even in the most materialistic minds that exist or have existed on planet Earth.

Even though we have a material side that can be heard, seen and touched, we want to be treated as spirits. When we are touched, we want to be touched as humans with respect and empathy. When we are looked at, we want to be looked at by a humane eye. When we are seen, we want to be seen as spirits, not as a collection of atoms or second-class humans. We could lecture all day long about materialism, neuroscience, and advancement in nanotechnology to treat brain diseases. We could discuss the concept of evil and prove that God is hard to be there because of all the evil that is in the world. We could write a ton of books guided by sophisticated philosophy to prove the concept that material is all that there is. But deeper in our hearts, we believe we are souls. When people are talking to us, we do not only hear the words and the sentences, but we feel them and actually dive into the meaning of the words and we feel how hard they are hitting our soul.

We can lecture people about materialism, but we demand to be treated as spirits: what an obvious contradiction. When we lecture, we are assuming that the audience is like us, spirits, and they take things to heart. We also assume that they can process ideas and concepts. They are not questioning what the word "concept" means. Advanced neuroscience can go far enough to tell us which part of the brain has to be functional and active while we are experiencing qualia down to the level of the electron and which is the final product of the chemical reaction. But do you think this is going to solve the problem of who we are? When you wake up in the morning and look at yourself in the mirror then ask, “Who am I?” is materialism able to give you the answer to that?

STOP 15

THE COMPLEXITY OF THE HUMAN BODY

How complex is the human body? You can divide the complexity if you would like to separate areas, which may include the designs and the shapes of the structures of the body.

This design allows the parts to work together to perform certain functions. For example, when we study the structure of the foot, we see that it is designed to enable us to move and lift our bodies. Then we find ourselves studying the architecture of the bones and muscles, the connective tissues, including the blood supply, then the nervous system, and others. Next, we look at the mechanics of the cellular interaction between different tissues, like the connective tissue and the bone for example. We then look at the cellular design, meaning the inner structure of the cells.

These elements come together to make a functioning human. How complex is this? I did not appreciate this complexity when I was a medical student concerned about passing the exam and graduating. During the years of my residency, my concerns were to finish and have a decent ability to deal with my patients. After a while, when asking a patient to open his/her mouth, the picture of the oral cavity started to look different to me. I started to appreciate the complexity of what I was looking at. One day I felt, oh my God is this real? How is this embryo able to become a human? I concluded this is the largest and most complicated construction project ever built on Earth; it is actually the construction of the embryo.

While reading in biology class about the subject of egg fertilization, it is very common that we read this statement about the sperm; the sperm moves from the cervix toward the uterus cavity, then to the fallopian tube until it reaches the egg and fertilizes it. This statement is clear; our brain accepts the description without much questioning. If you happened to be thinking of the space shuttle traveling from Earth toward the moon, for example, the background of your thinking is visualizing NASA's scientists working hard on this task.

NASA's projects, like the space shuttle, require massive efforts. Behind NASA, there are thousands of collaborative efforts and engineers. In addition, behind these efforts, there are the minds of the humans working on these projects. However, we do not think of the process of sperm moving around as a very complicated process, even when we listen to the lecture explaining the biomechanics of the movements of the sperm. The explanation is typically simplified. An example of that is the sperm following a chemical grading of a substance secreted by the egg. In other words, the egg is secreting a chemical the sperm is attracted to, and the sperm is able to move toward the higher concentration of that chemical, a process that is easy to understand.

The over-simplification that is used by biology often gives us a false feeling that we know how, even though we do not know how or why in biology. To be fair there is a benefit from this way of thinking. The benefit is to be practical and create a solution to medical problems without diving into the details. Biological applications are fruitful and massive. We can make useful medications to treat illnesses, sequencing the DNA and figuring out the genome. Discovering the signaling proteins that have critical effects on the biological function allows biology to move from the descriptive state to becoming a bit more mechanistic. However, I see that the oversimplified way of thinking is very delusional as it gives us the impression that we know how biology is functioning.

Living in a state of knowing it all is depriving the mind out of its ability to behave with vast curiosity. It is depriving the reality of biology from the wonder and beauty that it has, and I feel this has side effects. We know it all and we figured it all out for you; we will relay the message to the students in the classroom that you do not need to be curious about anything anymore. The scientists and educational system have figured it out for you.

The educational system needs to present the subject curiously to students to make them more interested psychologically in these topics and make the material way more enjoyable. Bombarding the students with massive amounts of dry material with deadlines and exams leads to a lack of interest and even a stressful life for students. Being in a school should be a very enjoyable experience and not a place to smoke weed.

How we are programmed in school to think will dictate much of our way of thinking. When we feel that the process of thinking is fun and curious, it will sharpen our thinking and the result of that will enhance our social, business, and academic life. We are going to discuss together a few examples.

The Structure of the Finger Bones

If we look at the structure of every bone in the body in different people, we will obviously find similarities in the shapes of these bones. Let us take a look at the distal bone of the index finger, for example. You can see that it is a three-dimensional structure, and we are going to shed a bit of light on the process of constructing this structure in our embryonic life. Among many cells working on this project, chondrocytes are the key elements in this manufacturing. Let us consider the chondrocytes as construction workers in this process. We are going to compare the construction project of building this bone to the project of building the Sears Tower in Chicago, side by side. So, we have two projects, one is building the Sears Tower, the other is building the distal bone of the index finger.

Now let us talk about the complexity of these projects. If we look at the blueprint of the Sears Tower it may not look very complex. We see a drawing on a piece of paper showing many levels. Each of these levels may not be more sophisticated than an average house. An architect may draw the blueprint in only a few hours. Now let us take this blueprint and give it to the construction company; from there the blueprint will go to the civil engineering department and the project will get started and the details will be figured out. I am going to list just a few examples of these details: the number of support steel beams, the shape of the wood trims used to finish the windows, the electrical wiring and the plumbing system.

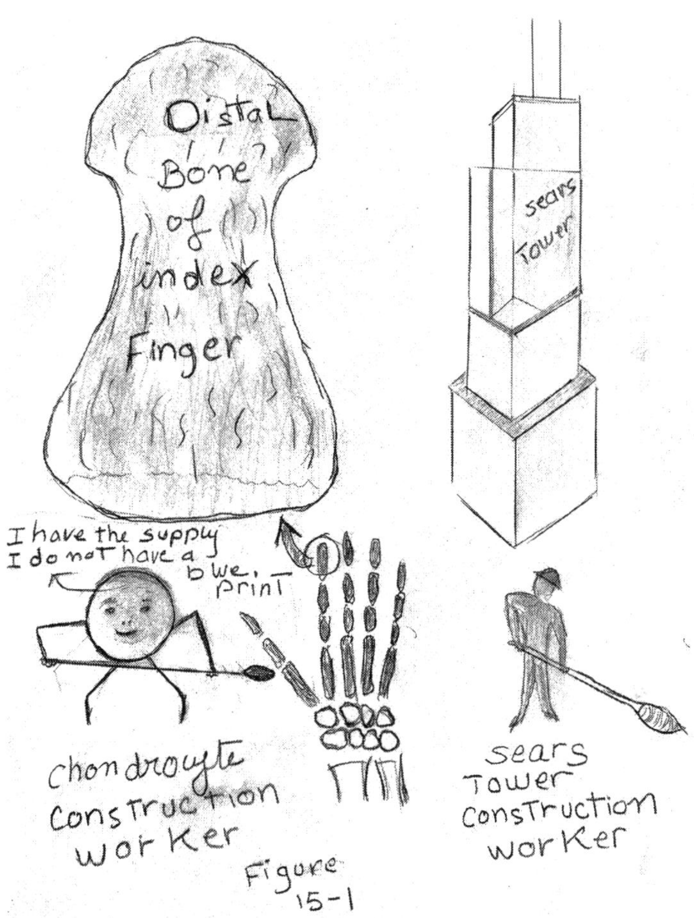

Figure 15-1

To complete this project, each one of these construction workers has to come to work for a number of days. A question to ask is how many movements a worker does every minute of every day? Could you count how many words this worker should say to communicate with other workers and managers during the time spent on this project? How many words do the carpet installers need to use to lay the carpet out on every floor?

Someone may say you can reduce the number of words to zero if you have a robot doing the project. The answer to that would be that each robotic machine was manufactured by using words in another facility and software engineering is involved which means, in reality, using more words. Imagine the carpet installers come early to do their work and they are sent back by the manager because the floor is not ready to lay the carpet. Imagine that a whole bunch of wood pieces are left at the entrance of the building and are now blocking its entry in the middle of the project. How could the project get completed in that case? Why do their tasks have to be done in this order? Could this order of events happen through trial and error? Is there a mind in the brain of these construction workers that would allow them to finish this job?

Now let's look at the second project, building the distal bone of the index finger; the information required for this manufacturing, from reading the blueprint through to completion, is potentially larger than the genetic DNA components assigned to create the finger. It is estimated that we have about thirty thousand genes in our genome, according to our current naïve and primitive understanding of how the DNA works.

Consider that there are close to about a thousand genes assigned to our sense of smell. A large number of them are not functioning in the human, as we understand their function at this time. These one thousand genes are functioning in dogs because dogs need a sophisticated sense of smell. This means that one out of thirty of our entire genome happens to be sitting doing nothing, which gives the impression that we have redundancy in our genome! If this is the case, how many genes are left for the design of the blueprint of the bone of the finger? To make the situation more complex, we have right and left fingers. Even though the genetic materials are the same for both hands, somehow the constructing cells figured out that the grooves and the curves of these two bones of the right and the left index fingers are going to be a mirror version of each other! How do these cells figure this out? How are they signaling each other?

When we study the human genome, we can classify the genes into categories. The two main categories are the enzymes, which are proteins that facilitate chemical reactions, and the building blocks of cells and tissues. Of course, we have miscellaneous proteins, like hormones and messengers, as well as proteins that perform the work of these two categories at the same time. An example of that is the proteins that control the transport systems in the cell wall.

Now going back to the three-dimensional manufacturing of visible structures in biology, as in manufacturing the distal bone of the index finger, for that to happen we need a specific gene to give the order to orient the chondrocytes and other cells like osteocytes to stack the manufacturing materials like calcium crystals in this way or that way. How many genes do we need for that? If we need a gene to do every mechanical move the chondrocytes are doing in this manufacturing project, then the entire human genome is not enough to manufacture the distal bone of the index finger! In fact, we may need one billion genes to manufacture the distal bone of the index finger. Do you think there are more than one billion detailed orders to manufacture the Sears Tower as the construction workers do their work, day after day for one or two years to finish the project?

We obviously are still in the early phases of discovering how DNA works, and maybe we will discover another information system working side by side with the DNA system, interacting with it and performing these mechanical tasks of construction. This system is likely electrical or electromagnetic, performed by the Glycoproteins, and we may never find this system.

This will give you an example of the complexity of biological manufacturing. Biological manufacturing is not simple. Even though we have made advancements in tissue culturing, when we are playing in the bacterial genome and stem cell genome to serve humanity and heal diseases, we are really relying on the cells, in the end, to do the manufacturing without us understanding how it's being done. We are harnessing the bacterial capability to take genes from their surroundings, effortlessly, to manufacture biological material like insulin.

Even though we have made advancements in nanotechnology, embryological manufacturing, creating a creature from a fertilized egg or even a cloned creature is not only beyond our reach, it is beyond our intuition and our questioning mind. We take for granted that when the chicken lays a fertilized egg the majority of these eggs are going to hatch chicks. Please remember the Sears Tower when you look at a face or an eye. The examples of the complexity are endless.

I would like to give you a few other simple examples, from the anatomy of the human body:

First, the long plantar ligament of the foot.

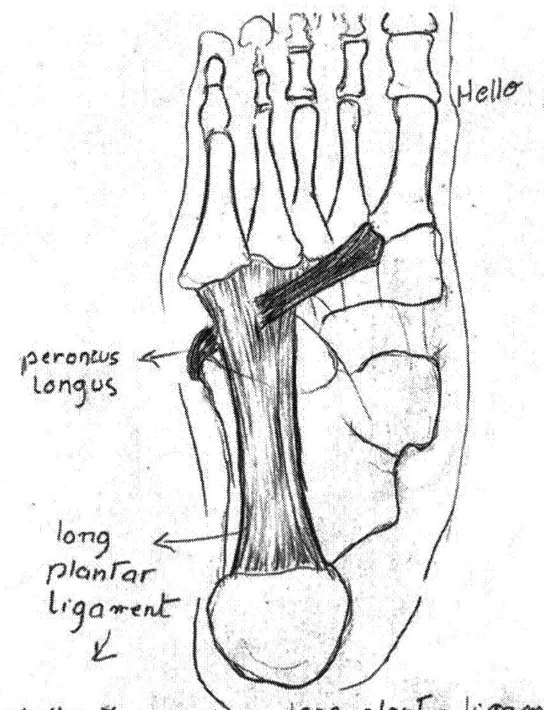

Hello, I am your long plantar ligament. during my embryonic formation I ran into a muscle called peroneus longus, creating a traffic Jam situation. To be nice I made a tunnel for the Tendon of this muscle to pass through the front end.

Second, the posterior circumflex humeral artery.

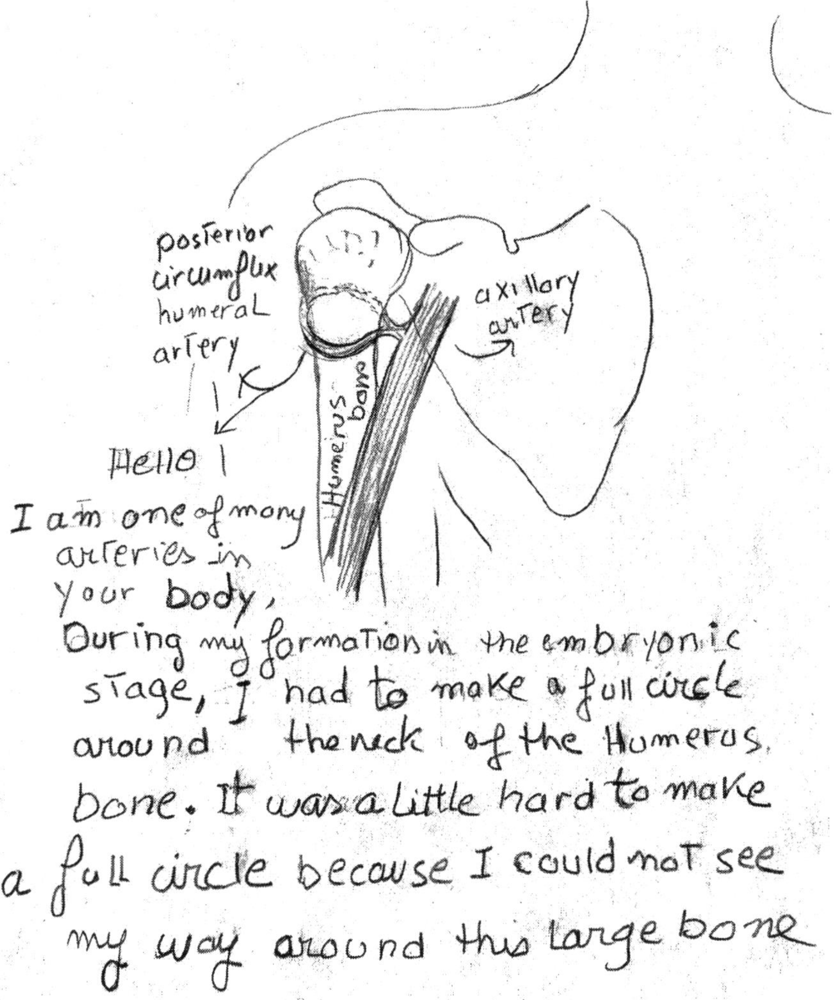

Third, from intracellular structures, the motor protein.

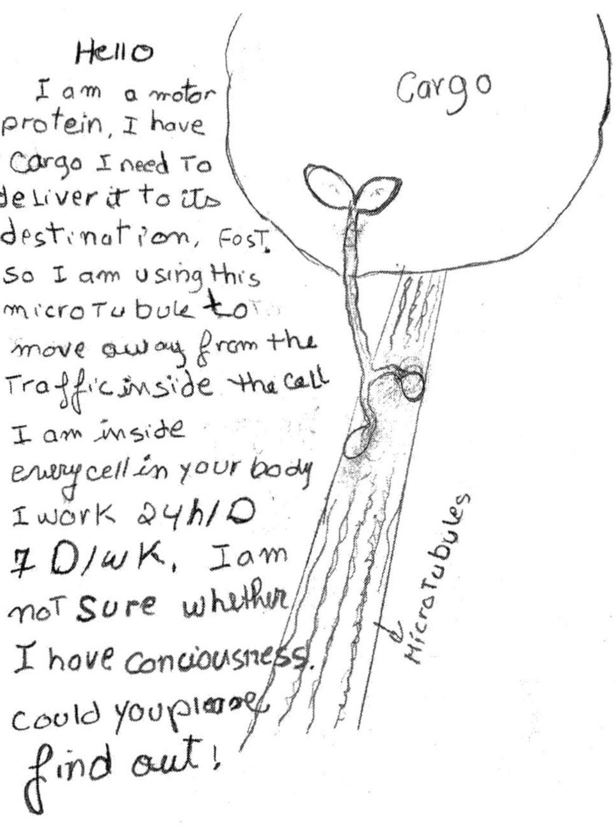

Just to try to imagine …

If we are going to make a blueprint for an embryo to manufacture a baby, in my humble opinion we need over a trillion genes to finish this project, because a simple biological model, like the genetic system, per our understanding of its function, is not capable of producing a blueprint for manufacturing. The design of the car we drive is made by the intelligent conscious being called human, even though the car is relatively simple compared to the human cell.

In building the bone of the tip of the finger, are we going to ascribe intelligence to the chondrocytes? The chondrocyte seems to have the intelligence to be able to do its job! It cannot rely on its genome to make its blueprint! The bizarre examples in the biological world are chilling and countless, beyond the thirteen billion years of the age of the universe. Yes, we are using key components in the bacterial genome to produce proteins, but the details of that are still hidden from us. The mechanisms controlling the full manufacturing are too complex.

If we take x-rays of the tip of the finger for twenty people and show them to a radiologist, do you think she/he is going to see the difference between any two x-rays? This similarity cannot be attributed to a chaotic system. You would think there is a reductive system that is in use to make the bones of the tip of the index finger belonging to two different humans look alike. This system has to account for every minute detail to give a similar product in the end! This design has to have a blueprint. The mechanism of the genomic expression by manufacturing proteins alone is incapable of giving us this blueprint.

Genes do play a role in signaling the initiation of building an organ. For example, fruit flies are often used in a laboratory to study gene expressions. Researchers can modify a gene in a fruit fly and the product can be a fruit fly without wings or with four wings. Nevertheless, when the wing is formed, where is the blueprint of the wing manufacturing hiding?

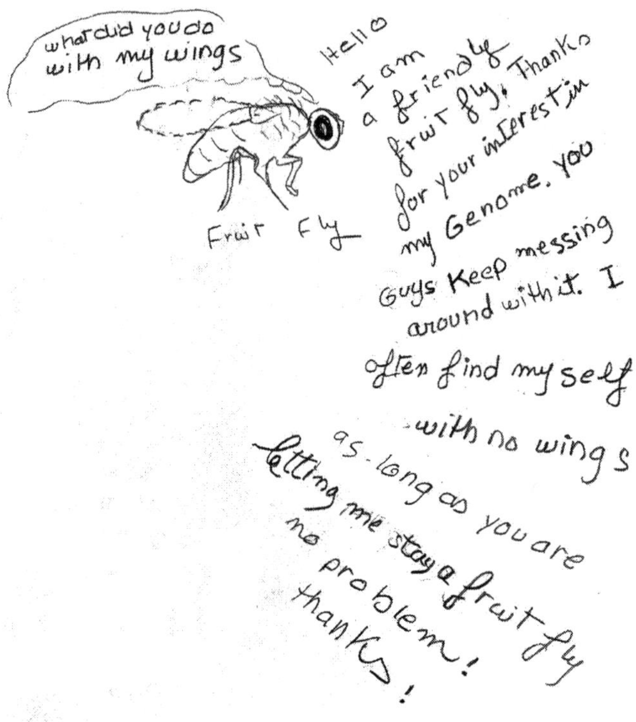

We use syntax to put sentences together in meaningful ways to make a nice long story that we can enjoy reading. Something similar must exist to put the genome together in a meaningful way to make an animal or human. This system is asking for recognition; does it deserve it yet? Are we too sleepy to wake up and look at it? Could the next one hundred years tell us more than we know now? What we know now is too primitive, even though it is useful in its application in medicine, agriculture, and genetic engineering.

The Complexity of Human Function

Let me give you a silly and simple example, like the behavioral ability of humans to be able to cross their legs when sitting down. It is obvious that this ability comes from the complicated structural connection between many parts of the motor centers in the brain. However, that structure has some blueprints that the embryo can create. What makes us different from apes in this regard? Logically we can answer by ascribing this ability to the uniqueness in the manufacturing of the human brain.

One day we may understand what gives us the desire to cross our legs when we sit down on a chair. We would like to know what gives us the ability to have the fear of death or not to have it. What about feeling fearful of failing an exam and the ability to differentiate between syntax and semantics? What happens when we understand the difference between operational memory and episodic memory? Are we experiencing a special protein synthesis when we say a word or when we hear a word of any language?

These are examples of the biological complexity I can keep counting, not only exceeding the number of genes that we have but also exceeding the number of tiny units that make the elemental structures of our DNA.

STOP 16

OPINION AND ARGUMENT

How do opinions form? The origin of opinion likely starts in the neocortical neurological circuits. Needless to say, it has strong ties to the limbic system and the reward center in our brains. The neocortex is the home place of thinking and imagination, and likely the place of inquiry for any idea. When we voice our opinion to others, we try to influence the circuits in their brains that are similar to ours, whether they are related to the neocortex or the limbic system. We mainly aim at creating synchrony between our brains and other people's brains. Achieving this synchrony tends to put our psychology at rest and stimulate the reward system.

Compared to the neocortical centers, the social centers in the limbic system have way more influence on our views and behavior. The end target of the limbic system's neurological output is the reward system and the hypothalamus. The limbic system has a direct connection to each. It has the most influential effect on our sense of satisfaction and comfort. For this reason, it is very hard for human beings to be purely rational creatures.

While the neocortical centers are concerned about looking for facts, the deepest part of the limbic system, the hypothalamus, is usually concerned with emotions. The hypothalamus is strongly subjected to the output of the rest of the limbic system and the reward center. But it could be concerned with facts in some of us! Between these two worlds of emotions and facts comes the birth of reason. Reason finds a home somewhere in between. Reason is often the tool that we use when we voice our opinion. It has the potential of being a factual neocortical tool, or it may simply stay as a psychological emotional response, but beware! The deep social centers will try to trick the neocortical centers into skipping verification and considering its position as the ultimate truth. The verification comes from the work of our senses and direct experience. Experience is from direct observation using our senses of vision, touch, auditory and smell. Often opinion sits in the roam of reason, unable to be tested and verified, since testing is often very hard and impractical. Frequently, our opinions are influenced by other people's opinions, leaving the neocortical centers subject to the influence of our emotional centers.

Can you imagine the pulse coming from the interactions between the cortical centers and the limbic system? This delicate rhythm is what allows the human being to use his/her brain and claim that he/she is a rational creature! You can judge, evaluate, and make conclusions. Look at a patient with schizophrenia. In this case, the interaction between the two systems is disrupted and the outcome is dominated by delusion and grossly unverifiable conclusions. This outcome will cause the schizophrenic patient to do threatening behaviors to themselves and not to others. Compare this example to patients with antisocial personality disorder, commonly called psychopaths. In these patients, the interaction between these two systems is intact, but both systems are independently dysfunctional. In psychopaths, the neocortical centers are paralyzed and unable to make sound judgements, and the social centers are intoxicated with the physical self, which numbs the human and makes he/she behave like a zombie. This state will cause the loss of ability to see others as no more than materials to consume and prey upon. Soon this behavior will lead to the demise of the psychopaths themselves.

When we are faced with another human who does not agree with our opinion, our reaction is going to be dependent on how our reward system is programmed. We, as humans, find pleasure in finding others who agree with our opinions. The opinion may have humane implications. For example, finding people we agree with is an important goal we strive to achieve. It tells us about the degree of empathy others have toward us and how friendly the social environment is. Agreeable people constitute important elements of our social atmosphere. This situation is critical when we are put in a place of leadership and have to make many decisions affecting others.

Inside the word "opinion," you can also find many philosophies and what people in general call "logic." The definition of logic is as complicated as the word consciousness. How can we define logic as the brain activity isolated from the reward center? Often, we manage to put it in a mathematical frame. Aristotle's deduction method is a prime example of this.

Are the opinions you cling to connected to your reward center or not? You can put this to test by using a simple method! When someone else presents to you a different idea that is not agreeing with yours, and they are backed up by some evidence or with sound reason, if it is very easy for you to consider the other opinion, then you can conclude that your opinion is not strongly tied to your reward system and your opioid centers. Changing your opinion, in this case, may not trigger the limbic system to be involved in the process. For example, the amygdala does not send negative signals to the hypothalamus and the nucleus accumbens. In this case, our emotions are not involved, and we stay calm.

When changing your opinions does not incur a financial or materialistic loss, this change is even more acceptable. In fact, if we take the matter a step further if changing our opinion results in financial reward, would we really care about ever thinking we had this opinion to begin with? Maybe in this case, there will be a swift and quick intracellular reprogramming in the reward system, mainly the nucleus accumbens and in the amygdala.

Using sarcasm to attack other people's opinions is a very common tool people use to support their opinions. Sarcasm is also used for retaliation. Retaliation has been found to lighten up the reward system. I have seen sarcasm used widely in scientific debates, and when you see it, you know exactly what it is intended for! What the debater is really saying is, "Please do not take it personally, this subject of discussion is strongly connected to my reward system and it has huge emotional baggage." When sarcasm is used in scientific debates, it is easy to see that both sides really have no clear facts on display here, and you know that both are swimming in the metaphysical sea. Otherwise, there would be no argument to start with! There is nothing wrong with displaying the facts as they are without adding a personal interpretation that will lead us towards an unnecessary debate and unverifiable opinions.

An opinion that is connected to a personal profit is even worse. A human sometimes may not understand his/her real intention and can easily fall into defending an opinion not realizing that they are trying to serve their own interest.

Sometimes an opinion can be so consuming that it takes over a person's mental faculty. When you examine this opinion, you have no idea how the person came to this conclusion because on one hand, you do not see a financial benefit for taking this opinion, nor does it make any sense. You realize this opinion is a mere reflection of the limbic system dominated by a dysfunctional ego!

Our society and culture can place mental and social spectacles before our eyes. These spectacles work as filters, allowing only a few colors to pass through and stain our entire mental views with them. During the process, they prohibit us from seeing the huge spectrum of many other colors. Starting from the time we are very young, these spectacles contribute to the design of our neocortical and limbic systems, which together help us create our opinions. These spectacles are usually harmless and aid in supporting the foundation of our cultures. I see no problem in using these spectacles as long as they do not contradict any ethical principles agreed on by all of humanity. In fact, all of us are wearing them without paying attention to what is resting on the bridge of our noses.

The Argument

Can we argue about anything? Probably yes, except for a few situations. In math, when we say 1+1=2, there are no questions. You will never see anyone argue about this reality. You could also think of a statement we could verify easily. For example, when I tell you that in this book if you go to page number 55, the first word is going to be "water." This is a simple statement that is easy to verify. Simple deductions are hard to argue about as well. This is summarized in the famous example which says, "Humans are mortal, Socrates is human, and therefore Socrates is mortal." No one will argue about this.

It is also hard to argue about all the principles of math and physics because they are based on definitions designed to build science accordingly. These definitions are the foundation of theoretical sciences.

But generally, who would win any argument? Whoever studied the subject better or whoever studied the nature of the argument of the opposite side, because that person understands the rationale of the opposite side. The winner will be whoever can experience the entire essence of the opposite side. They will be self-confident and will smile more during the argument. They will be less emotional but at the same time very passionate about their opinion while finding a variety of supporting ideas about the subject of the argument. The winner will be whoever is presenting themself as the empathic side to the audience and able to capture their hearts. This skill makes them more socially intelligent. The winner will be whoever has more processing power, better attention and higher critical thinking. Unfortunately, the winner will be whoever can supply a series of lies to support their position, which will be unverified during the presentation of the argument.

But in any argument, how can we tell who is truly right? All of the above is not going to tell us who is right. The reason I am discussing this matter is to give you some tools to help you control your reactionary mind. We always allow our emotions to be the judge of everything we do. Our emotions interfere with the majority of our decision-making process. This is also true for scientists when they are really doing metaphysics and they think they are doing science.

Mentioning God in Universities

While dealing with complicated biological phenomena, such as the origin of life on Earth, a scientist may find it very complicated. She/he may suggest that God must have interfered here and put things together. A response might come from another scientist that if they cannot find a naturalistic explanation for a phenomenon, it is not right to attribute it to God, and what they are doing is not science. One side says it is God behind the scenes, the other says it is the law of nature behind the scenes. In my opinion, both sides are relying on their emotions and feelings to supply them with these opinions. Both sides are doing metaphysics, not science. They are trying to explain the nature of reality, which is beyond our reach. The atmosphere in the universities will be more rational when we understand this notion. It is necessary to give each other space to breathe and express our emotions since there are no neutral rules to govern this matter!

If you are really doing science, your project is not going to be affected by your belief of either God or the law of nature behind the scenes, even when either one is mentioned by the researcher who is working on the project a million times. How come? Because as I explained in the example of the grandmother who is making a burger, when you eat the burger, your taste buds are going to experience the ingredients of the burger, and you can open the burger and check what is in it. Whether your grandmother said God a million times or the law of nature a million times is not going to change the ingredients of the burger. If you are doing science, then take it easy. Isaac Newton often mentioned God when he was studying the solar system, and it did not hurt his project.

Objecting to someone's unverifiable opinion means that his opinion has triggered a negative emotional reaction in us. When we understand this concept, it will be easier for us to give people space when they tell us about their opinions. We can understand that their emotional views especially when they are connected to their theological beliefs as long as the subject does not contradict simple facts, like 1+1=2, or disagree with the senses. The objection to this relies on the concept that it is just a matter of time before we know all the details of natural sciences and reduce everything to simple measurable elements. I think the answer to that is that we are always going to be relying on abstract concepts. We are always going to be relying on metaphysical rules that suit our reasons and emotions. The next section is going to give you an example of that.

Theistic and Atheistic Brains

I hinted in this book about this topic on multiple occasions, so you can realize by now that I see religion as playing an immense role in structuring human cultures. This important element of our psyche can be constructive in many ways, such as decreasing the depression rate and fulfilling our spiritual needs. There is a mounting amount of evidence supporting this claim. Another way is by creating a liability system in our mind that reminds us that it is not only the legal system that is monitoring our behavior, there is a higher eye that is looking into our consciousness and actions. This will aid us when applied rationally, to avoid cheating, lying, stealing, and abusing others. Also, it is suggesting that the real liability is the liability before the Almighty God who can examine our soul and intentions. This belief when taught right from early childhood, demands us to be conscientious humans. God demands us to have a good ethical will and this ethical will gives us dual benefits. The first: our belief in God makes us act in ideal ways and gives us psychological comfort. The second: the benefit we receive when others are dealing with us when they are using an ideal ethical standard, like super honesty and fairness.

Atheistic cultures are capable of teaching children idealistic and high ethical standards. Examples are plenty. Some of these cultures earned a great recognition from the rest of humanity for their ethical standards and empathy that they adopted.

Atheistic cultures, however, may not enjoy a reduction in depression and other psychiatric diseases compared to the theistic ones. The saying "religion is the opium of the masses" is not far from the truth. There is a spot in the hypothalamic area that fires internal endorphins when we practice our rituals, and some human beings, when they discard the rituals, have to replace them with street drugs like heroin. When this spot becomes ignored by the rest of the brain, the brain becomes restless. Then we seek drug use, and we become addicts.

Adopting a theistic or religious approach in teaching our children has to emphasize the idealistic ethical standards application in their life. When we are working and doing tasks, the existence of God to monitor our behavior, our attitude, and be supportive of our hearts, will magically boost the level of acceptance of the difficult conditions that may not be to our liking. This has tremendous positive ramifications that make human life to be in functioning conditions.

We can try to shed a tiny bit of light on the matter of belief in God and what we know about the social brain, but this is not going to be optimum. We as humans are looking for answers to questions related to our origin. Where do we come from? Another hard question is why do we tend to ask these questions in the first place? What causes the hypothalamus to respond to the idea of a creator in one way or another? How did we arrive at this point in our life to question our beginning and our end? For some, we find tremendous comfort when the issue is discussed and when we are involved in a ritualistic religious activity. Some of us have difficulty accepting the idea that we came from nothing and after we die, we become nothing. Some of us have no problem accepting this idea that it is all about chemical reactions from gases and water on the surface of the earth, and this leads to the formation of a human. This chemical reaction happened to be a special one, and it led to creating the sophisticated machine we call the brain. Some of us may not really care about the entire subject during our lifetime or may not pay enough attention to it. All these positions have to be respected by the rest of society. Unfortunately, I still see bullying and disrespect when this matter is brought up, even in the developed West.

When theists examine the idea that it is all about chemical reactions that created all the creatures, he/she may see that the atheists are living in wishful thinking, and the atheists also may consider the theists as living in wishful thinking. Of course, each side will try to rely on reason to support their position.

The area in the hypothalamus that is concerned with religiosity does not have the curiosity to know how biology works. The hypothalamus is looking only for conclusions. We want to live the conclusion. We are all looking for short cuts. We pretend that we know the details of how things work, but in our deep hidden reality, we know that we do not know how we are formed and where we come from. The biological complexity simply is beyond our brain capacity to comprehend.

When we involved thinking about the issue of biology, the subject turned philosophical by nature and it is no longer in the range of science. We like to say that our conclusions are based on evidence, but as soon as somebody presents us with different evidence, we start to sweat, and we may go into an anxiety or panic attack.

Many unbelievers came to their conclusion that there is no God at the age of fifteen years when they look at the picture of the world; it made more sense to them to see it through an atheistic eye. Others took longer to reach this conclusion. Others were overwhelmed by the surrounding complexity on planet Earth, they felt that they have a soul and they concluded that there is a God. I have to admit here that during our time, where the social atmosphere in schools and universities is siding with the metaphysical position that there is no God, the belief in God requires harder work and it is actually becoming a challenge. The way to it goes through mud and clouds. This chaos is created on one hand by the corrupted religious systems with their unqualified representatives, and on the other hand by the claim that the majority of scientists are unbelievers! What a difficult situation. I was told on multiple occasions from the media and from listening to lectures discussing evolutionary psychology, that the majority of people walking on the street believe in supernatural entities like spirit and God. I have to admit that this belief is not endorsed by the prevailing social views of the educational system. This situation is creating internal turmoil for many of us, especially in people who say that they believe in God.

If you keep going through the mud and the clouds, you may find that understanding the concept of what it is metaphysical and what is physical or scientific could be of some help. This not going to help you find God, but it will allow you to look at the scientific evidence on open-minded nonbiased ground.

Now, let us look at a likely scenario in the neuroanatomy of the brain and how it works in having a feeling about the existence of God.

Is there a creator? Where did this thought come from? The probable location of this thought in the brain has to involve the neocortex; after all the neocortex is the problem-solving center of the brain, the home of ideas, and curiosity.

Another location for that is the prefrontal cortex and cingulate gyrus. God has created us to be programmed to look for warm interaction with the environment while we are alive and after we die.

The inquiry may start in the neocortex, but the prefrontal cortex will help us pay attention to this matter. With a quick connection to the cingulate gyrus, it will help us consider a calm, thoughtful, warm focus on the matter. It seems logical also to think that the cingulate gyrus is a probable location for this inquiry since our empathy drives our thinking to some extent.

The idea then goes down to the amygdala. There, the idea will be evaluated, and according to its programming, the feeling of comfort or discomfort arises, likely through signaling the hypothalamus. The amygdala also sends signals to the nucleus accumbens. If the nucleus accumbens has a powerful response to this matter it will give us further enthusiasm and excitement to keep going with this line of thinking. Now the hypothalamus by itself has a heavyweight on judging any matter, which is going to give a near ultimate response to this idea. If favorable in that case, endorphins are released, facilitating the approval state. In the end, we or consciousness will make the final decision. As you can see, this book is an attempt to make a case for this notion. If these centers are working in harmony with each other, the neocortex will calm down and the thinking will be settled. A world view is now taking place and after that, we tend to have psychological comfort.

After reaching a positive conclusion for the idea of a deity, we will see that opposite ideas would not have any logic to them. An example of that is the idea that we are the product of a chemical reaction. This will have uncountable flaws. When we look at the fossil record, the movement from the single-cell organisms and simple form of life, such as sponges, to the Cambrian era of complex creatures that could swim and move, should take more than eternity to be accomplished on its own, without divine intervention. The fossils are always reflecting our heart's desires. We start creating endless questions. One of them is why didn't dinosaurs change themselves over time to become intelligent dinosaurs and create civilization or have intermediary forms between their different species? Didn't they have enough time to become intelligent creatures and build a civilization? Intelligence does not hurt overall. It looks like they were waiting for an asteroid to hit the earth, or a flood to destroy them to bring on their extinction. In many theistic brains, life has no meaning without life after death.

What about our atheistic friend? In that case, imagine the opposite of all that we discussed, about what happens in the limbic system and the neocortex of a believer. This opposite will lead to creating a vacuum in the production of endorphins and dopamine, for example. Then negative feelings will surface, and the neocortex will receive the news from the hypothalamus and the nucleus accumbens. All of a sudden, and it becomes comforting for us to say there is no God. We look at the world and see it is full of reasons to adopt this view. An example would be when we say none of us has seen God.

When we try to date fossils and we are unable to do so, we have no problems whatsoever to find strange ways to date them. For example, we will look for a volcanic rock, sitting nearby the fossils. We can date this rock and then conclude that the age of the fossil is the same as the volcanic rock.

The idea of evil becomes huge enough to the point of making it hard to consider God to exist. All of a sudden, you look at the biological design and you find it full of problems and conclude that this design is only created by a chaotic process. How about consciousness? There is no such thing. It is a matter of time and the computers will have consciousness. Who knows it all, our rational brain or our emotions?

But who is right? You are right! This is one of the conclusions of this book if you read it carefully. You are right. Regardless of your level of education, do not believe that scientists or theologians are more qualified than you to tell you the answer. It is your responsibility to come up with your own conclusion. If you try to look into the evidence and reason, you are welcomed, but you will be disappointed because you are not going to find direct answers. Work concerning this matter is all about emotion and stories designed to force notions on our minds. The necessity of explaining the origin of life forces us to adopt speculation and assumption. Scientists must have some philosophical understanding, and it is about time they hatched out of the shell of sophistry and illusion. Science is only about direct empirical findings; it has nothing to do with inventing stories describing what happened millions of years in the past.

Adopting the materialistic view concludes that there is no such thing called "mind" because the brain function is all about chemical reactions. These notions give birth to determinism. If my opinion and yours are both determined by the laws of physics, who is right? The word "right," if we accept materialism and determinism, will absolutely have no meaning at all. I hope the idea is clear. Many philosophers discussed this matter, including Emmanuel Kant in his famous book the *Critic of Pure Reason* and David Hume in his famous book *An Enquiry Concerning Human Understanding* did a very good job of explaining this concept.

The problem of the origin of life is happily joining other metaphysical dilemmas like how gravity works, how the electron is attracted to the proton in atoms, what infinity is, how we think, what consciousness is, and all the unexplainable problems related to quantum mechanics.

As David Hume, who himself is not a theist, said that there are things that we know and things that we cannot know, because simply they are out of our sense of experience, sense of vision, hearing, taste, or touch. How logical to say that this accidental collection of atoms which is us, must, and I am going to repeat the word must, know its origin! Really!

We will do much better if we take the issue out of the discussion, respecting each other's opinion on this matter because opinions here are only about creating a psychological comfort. This opinion is what produces dopamine and endorphin in the reward system and the hypothalamus. We are using our limbic system to judge other people's opinions, not understanding that this system has been tampered with by the environment from the time we are born, and this system is mirroring our emotions.

Why can there not be something better than adopting the practice of pushing each other to follow our views because we think we are right and others are wrong? Why not use science to save Earth from destruction, instead of setting it to become like planet Venus, which has an average temperature of about seven hundred degrees Fahrenheit? Why are we marketing our emotions and egos to the public? We are selling our power struggle to the public no differently than any salesperson, using marketing techniques, no different from any other past age of humanity when we lived in our dogmatic views.

If a scientist wants to bring God to their lab, please give them space and let them say what they want; it is only a mere emotional expression. The scientist is not going to mix God into the recipe. When I am going to buy a burger, and the cook tells me that he/she prayed on the ingredients and they become a burger, I am not going to accept this story. I will return the burger to the cook. But if the cook tells me that they were praying while making the burger and they were admiring the structure of the bread or the tomato, and says that God must have created them, I am not going to make a big deal of that as long as the cook opened his/her eyes while making the burger and followed the right steps in making it.

Being an atheist or theist is not going to conclude whether someone is a good biochemist or not, and it is not going to hurt anyone's research or project in any way. Please do not do what the

Drawn by Al-Ado, inspired by a painting
of Galileo by Justus Sustermans

the religious institution did to Galileo. This system considered itself to know more, and it suppressed the freedom of speech of anyone who disagreed with it. Whether Galileo was right or wrong is not the issue here. The religious system was the powerful predominant system at that time. Just imagine that Galileo was left alone saying what he wanted regardless of whether he was right or wrong. I can assure you that the religious system overall on Earth would have been in better shape in our time. It would not have the stigma that it had in the Middle Ages as a suppressive negative force in society. What is wrong with us being open-minded and accepting the other's opinion, especially at this time, the time of neuroscience when we are discussing what it really means to have an opinion?

These institutions have other jobs to do in society other than going after people for their views. If you are comfortable with a chemical reaction being the explanation for what you see in the lab, there is no reason for you to have any discomfort when someone says I can see God's hand in the matter. Both opinions are relying on a metaphysical philosophy, and we need to understand there is no such thing as neutral rules when we judge other's opinions. We are operating every single second of our life, being soaked in our emotions, and we use our emotions to judge all the ideas around us. We are at the mercy of our reward and endorphin systems until we understand this concept very well.

We better wake up and let people live in their own culture and religious beliefs if they choose to do so. Sound cultures will give us mental and emotional stability. Please do not describe religious cultures as unscientific, inferior or unenlightened. Let us get to know each other and enjoy the diversity of human culture without forcing our views on others.

Maintaining this variety of human cultures, especially the positive elements of every culture that the majority of people agree on, is a realistic and fair goal to achieve. It is better to aim at having a population with an extremely low level of depression of about one percent. This is a rate that society can handle. The families of these affected patients will have reasonable support from the medical system and the rest of us. Also, society will not feel overwhelmed by this low rate, as we are experiencing in the West currently.

The variety of human cultures, including their belief systems, have to be accepted by all of us. We should avoid becoming bullies to each other, especially when we discuss other cultures' conditions. This is a necessary tool to know each other and this process, when used with open-mindedness, will enrich our lives without the feeling of anxiety about abandoning our cultural essentials that are embedded in our reward system from the time of our childhood. If we happen to see what we consider inhumane practices in some cultures, we can try to approach that by discussing this matter with the governing resources in these cultures and help to fix them.

Who is Our Friend?

Our views and opinions are stable as long as the internal and external circumstances are stable. Let us take this example:

Let us suppose we have two friends who share atheism as a social bond, and one of them betrayed the other or mistreated the other in some way, and this friendship has ended. Then the betrayed one happens to run into a neighbor, who is a theist or religious.

The theist then invites his new friend the atheist to his home frequently, and they become close friends. The theist shows real genuine empathy and excellent friendship toward him. He treats his new friend in a manner that the atheist has never seen in his life.

The next thing to happen is the atheist gets to know other friends and they are all religious. They all treat him in an excellent way. Let us take this matter one step further. Suppose that the atheist has a serious financial problem and his religious friends come to him and give him enough money to solve this problem. Do you think his scientific views regarding the creation of Earth are going to stay scientific?

Let us take it another step further. The religious friends come to their atheist friend and tell him they want to pay off his mortgage and buy him a new car! Do you think that this guy is going to look for his old atheistic friends anymore? The resistance to adopting new friends is going to go down and, at some point, his mental structure might collapse. These friends in theory were able to tackle every spot in our friend's brain and brought happiness in every aspect of his life like he had never experienced before. This group was truly presenting the right example of how religion should be presented to each other. This group has abandoned the traditional way of presenting a religion, which is maintaining fat bank accounts under a religious umbrella, and it has adopted what would elevate religion to the status that it deserves.

If you are a materialist or naturalist, this should make absolute sense. After all, our behavior is influenced by complicated nervous electrical circuits, and these circuits are formed during our life experience and influenced by our genetic makeup. Often the environment has the upper hand in shaping the outcome of the interaction.

You can imagine other scenarios regarding our loyalty to other psychological entities which is becoming a fragile mental structure when tested.

Similarly, a theist who is living through atrocities and evil acts done in the name of religion will have difficulty adhering to his/her religious views, especially, if his/her neighbor is a naturalist, who is treating him/her in the exact same manner, the theist neighbor has treated his atheist friend, in the example, I described above.

I heard from my atheistic friends that to be religious you have to have a special gene, and the expression of this gene will make you have religious feelings. My answer to that statement is the following question: What formed your opinion or your choice of atheism? Did that happen because of the lack of this gene? Or maybe having a different copy for that gene! Is that what influenced you not to have religious feelings? Why do you think that your gene is better than someone else's gene? Did it make you consider your opinion to be rational, and the opposite opinion as irrational if both opinions are just expressions of some sort of genetic makeup?

You can argue about this point endlessly, and you can say our views are based on a genetic determination, then I am going to say our entire discussion makes no sense at all because this discussion is the product of genetic expression and our social interaction is just a chemical reaction. We still need a mind to understand this concept, because the mind governs understanding, and chemical reactions have no understanding. I hope the idea is clear. I tried my best to explain it.

STOP 17

EARTH MATTERS

How realistic is it to say that it is a matter of time before we are going to leave the solar system by inventing a new space ship able to go to the nearest star in the Milky Way while we are bombing Earth with rockets every day using the excuse of the necessity of war against the other ones? We are dreaming about leaving Earth and colonizing Mars by seeding it with the right bacteria to changes its atmosphere. How come these sophisticated brains are not working together to save Earth's atmosphere from depleting all the oxygen on Earth and turn it into carbon dioxide?

It seems to me that humans harbor mistrust and fear from each other and want to leave Earth! Maybe on another planet, we can have true civilization. The reality, if we cannot save the jewel of the universe, Earth, we are not going to be changing Mars. NASA decided to have the spacecraft Cassini dive into Saturn's atmosphere and get burnt in order for it to not seed Saturn with bacteria and change its atmosphere! It seems to me very strange that we have this great worry about changing the atmosphere of Saturn. Why do not we show the same worry about the atmosphere of planet Earth?

We get excited about the potential ability to build a new civilization capable of warping space and time and improve our ability to travel with the speed of light looking for other planets similar to Earth.

We hear about levels of human civilization able to escape our universe when the universe is going to collapse on itself. And the big bang becomes reversed! We dream about a civilization that gives us the ability to run through the wall of a building as if the wall does not exist! it sounds to me like we are describing the function of angels, but we do not like to believe in angels.

The new age we are living in is different. Our challenge now is not about launching successful wars against each other anymore. Wars, expansion and supremacy are going to be problems of the past millennia; they are not our real problems now. Our real problems are global warming and climate change, the destruction of Earth's atmosphere by depleting the oxygen and turning it into carbon dioxide, destroying the topsoil and creating new extinction that may have us on its menu!

Ego-driven politics should be a thing of the past because they are out of touch with reality. All human beings should partner in dealing with these problems. What is going to help deal with these problems is partly adopting green technology. But way more important is adopting a green conscience and green social harmony. A green social environment will allow us to live close to where we work, and we do not have to drive. This will mandate us not to throw away the leftover food which will end up in landfills and create more methane and carbon dioxide. Green technology should mandate cities to adopt new building codes. Among many new ones, it should mandate placing solar panels on every roof. The housing and landscaping codes should be environmentally sound. These codes should mandate planting native trees and shrubs on every tiny piece of land and eliminate the use of pesticides and herbicides in the front and back yards of houses. We can create smarter ways to keep the look of these houses appealing. New trees should be planted in every possible spot on the side roads. We should not allow the building of large houses for no reason. This attitude should start at home. Our behavior should reflect our understanding of these concepts. We should worry about how we use energy and what we are doing with our waste. Our waste should be reduced by one hundred percent. Landfills should be closed down. The use of fuel, coal and natural gas should be deserted. These chemicals should be left in their reservoirs and not touched. Transportation should be prudent and should rely on the use of renewable sources of energy only. New technology in agriculture should be adopted to limit the land available to agriculture and avoid further expansions. It is time for the media to mature and show that it is in touch with reality. It is time to become intelligent and not clever.

The social environment should promote modesty, respect and love for nature. Schools should teach honesty and ethics every year according to the level of the students. Fairness, justice, and integrity should be advertised on TV. The naïve old human history that is taught in schools is not for us anymore. We proved anyway that we do not learn from history. We live in a different era. Wars and revolutions are going to be something of the past. Every time we throw a bomb on the surface of the earth, we are tightening the rope around our neck closer to the point of strangulation. We can win a war, but in reality, we are destroying every hope of our survival on planet Earth. We should mature and face reality. The new reality is that us, Humans, must live in harmony with every other species on planet Earth. We, supposedly the rational creatures, should live up to this term. We should show other species on this planet that we are trying to mature to become friendly creatures! We should show Earth that we do appreciate this great gift. We should end the aggressive assault on forests, temperate zones, seas and other creatures' habitats.

Social modesty, humbleness and cooperation with each other are going to be our survival tools in the future. They are as important as adopting green technology and environmental engineering.

Global warming and pushing Earth to explode on us will change all the rules of human views about what civilization is all about. Global warming will change our views toward culture, art and technology, and it is going to change what philosophy is all about. It is the new monster that is going to destroy every bit of our history and make us wake up from dogmatic ways of living. Global warming is going to force us to use our intelligence effectively, and not only for greed and mischief.

STOP 18

THE BRAIN OF ISAAC NEWTON

Isaac Newton

Isaac Newton was one of the most influential minds in science. By choosing his brain for this discussion, I am not by any means trying to belittle the work of the numerous scientists who lived in the past or present who have done great achievements and whose brains are as organized as Isaac's. Since I am writing this book in the West, I find him an ideal example for this book.

Isaac Newton's life and achievements are undoubtedly amazing. Our interest today in this section is not to count his achievements, but to shed some light on how he achieved them and to make it a fun exercise to test our comprehension of the social centers of the brain.

If Isaac Newton were living among us today, it is logical to think that he would be working with a team of scientists. As we are living in the quantum physics era, he would likely be working on an area in this field. He might spend fifty years of his life, as many quantum physicists do, working on understanding the inner structures of atoms. His achievements may turn out to be relatively modest or could be substantial because the closer we get to the atom the more complicated the physical matter becomes and starts to make no simple sense.

Isaac Newton managed to break away from conformist researcher roles on many levels. He even got himself involved in chemistry, a branch of science that was not popular in his time. Obviously, he was not interested in becoming rich. Even though he managed to write about most of what he did, he did not put all his work on display. He contributed to public life but lived a simple life. For sure, no one described him as having affairs with women, even when he was a young man.

I find his brain worthy of dissecting to make a model for our youth who would like to pursue a scientific future. Our youth seem to be stuck on the idea that they have to work hard, go to a great university, take out a large student loan, and later, make a lot of money.

Fame, power, and luxury were not on Isaac Newton's mind. Fame and money are items mentioned frequently in the world of science in our time as goals worthy of pursuing, not realizing that they are poisoning our life.

Through his great vision, Isaac Newton took humanity with him out of the earth and into outer space, the first trip ever available to everybody. It is very interesting to try to imagine how the brain of this interesting man was constructed. We can imagine this scenario in the brain of someone who is able to spend many hours working in science without boredom.

When the scientific inquiry in the neocortex reaches the amygdala, the amygdala has a favorable response to this neocortical activity, and when it reaches the prefrontal cortex, the prefrontal cortex stays calm and supportive of the neocortical areas. The prefrontal cortex and the amygdala work in harmony to decrease the effect of environmental factors that cause distractions from work.

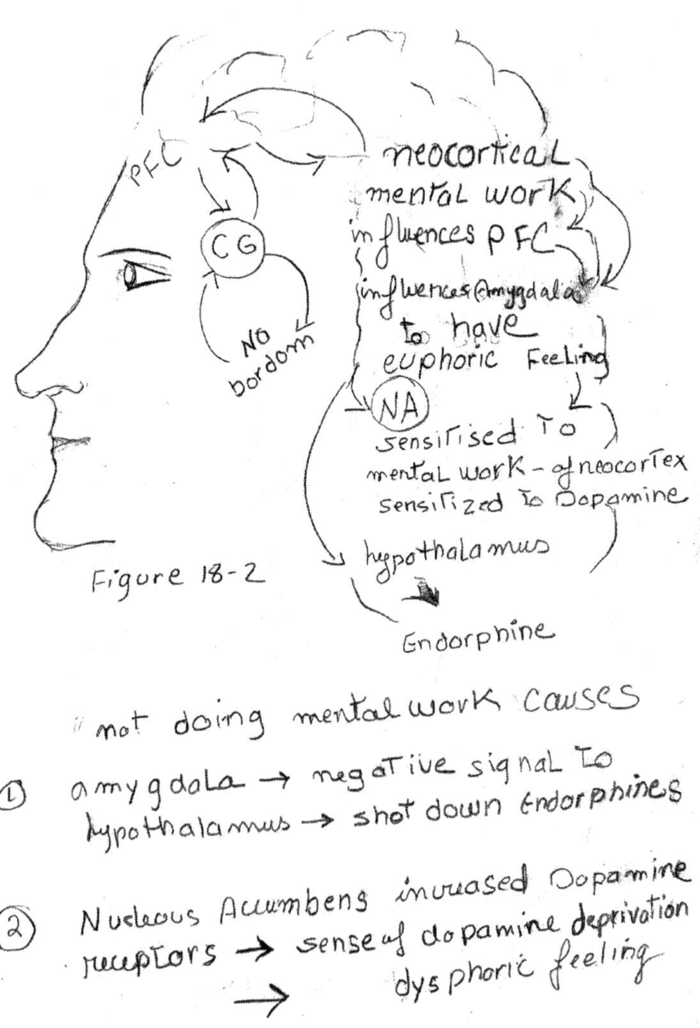

Figure 18-2

The amygdala influences the nucleus accumbens to increase the dopamine receptors. Dopamine release which is targeting the nucleus accumbens is influenced by the neocortical activity.

The amygdala after a while ceases control over the nucleus accumbens, and the nucleus accumbens takes an autonomous role. The nucleus accumbens is receiving dopamine around the clock from the arousal area, namely the ventral tegmental area. The hard work on science, in this case, becomes a very easy task.

The amygdala becomes a hub to transmit the neocortical activity back to the nucleus accumbens. The amygdala may be very quiet during the whole process or it is assuming a different role, which is to keep sending favorable signals about the neocortical activity through its connection to the hypothalamus. This, in turn, releases a small amount of endorphins. The amygdala and the hypothalamus influence the arousal system to activate it and keep the brain awake.

The cingulate gyrus is influenced by the amygdala and the prefrontal cortex. The cingulate gyrus helps the brain avoid boredom and contributes the ability to work for many hours.

The amygdala influences the hippocampus to respond favorably to all the sensory stimulations and its size increases with more cell proliferation, which is a unique hippocampal ability. The neocortical connection influences the imagination to go on a journey to space while a person is sitting in her/his chair, working by using her/his imagination and math.

Extreme harmony was formed between the neocortical and the social centers of Isaac Newton's brain and this harmony was out of the ordinary. It allowed him to work obsessively for eighteen hours a day! Despite his illnesses, he lived until he was eighty-four years old.

Isaac Newton was very lucky when it came to two things: the first was biology, which did not interest him much. A feeling I get is that if Isaac Newton were stuck in biology at this time, he would not have achieved as much in his life. The second thing he was lucky with was that he was not living in our lifetime.

What Isaac Newton Did Not Do

Isaac Newton did not listen to people criticizing him. He did not carry his childhood trauma and the difficult life that he had as a child. Isaac did not look at large houses and mansions of his time and seek to have one of them to himself. His brain was immune to the toxic effects of money that seem to be poisoning our life. Look at how many people are wasting their brain cells playing the lottery regularly and living in a dream world. Look at how greed is dictating our lifestyle.

Isaac Newton did not ask the religious community to tell him who God was and how to have a spiritual life; he figured this out on his own. He did not ask God to speak to him personally! He did not ask him if he was real or not. Isaac Newton did not ask God to tell him who he was. The social environment received him favorably, despite the man's somewhat unusual characteristics, either because of his achievements or because of his modesty and childish ego. Isaac Newton did not have any affairs with women, and he excelled in sexual transmutation. This is how he achieved what he achieved. He had a regular brain like yours and mine, but it was put together the right way to endure hard work.

This is setting rules for our youth for how they should live their life and utilize their potential to be productive people for themselves and society. The productive lifestyle that humanity needs these days is to save other creatures' habitats and avoid mass extinctions created by mindless human activities. One of these activities is war, which has a massive chemical, physical, and psychological polluting effect on Earth. Other creatures are looking at us and may be wondering what we are doing. They are saying that humans are doing a heavy bombardment on Earth when they throw rockets at each other. When we throw them at Earth's surface, we are destroying our habitat. What do rabbits and squirrels say about us when they are watching these scenes? They may say these creatures must be aliens without an intellect or maybe their intellect is under siege by their ego.

In the end, I tried to make this book as interesting as I could, to keep it beneficial for the readers who want to have an idea about how the social brain works, and for the ones who are looking for self-improvement. I tried to show that consciousness or the spirit is the center of our thoughts, whether we feel it or not. Without it, any biological system, like the human brain or a single cell, will break down. I also tried to give the reader a taste of the complexity in biology and increase the reader's curiosity. I attempted to show that the social brain, in reality, is influenced to an extreme extent by our social surroundings and the prevailing views of society. I tried to show that spiritual life and having a religion is an essential pillar in building the structure of a functioning human society that has a low rate of depression and other psychiatric diseases. I tried to show that the majority of the cases of depression are caused by society. I also tried to put sexuality in its place and bring it down from the elevated and exaggerated status created by the media, and I wrote in detail about sexual transmutation.

I think I did a very good job explaining decisively the concept of science in a clear language and using simple examples to help the reader organize the faculty of her/his thoughts when examining any human work.

I tried my best to show that fixing the problem of disfunctional social interactions between humans is a very important component of fixing Earth's environmental problems.

I hope that I was able to express my thoughts using words since this process cannot be perfect and the goal of all that is to try to ease some of the self-induced artificial pressure off my fellow humans.

The End.